Guided by Spirit

Guided by Spirit

◆

A Journey into the Mind of the Medium

Charles F. Emmons
and Penelope Emmons

Writers Club Press
New York Lincoln Shanghai

Guided by Spirit
A Journey into the Mind of the Medium

Writers Club Press
an imprint of iUniverse, Inc.

For information address:
iUniverse, Inc.
2021 Pine Lake Road, Suite 100
Lincoln, NE 68512
www.iuniverse.com

ISBN: 0-595-26805-6

Printed in the United States of America

Contents

Part III   CHARLIE'S JOURNEY

(a sociologist's participation as a late-comer to mediumship, grounded in lifelong curiosity about science, religion and the paranormal)

Part IV "SO WHAT?"

(possible purposes for mediumship, including counseling and healing, proving the continuity of life, entertainment, and practical magic; distinguishing mediums from psychics and fortune tellers)

Part V   ON BECOMING A SPIRIT MEDIUM

(an analysis of how spirit mediums have survived the ridicule generally directed toward their work in this culture and have learned to make sense of what they do)

Part VI   HOW MEDIUMS GET THE MESSAGE

(the variety of ways mediums cultivate their abilities and receive information clairvoyantly, clairaudiently, clairsentiently etc.)

Part VII THE MEANING OF MEDIUMSHIP

(how mediumship has been viewed in social sciences, scientific debunking, parapsychology, and spiritual traditions)

Acknowledgments

We thank the following organizations and people, living and "dead", for their inspiration, editorial assistance, practical advice, and love and friendship. Without any one of them this book would have been less than it is. We appreciate so many people; we apologize to anyone we have left out who would like to have been named. Thanks also to the many anonymous individuals who were interviewed and observed. Special thanks to Gettysburg College and the Faculty Grants Advisory Committee for funding this study.

Thanks to The Christian Spiritualist Church of Erie, The Church of the Living Spirit, Earth Light Institute, Fellowships of the Spirit, The First Spiritualist Church of Erie, Lily Dale Assembly, The Lily Dale Spiritualist Church, The National Spiritualist Association of Churches, The Spiritual Center of Gettysburg.

Thanks to George Anderson, Stephanie Andrews, Jack Boland, Kim Breighner, Sherry Lee Calkins, Beverly Burdick-Carey, Chris Chaffee, January Chaffee, Dr. and Mrs. E.H. Cosner, Ellie McCabe-Cratsley, Tom Cratsley, Pearl Curran, Gilles and Liliane DesJardins, John Edward, Celeste Emmons, Frank Emmons, Joanne Emmons, Lee Emmons, Mildred Emmons, John Fleming, Jessie Furst, Anne Gehman, Connie Griffith, Patricia Hayes, Martie Hughes, Heather Karki, Pauline Kay, Rose Klassen, Gretchen Lazarony, James McClenon, Bill McDowell, Jack McNab, Lynda Kaiser Mardis, Mark Nesbitt, Janet Nohavec, Kitty Osborne, Ozzie Osborne, Susan Paddock, Nancy Parker, Betsy Phillips, Katherine Ramsland, J.B. Rhine, Thomas Rugani, Neal Rzepkowski, Barbara Sanson, Barbara Savelli, Gary Schwartz, Marilyn Stafford, Virgil Stafford, Isabelle Swantner, Leonard Tatt, Elaine Thomas, Mark Thomas, James Van Praagh, Pamela Tate, Lynda Terry, Raymond Torrey, Kalin Vasilev, John C. White, Lynn Wiltsie, Patience Worth, Leonard Young.

Many spirit mediums, whether in this study or not, can be reached through the Lily Dale Website: *www.lilydaleassembly.org* The Church of the Living Spirit Website is *www.livingspiritlilydale.org* The Fellowships of the Spirit Website is *www.fellowshipsspirit.org* The National Spiritualist Association of Churches Website is *www.nsac.org* You may contact Lynda Terry for her meditation CDs and tapes at *lyndaht@superPA.net* You may reach us, the authors, by e-mail at *penelope@superPA.net* or *cemmons@ gettysburg.edu*

Cover designs and front photography(view of Cathedral Rock near Sedona, Arizona): Penelope Emmons. Back photography (path into Leolyn Woods and Inspiration Stump; Lily Dale, New York): Ellie McCabe-Cratsley.

1

An Invitation

We wrote this book for anyone who is curious about the phenomenon of spirit mediumship, the process of allegedly contacting spirits of the dead and bringing their messages to the living. Currently in the United States this subject has a most peculiar status. Spirit mediums like John Edward (who appears on the Sci Fi Channel) are very popular on television and in best-selling books. At the same time sociologists wonder what the popular revival in such paranormal and spiritual subjects (if not in organized religion) means for this technologically advanced society. Some debunkers ridicule mediumship on scientific grounds; some believers fear it for religious reasons.

On a world scale, spirit mediumship is very common, but its form and especially its meaning vary significantly by cultural context. In ancient Greece the oracle at Delphi involved women in an altered state of consciousness bringing through messages of great political significance. In Great Zimbabwe in East Africa the most important people used the highest ranking mediums to communicate with spirits of the highest status. For thousands of years Chinese have been consulting spirit mediums in order to discover what their ancestors require in their parallel lives after death, so that they may help them by burning paper models of those things (including money and houses). In turn the ancestors are expected to improve the lives of those who worship them.

What could spirit mediumship possibly contribute in a modern, rational culture like the U.S., where practical matters are dealt with scientifically and bureaucratically? Even in most American religions there is little support for such a practice. We need to look back a century and a half for pieces of an answer.

The main identifiable origin of spirit mediumship among European-Americans involves the Fox sisters who interpreted rapping sounds in their parents' cottage near Rochester, New York in 1848 as messages from the spirit of a peddler who had allegedly been murdered there and buried in the cellar. People in western New York State and elsewhere were already familiar with such ideas, because some individuals had been known to bring through spiritual or psychic messages under hypnosis (known then as Mesmerism). News of the Fox sisters and of other mediums provoked both strong positive and negative reactions but also spread the phenomenon throughout the U.S. and Europe by the 1850s.

Here we must distinguish between mediumistic practice and the significance of Spiritualism as a social movement. Practices included seances or home circles around a table, communicating messages to the "sitters" through the medium; and "platform" mediumship in churches or assembly halls, where the medium would give messages to people in the congregation or audience. There was also "physical" mediumship (as opposed to the "mental" mediumship above), in which the table might tip or rise, musical instruments and other objects might appear or fly through the air, or paintings might appear on canvases and writing appear on slates. Some of these feats came to be performed in elaborate traveling shows, which not surprisingly were often attacked as frauds.

As for the religious social movement of Spiritualism, it was diffuse and eclectic, often resisting formal organization into churches or national assemblies, at least until the late nineteenth century. Although Andrew Jackson Davis wrote about natural law and other Spiritualist ideas from about 1850, based largely on the mystical works of Swedenborg, there has never been much in the way of Spiritualist dogma. The freethinking theology of Spiritualists brought them close to other reform movements in the nineteenth century, especially those for women's rights and the abolition of slavery. Most prominent families in the North contained at least one Spiritualist.

It is not easy to characterize the significance of mediumship and of the Spiritualist movement, because surely they must have been many things to many people. On one level mediumship was an amusement or curiosity, almost like a parlor game, similar to playing with a ouija board at the dining-room table in later years. Many people consulted mediums to be reassured that their dead relatives were peaceful in heaven, especially during times of war and high infant mortality. Still today a major focus of popular books on mediumship is grief management.

Of course there have been other developments in spiritual thought in the U.S. since 1848, including Theosophy in the late nineteenth century, a movement to "upgrade" Spiritualism by importing Eastern mystical philosophies and by concentrating on higher spiritual guides, not just contacting one's dead relatives and friends. The New Age movement has roots in both Spiritualism and Theosophy but also in other alternative spiritualities. New Age "channeling" is similar to spirit mediumship but also allegedly involves communicating with highly evolved spiritual teachers and angels, or even with aliens. Clearly the new spirituality in America is broader than Spiritualism or spirit mediumship, and this is only one book on one corner of the subject.

What, then, is especially significant about the phenomenon of spirit mediumship in the U.S. (and in some other Western countries) today? We see it as both a popular and a scientific wonder. Films like "Ghost" and "Sixth Sense" illustrate the popularity of mass-media themes dealing with contacting spirits of the dead. Gallup poll data indicate an increase in belief in mental communication with the dead from 18% in 1990 to 28% in 2001; belief in haunted houses is up from 29% to 42% in the same period.[1] By age, belief is much higher in the 18–29 year-old group, and younger people are the prime audience of media culture.

It is always difficult to locate original causes in correlations between media content and popular belief. It is also beyond the scope of this study to analyze the wider social context in which spirit mediumship has made a popular revival. However, it is worth contemplating the possibility that the current growth of popular involvement in spirituality and the paranormal is partly a consequence of the continuing decline in community in mass society. In spite of, or perhaps because of, the great legitimacy assigned to science and technology, there is widespread and growing disenchantment with authoritative institutions, not only politics and the economy (including the stock market) but established religion as well. Finding meaning in such a postmodern society might include personal spiritual experience and involvement with or fantasies about the paranormal.

As we shall discuss later in the book, scientists of different types have varying reactions to this popular involvement in mediumship and other paranormal or spiritual subjects. CSICOP (Committee for Scientific Investigation of Claims of the Paranormal) and other debunkers express dismay over what they see as dangerous gullibility and lack of scientific thinking in the general population. Social scientists often analyze practices like mediumship in terms of their social functions and try to avoid commenting on their scientific validity.

Parapsychologists and some other renegade scientists, however, have actually done some serious studies of mediumship for over a century, with varying results. More recently there has even been a tendency for some anthropologists and sociologists to consider the possible reality of spiritual phenomena and to describe their own paranormal experiences in the field.[2] The investigations of both the parapsychologists and these social-scientific "radicals" represent departures from "normal science."

In studying spirit mediumship, parapsychologists seemed to be violating the boundary between science and religion. Today some scientists and philosophers actually want to combine rational and mystical sources of knowledge in a single theory of a united universe connected by nonlocal consciousness, in which spirit mediumship would have a normal rather than a paranormal explanation.

Social scientists who participate fully in the spiritual experiences of the people they study (for example, by actually doing spirit mediumship themselves) are challenging another normal-science principle: "objectivity" (being an external observer with no attachment to any bias). Instead of "participant observing" in a semidetached way, they are participating to the point of "going native", as they say in anthropology. They may also be getting information in an altered state of consciousness, which is not considered a scientific way of knowing.

However, this deep involvement makes some sense under new standards of postmodern ethnography. Postmodernists question notions of objectivity and favor the appreciation of multiple perspectives on reality. What better way to understand the perspective of spirit mediums than to observe them, interview them, and finally to learn to do what they do, and describe how it feels? This is precisely what we have done. However, we also appreciate the dangers of "going native" and of substituting one bias for another. Although we are skeptical of the concept of objectivity, we are careful to consider multiple perspectives, in order to avoid excessive attachment to any single set of biases.

This book was written by two people who are in about four or five different minds on the subject. Charles is both social scientist and experiencer. "As a sociologist I try to stand back and ask 'objective' questions about all the data we have collected from 40 depth interviews with spirit mediums, from library materials on 80 other mediums, and participant observation from 1994–2002 at the Spiritualist community in Lily Dale, New York and elsewhere. But I have also taken many classes and workshops in mediumship, and performed as a 'student medium,' which gives me an insider's view as well."

Penelope can also entertain multiple views of spirit mediumship. "I call my various perspectives 'The Committee,' which refers to how I view mediumship through my roles of spiritual seeker, healer, minister, medium, and clinical social worker/psychotherapist.

"I have always been intuitive. In fact I recall (and I have been told by relatives) that I saw auras around people, saw spirit people and gave messages with my grandmother as early as age three or four.

"As a teenager and college student I was interested in learning and writing about various religions and philosophies. In my twenties and thirties I learned and practiced many spiritual paths: Unity, New Thought, Transcendental Meditation, several Hindu and Buddhist schools of thought, Siddha Yoga, Vipassana meditation, and the Course in Miracles. Later on I studied and practiced Reiki, therapeutic touch, reflexology and yoga. I was attempting to compare and to find links among the paths, and to integrate metaphysics and spirituality into my daily life.

"With this background I encountered formal mediumship in 1987 and became an ordained minister in 1991. When I began to offer 'public' messages and spiritual counseling, I soon discovered that many clients also needed healing for complex psycho-social and psycho-spiritual issues.

"I then added another 'committee member': the psychotherapist, with a Master's in Social Work. I believe that as a theorist and practitioner who works in a challenging world with well-developed psychic senses I can effectively discern and facilitate balanced living. As a medium and healer I am also hopeful that this book will assist in expanding our possibility thinking about the dimensions of the mind."

We approach this subject openly and with an appreciation for different perspectives. We do not attempt to test mediums as a parapsychologist or debunker might. With due respect to those who either reject or discount evidence for spirit mediumship on either scientific or religious grounds, we emphasize that our main purpose is not to "prove" anything about mediumship but to show how it looks and feels from the inside. We believe that skeptics and even debunkers can learn much about the phenomenon of mediumship from this insider's point of view. However, insofar as spirit mediums themselves are skeptical about their own work, we do pay attention to how spirit messages sometimes evoke "confirmations" of their validity. Although we have both seen enough evidence to convince us that something "paranormal" often happens in this work, this book is not put forth as scientific "proof" of spirit contact.

What is special about this book? It is neither a parapsychological study of mediumship nor a single medium's biography. Of course it presents a sociological/anthropological ethnography and analysis, but one that relates the stories of many mediums, including our own stories, brought together to reveal patterns in the perspectives of mediums themselves.

Although some people in this society regard mediumship merely as an interesting oddity or as entertainment, it is clear that there are greater issues. In Part Seven we consider a variety of interpretations of the meaning of mediumship: social and psychological, debunking, parapsychological, and spiritual.

We think you'll enjoy the journey!

PART I

A MEDIUMISTIC SAMPLER

This section contains some of our favorite examples of the experiences of spirit mediums. They are selected to demonstrate a wide range of phenomena associated with the role of medium. We cannot verify them all, but none of them are evident fabrications as far as we know.

Remember that "spirit mediumship" refers to using a sensitive or psychic person (the medium) to bring through messages from the spirit world. However, mediumship is also connected to a variety of other paranormal experiences like apparitions (ghosts), telepathy (mind reading), clairvoyance (being able to see or know things through ESP, extrasensory perception), and precognition (knowing the future). It is often difficult to distinguish among these different phenomena, or to know for sure if they are "real" or imagined. Some cases are "evidential" however, when there are multiple witnesses to a paranormal event, or when the information brought through is later confirmed through normal channels.

Probably most mediums could give at least a few remarkable examples from their own work. You should not conclude, however, that everything in the lives and spirit readings of these mediums is so remarkable. What the following cases *should* do is to whet your appetite for the subject and to demonstrate the kinds of events that are most significant, though often troubling, to mediums themselves.

2

"Queer, Very Queer:" Childhood Mediums

Mrs. Cecil M. (Ellen) Cook (American, born late 19th century). Most spirit mediums in this study have had significant paranormal experiences in childhood.[3] Except for cases of mediums who are born into supportive Spiritualist families, most of these experiences are ignored by others or provoke ridicule. At age 4, Ellen started hearing voices "coming out of the thin air."[4] Soon she could see apparitions of gentle, considerate children to go along with the voices, telling her that other children couldn't see them. In Sunday school she was scolded for her impudent remark that angels were not just "way up in the sky;" they were all around them. Neighbors commented that she was "queer, very queer."

At age 6 both she and her mother heard a voice coming out of an old stove-pipe hole in the ceiling. Neighbor ladies shared this "collective apparition" (a "ghost experience" happening simultaneously to more than one person), hearing "some very abrupt and blightingly truthful things about their conduct" from the hole. Some of these women said that it was the Devil, or that the house was haunted, and that Ellen was possessed.

By age 7 she began to be "controlled", going eventually into full trance, feeling as if someone had entered her body while her own consciousness went elsewhere, unaware of what she was saying. At age 15 she did her first sitting for another person, on her way to becoming one of the most famous mediums of the early twentieth century.[5]

Mrs. Cecil Cook, as she was called, commented on how she was shunned and isolated in public often by people who sought her out in private. "Alone, in the dark, so many seemed eager to talk to their loved ones in spirit. Out in the light, when talking to others, they openly ridiculed that which alone brought them comfort and sustained them."[6]

9

Estelle Roberts (British medium, born 1889). From her earliest recollections, Estelle heard voices and was spanked by her father with a leather belt for saying so.[7] She was told that "such things were evil;" and having no knowledge of Spiritualism, she feared that she was crazy. Her brother Lionel, who had died before she was born, was one of her earliest spirit visitors. In fact she watched him grow up in his spirit form over a period of years, which is something that Spiritualists claim happens.

At age 7 she had what she considered her first major psychic experience. She saw a vision of a White Knight outside her window, pointing his sword at her in salute. This is another example of a "collective apparition", because her sister Dolly saw it too and fainted. Years later, just before speaking at a meeting and doing her first "platform" work as a medium, she saw the White Knight again, suspended above the auditorium. Into her mind came the words "to serve and not to yield."

Estelle Roberts told of her tendency to edit out information she received as a medium, a very common issue for mediums. At one sitting a spirit kept saying "Not bloody likely."[8] She didn't want to pass along such "strong language", but she finally did. The sitter (the person who comes for a reading), a woman, laughed and revealed that it was from her fiancé. The two of them had agreed that whoever died first would try to come through with this phrase from Shaw's *Pygmalion*. Many people, famous and otherwise, have made such arrangements, as in the Houdini case, which we will examine later. From Roberts' point of view, this experience represented a "confirmation", something very important to most mediums in our skeptical, scientific society.

D. D. Home (Scottish-American medium, born 1833). Little Daniel's cradle allegedly often rocked by itself, a claim that has been made about the infancy of other mediums. At age 4 he had a vision of his cousin's death, later confirmed. However, the first "vision" he distinctly remembered happened when he was 13.[9]

A darkness came over his room, and then he saw a gleam of light. It was his friend Edwin pointing his right arm up and making three circles in the air. Daniel knew then that his friend had died three days before. A month earlier they had both agreed that if either should die, he would appear to the other three days after death. A few days later a letter arrived confirming that Edwin had indeed died unexpectedly of dysentery.

Home said that his mother was a "seer", with "second sight", prone to visions or apparitions. She had precognitive abilities (could tell the future) and had a premonition of her own death. Daniel at age 17, a few months after his mother's death, received spirit raps on a table, which upset his aunt.

By the time he died of tuberculosis in 1886, D. D. Home had traveled to Europe from America and had amazed royalty with his table-rapping mediumship (each letter represented by a certain number of raps). He was also a renowned "physical" medium, levitating tables and even himself.

Sir William Crookes, inventor of the x-ray tube, reported to the (British) Royal Society of Scientists that he had seen Home (pronounced "hume" or "hoom") "raised completely from the floor of the room" on three occasions.[10] When Crookes was elected president of the British Association for the Advancement of Science twenty years later he reiterated that he had "discovered no flaw in the experiments then made" on Home. Home was seen levitating on many other occasions as well, the most spectacular and controversial being the time he floated out of a window seventy feet above a street in London, reentering another window over seven feet away.[11]

Eileen J. Garrett (Irish medium, born 1893). Eileen, an orphan brought up by an aunt and uncle near Dublin, from at least age 4 could see children whom others called "imaginary". Regular people and other living things were surrounded by light that revealed their personality and state of health. What she called "surrounds" of light, we would call "auras" today. But "The Children" of her "imaginary" world consisted entirely of this light.[12]

Jeannie (her childhood nickname), sitting on the porch one day, looked up from her picture book to see an apparition of her favorite Aunt Leon with a baby in her arms. When the woman said, "I must go away now and take the baby with me," Jeannie ran into the house to get her Aunt Martha (with whom she lived). Aunt Martha found no one about the house and punished Jeannie for making up the story and for claiming not to have known about the new baby.[13]

Angry at Aunt Martha, the next day Jeannie drowned her aunt's favorite ducklings, then saw "a gray smokelike substance, rising in spiral form" from each one (their life energies?). At this point her aunt told her that she was so wicked that she would have to be sent away. Shortly after being sent to bed without supper, Jeannie was awoken by Aunt Martha with the news that both Aunt Leon and the baby had died in childbirth. Jeannie was told never to speak of the things she saw again lest they come true. Many mediums or psychics have been afraid, especially in their youth, that they were somehow responsible for causing the events they had foreseen.

In later life Eileen (Jeannie) reported that she had learned from an early age that she could go into trance and tune out her aunt's voice, "to sleep away from it."[14] Today a skeptical psychologist might call this "dissociation", a "pathological" defense mechanism for escaping unpleasant experiences.

Interestingly, Eileen Garrett herself was very skeptical when she worked with parapsychologists who studied her mediumship, which was considered by many to be the best of the twentieth century. She was not at all sure that the spirit guides or "controls", like Uvani and Abdul Latif, who came through when she was in trance, were real. She thought that they might be parts of her own consciousness; that is, a case of multiple personality. She even wrote that she was uncertain that her spirit messages were evidence for life after death, and said that there is no definite scientific answer to the question of whether there is survival of the spirit after death.[15]

Such skepticism on the part of a woman with such evident mediumistic ability is intriguing. For one thing it tends to lend credibility at least to the subjective reality of her childhood experiences and to those of others who have had quite similar ones. It also shows how dominant the scientific attitude of Western society in general is, when even prominent spirit mediums have it in spite of their own powerful paranormal experiences. Imagine how difficult it must be for mediums to accept their mediumship when it begins not in childhood but in later years.

3

"Hain't I a Real Dreamer?:"
Skeptical Mediums

Andrew Jackson Davis (American medium, Spiritualist writer, born 1826). As a little boy in a poor rural farm family in Orange County, New York State, "Jackson," by his own account, became a skeptic. Once, he saw a hoaxed apparition by the side of the road consisting of a sheet covering a bundle of straw, topped by a hat. In his 1859 autobiography, *The Magic Staff,* Davis states, "Methinks Providence could not have better prepared my mind for investigating and discriminating between genuine spiritual personages and fallacious apparitions than this midnight encounter with the phantom-man of straw."[16]

He was also skeptical about the Santa Claus story and spied on the stockings hung up for Christmas. He caught his mother putting some things in them, and she confessed. "A vigilant credulity regarding the existence of invisible personages was, by this human solution of the mysterious Santa Claus, made very easy of subsequent development."[17]

By contrast his mother was very much a believer in things paranormal. She was thought to have "second-sight", claiming to see a strange man walking solemnly outside as a portent of death in the community. Sometimes labeled a witch for her ability to find lost items, such as an ox-chain, she was nevertheless popular among neighbors who came to hear about the future, partly through the reading of tea leaves. She believed in bad omens and in her precognitive "bad dreams."[18]

One day the young Davis used profanity, then heard a reproachful voice say, "Why Jackson!" It sounded like his mother, but she wasn't there. Another time, in a cornfield at about age 12, he heard strange music and a voice saying, "You may desire to travel." Several months later he heard music and a voice again saying, "To Poughkeepsie." In 1839 the family did move there, where he attended Quaker school. He said that he learned very little in school (a total of five months in three places), and that his geography book was the only one he liked. Set up by his father to run a grocery store, he did poorly at that as well.[19]

In 1841, after his mother died, he went into a trance-like state, blinded by something like a black veil dropping over his face. He heard his mother's voice say, "Come here, child: I want to show you my new house." He saw a flowery scene, then a vision of his mother's "bright holy home." The black veil came down again, and then he witnessed the death of his mother (which had happened earlier of course). He wrote that it was as if he had been born again spiritually.[20]

Even after this he retained a rather skeptical perspective. When he heard a voice coming from a large tree saying, "Eat plenty of bread and molasses," he thought to himself, "Hain't I a real dreamer?...Why, I can make myself believe that I hear a voice. How funny." And yet later he thought that developing a big appetite for these foods helped "purify (my)...sanguineous system...(and equalize) my nervous forces."[21]

Subsequently Davis met a traveling "expositor of Phrenological science [reading head bumps]...and mesmeric miracles." This Professor Grimes was unable to mesmerize or "magnetize" (what we call today "hypnotize") Davis. In 1843, in spite of the previous failure, William Levingstone managed to mesmerize Davis, who went into trance and amazed those present with his clairvoyant power, reading a newspaper placed against his forehead and describing people's diseases.[22]

Thus began a series of allegedly remarkable and controversial occurrences in his life, including a clairvoyant "flight through space" (an out-of-body experience or OBE?) in which he saw the surface of the globe (in 1844), the ability to see flames of light coming from people's internal organs, and visions of the future. Also in 1844 he had a vision when beckoned to a vacant lot by his deceased mother's voice. There he was given a spirit guide and a "magic staff" (which was taken back when he got impatient), and he met the ancient Greek physician Galen and the 18th century Swedish mystical/spiritual philosopher Emanuel Swedenborg.[23]

At that point he moved from giving psychic messages and diagnoses to actual healing, by examining people and prescribing unusual remedies, like curing deafness by putting warm rat skins over the ears. This and the fact that he often performed in trance (called "somnambulism", literally "sleep walking") show a similarity to the 20th century "sleeping prophet" Edgar Cayce, who prescribed cures in his sleep.

In 1845, at the age of only 19, Davis began to turn to lecturing in trance (called "channeling" today) in New York City and elsewhere. His language was seemingly too sophisticated for someone with his background. Between 1848 and 1850 he produced two influential books: *The Univercoelum* and *Harmonia*.[24]

George Bush, a New York University professor and America's top expert on Swedenborg at the time, examined Davis and decided that he was an authentic marvel. He verified that Davis could dictate in Hebrew, Arabic, and Sanskrit, languages Davis could not have known, but that he might be channeling from Swedenborg or others.[25] Present-day social historian Whitney Cross takes a less charitable view, referring to Davis as "a yokel from Poughkeepsie," and saying that "with Bush's aid (he) in considerable measure plagiarized Swedenborg's writings."[26]

Whatever the case, Davis is a major figure in the Spiritualist movement. In a nutshell he stands as a bridge between the religious fervor in upstate New York that he was born into and the mediumship that took off after the Fox sisters began to get spirit rappings in their cottage in Hydesville, New York (near Rochester) in 1848. For more on this history, see Chapter 55.

Emma Hardinge Britten (19th century British-American medium and lecturer/author). Emma Hardinge had just as strong a skeptical streak as Andrew Jackson Davis, probably moreso; but unlike Davis she also had many unusual experiences in early childhood. It was the way she interpreted those experiences that left her dubious in her first encounters with Spiritualism.

Born Emma Floyd, she was "descended from the renowned 'Welsh wizard,' Owen Glendower," and had a father who was a sea captain and "a man of phenomenal powers of prevision (precognition)."[27] As a child she heard strange sounds and music and saw apparitions. Servants in the family thought that she had described their dead relatives and said that she could tell the future.

As a teenager studying piano she was found to be "a magnetic subject." "By the wave of the hand above my head (or by an unspoken wish from the audience) I could play any air desired."[28] In other words, she could be hypnotized (mesmerized or magnetized) and then channel her piano-playing as a musical medium. In the early 19th century, mesmerism was used as a way of tapping into psychic or mediumistic abilities, as we saw in the case of Andrew Jackson Davis.

Emma's mother and some of her best friends considered this to be a dangerous, evil, Satanic influence, and thought that it could lead to "permanent lunacy or death." So, her mother vetoed "my chances of being a professional somnambulist" (trance channel). Emma then became an actress, first in England and then in New York.

A married couple in her New York boarding house talked to her about spirits of the dead. Emma had seen ghosts and heard voices, but she had never associated them with spirits. In her musical trance-channeling days she had joined a society of occultists who had told her that ghosts were just "shades, vestiges" of the dead and not actual souls or spirits.[29]

Therefore, after attending a New York Spiritualist circle that engaged in table-tipping (in which spirits are supposed to move or levitate the table), she decided to investigate and to write a debunking article on the subject. She went to another medium who produced raps on a table that supposedly communicated the idea that Emma was a great medium. [30]

Skeptical to say the least, Emma lifted the table to look for machinery or a spring that might be making the raps. Then raps were heard all around the room. Baffled, she ran a pencil over a list of letters of the alphabet, recording which letter was indicated at each rap. After receiving two hours of information this way on her friends and acquaintances, "Doubt had been annihilated; skepticism crushed out."

After that Emma had many other table-moving experiences, heard voices whispering in her ear, and saw "bright faces (flashing) before me for an instant." Then she stopped getting raps on the table and just pointed to the right letters herself. Over the years she developed all forms of mediumship, including automatic writing, speaking in deep or light trance, and psychometry (getting impressions by holding an object).[31]

One of her benefactors was a wealthy merchant Horace H. Day who rented a building at 553 Broadway in New York and hung out a sign, "Society for the Diffusion of Christian Spiritualism," of which he was the only member, and he not really a Christian. He put out a weekly newspaper, *The Christian Spiritualist*, beginning in 1850, which Emma edited as a favor when she used the two rooms he provided free for her to give her readings and seances. Both she and the famous Kate Fox (one of the Fox sisters involved with the 1848 Hydesville rappings mentioned above) charged nothing to the public for their services, although Kate was paid $1,200 a year by Mr. Day.[32]

Emma wrote, "In the commencement of these sittings I was as great a skeptic as any of my visitors....One of the purposes effected by these curious experiences, therefore, was to bring indisputable assurance of Spirit presence and identity to myself."[33] This statement could just as well have been made by many if not most of the contemporary mediums we have interviewed, and indeed by ourselves.

Emma Hardinge Britten (she married Dr. William Britten in 1870) became better known for her Spiritualist lectures and writings over a 35-year period and attended meetings with Andrew Jackson Davis and seances with people like the Fox sisters, Horace Greeley, James Fenimore Cooper, Longfellow and Whittier.

4

"Rosabelle, Believe:"
The Houdini Controversy

Arthur Ford (American medium, born 1896). As an army officer in World War One, Arthur Ford had never heard of precognition or clairvoyance, and was astonished by his first significant psychic experience. One night he dreamed that he saw a roster of a dozen men in his unit who died of influenza. The next day he saw a real list with the same names. A similar precognitive dream occurred later but with a list of men killed at the front.[34]

Later he found out that his Aunty May was a medium, something rather uncommon for a Baptist family. In his early twenties, after the war, he took a college class in psychology and encountered information on parapsychology, the study of psychic phenomena. This led to more reading and experimenting with table-tipping. Having become a student preacher, in 1924 he visited a Spiritualist church in New York City. Then he met Fletcher, his spirit guide or "control". He said that he would feel Fletcher's face press into his, and he would lose consciousness.[35]

Ford often expressed doubts about mediumship, something that adds to his credibility and should be remembered when we look at the Houdini case momentarily. At one point in his development, "My mediumship was still somewhat sporadic and I never knew whether I would get results or not....Sometimes no relatives appeared."[36] Once he admitted to getting nothing for an entire year.

Ford got a very evidential reading from Eileen Garrett that contained information he did not know (ruling out telepathy). We noted Garrett's skepticism earlier. Ford said, "Eileen Garrett...was as puzzled as I over the nature of mediumship; and as unsure as I that she wanted to be a medium." It was Arthur Conan Doyle, the author of the Sherlock Holmes stories and an avid student of the mysteries of the paranormal, who convinced Ford to become a professional medium.[37]

What catapulted Ford to fame was the controversy over his alleged success in bringing through a message from Harry Houdini to his wife Beatrice (Bessie) in 1929. Houdini, who died in 1926, had demonstrated (fraudulent) physical mediumship in his own acts, such as making musical instruments play while he was supposedly tied up. Partly on the assumption that he could fake anything that mediums did, he went on a crusade to expose Spiritualist mediums.

Nevertheless, Houdini wanted to see if he could communicate with his wife after death, and the two of them agreed on a code and a message known only to them. No fan of Houdini, Arthur Ford seemed to bring through a message for Beatrice, first from Houdini's mother, then another from Houdini himself. Indeed, Beatrice agreed that it was their secret message: first "Rosabelle", a song she had sung in their early days, then "Answer, tell, pray answer, look, tell, answer answer, tell." The latter was based on a code used in Houdini's fraudulent telepathy demonstrations and meant "believe." Thus, the message, "Rosabelle, believe."[38]

On January 9, 1929 the *New York Evening Graphic* ran a tall headline, "Houdini Message Has Been Successfully Transmitted From The Spirit World To His Widow Bessie Through The Mediumship Of Arthur Ford." The next day they ran the contrary, "Houdini Message Big Hoax," and accused Ford and Houdini's widow of staging the entire thing as a publicity stunt for a lecture tour. The fact that the paper was a sensationalistic tabloid was not lost on other newspapers, which then carried the story in a more balanced fashion. It is odd that the *Graphic* accused Bessie of supplying Ford with the code for deciphering the alleged message, when it would be necessary and simpler to supply the message itself, perhaps an indication of the inept logic of the author of the tabloid article.[39]

This is a complicated story to tell, much less unravel. However, the simplest argument to make from a skeptical perspective is that there is no way to rule out telepathy, since Beatrice Houdini knew both the code and the final message. In other words, Ford could have read her mind rather than communicating with Houdini and his mother through Ford's control (spirit guide) Fletcher.

The issue is complicated by the possibility that the code was in general use among "mentalists" (magicians pretending to do telepathy).[40] Although Beatrice put it in writing in 1929 that Ford had brought through the correct message, she also stated six years later that she had never gotten a meaningful message from her husband through a medium. And although she had offered $10,000 to anyone who could bring through the secret message, this offer was withdrawn apparently very close around the time she had her sitting with Ford in which she received and verified the message.[41] Ford never received a penny of reward, but he received a great deal of publicity and came to be known as the medium of the century, if that title does not go to Eileen Garrett.

5

"Mistaken, if not Insane:"
Automatic Writers

Beals E. Litchfield (American medium, born 1823). The eleventh and last child in a family of strict, orthodox Christians in Chesterfield, Massachussetts, Beals was told about the devil and about the "boogars", monsters that lived in caves and under rocks and who caught bad kids. At age 4 he came to doubt the boogars and became skeptical in general.[42]

At age 16 he was an agnostic but went to revival meetings. This man was a seeker/skeptic, neither a debunker nor a true believer. The day after his grandmother died, he felt her presence and was puzzled by it. In short, this is a medium without significant paranormal experiences until his late teens.[43]

As an adult farmer in the 1840s he heard of magnetism (hypnotism) and considered it "humbug or delusion." Soon after, he heard about the "rappings at Hydesville" (the mediumship of the Fox sisters in 1848) and got interested because it might prove survival of the spirit, although he suspected that it was a fraud too. He said that he didn't believe in anything, but if he did believe, he would have been a Universalist (Universalists were very liberal and often became Spiritualists). In 1852 he read a book on Spiritualism and decided to try his hand at being a "writing medium" (automatic writing, in which some outside consciousness or spirit either physically moves the pen(cil) or gets the writer to move it).[44]

Litchfield decided to try it for seven nights, and got nothing until the final ten minutes of the final night. He felt his hand move, but he had his eyes closed and didn't know what it was writing, although he was thinking about his brother. Then the pencil stopped, and he looked down and saw the name William Curtis, his niece's husband who had died four years earlier, somebody he was *not* thinking of.

Litchfield asked if William was happy, and the pencil unexpectedly wrote "no". Litchfield states in his autobiography, "Here is manifested a force outside of myself, for the pencil has moved by the force being applied at the top of the pencil above my hand...." He later discovered that the writing was similar to that of the deceased William Curtis, and that convinced him that it was from the spirit.

The next night the pencil again moved without his volition, but the sensation of the force came from his hand and arm up to the elbow instead of just at the top of the pencil. In the first few sittings he didn't know what was being written, but after that he knew what it was as it was being written and then what the rest of the sentence would be. "Strive as I would to keep my mind fixed on something else, I could not avoid knowing what my hand was writing." Then he was afraid that "my thoughts would be conveyed to the paper through my arm."

Many things that were written through his automatic writing proved to be true in later years, such as that he would "preach the gospel of Spiritualism," which he doubted because he lacked the education and the interest. "After sitting...for a few weeks, the thoughts which my hand would write would be so easily impressed upon my mind, that they seemed to me very much like my own thoughts. I did not wish to be deceived or to deceive others." So, he gave it up entirely and thought that that would be the end of his mediumship. This is not only a refreshing account in terms of its honesty; it also provides fascinating self-reflective, detailed observation to help in the investigation of the phenomenon.

Soon he experienced other types of mediumship, including a type of spirit possession perhaps, when his whole body would "pass through a course of exercises." He received little support from neighbors and townsfolk who heard about his exploits. When he told a neighbor about his first automatic writing message, the neighbor seemed to think him "very much mistaken if not insane." He found Christians "most bitter in their denunciations," thinking that one should stick to the Bible as a source of revelation. Litchfield took comfort in the thought that Christians had criticized Ben Franklin for his investigations into electricity, which was considered quite mysterious if not supernatural at the time.

Over the next few years Litchfield's development in various types of mediumship was informal, mostly in home circles with friends, which was typical of most Spiritualists in those days. He attended his first Spiritualist lecture in

1858, and gave his own first lecture in 1861 with no previous speaking experience. He wrote poetry and gave many more lectures in support of various progressive causes into the 1890s, spending time at the Cassadaga Spiritualist camp, now known as Lily Dale, New York.

Cora L. V. Richmond (American medium and trance lecturer, born 1840). She was born Cora L. V. Scott in Cuba, western New York State into a family of religious free-thinkers. Cora claimed never to have had "any unusual visions or indications in her life," but that was because she had them all in trance or when apparently asleep.[45]

At age 10 Cora performed as a platform speaker in Lake Mills, Wisconsin, where she was studied by professors who were amazed "by her wonderful flow of language and the scholarship of her utterances." Today we would say that she was "channeling" her lectures.

At the age of 11 she fell asleep in the garden one day when she was supposed to be doing a composition for school. When she awoke she discovered that "the slate was covered with writing not her own."[46] It was signed with the name of her sister who had died in early childhood and whom Cora had never seen. Her mother was frightened when other children reported that they had seen Cora writing it in her sleep. This seems to be another case of "automatic writing", except that in the case of Beals Litchfield it was done while awake rather than during a sleep or trance state.

A few days later when Cora fell asleep in the daytime, her mother put a slate and pencil in her hands. Cora wrote various messages from dead relatives. This happened on various other occasions as well, sometimes once every two or three days. Although there was no knowledge of Spiritualism in the neighborhood, all their friends and neighbors started coming to see "Cora write in her sleep."

They found that they could ask questions and get replies. They identified two spirit "controls" or guides, one a son of a minister, and the other a German physician to help her heal the sick. All of this occurred while Cora was in deep trance. Following the advice of these spirit guides, Cora quit school at age 11, never to attend again. She was told to spend four years as a healer and then to concentrate on platform speaking.

At age 15 she began Spiritualist teaching before large audiences, her fame having spread from the small towns and local circles where she had performed before. In 1854 Professor J. J. Mapes of New York City came to see her for the purpose of investigating Spiritualism. He was astonished at her lecture on "primary rocks." It was a common practice in such demonstrations to have someone else pick a lecture topic, so that "spirit" would have to provide the information in the extemporaneous lecture. Mapes said, "I stand here this afternoon *dumb* before this young girl."[47]

Three years later a group of orthodox scholars tested her in Lynn, Massachusetts. One of them asked her to "give the diameter of a bucket that was filled to the brim with water." She replied, "The diameter of a bucket of water is probably as great as the diameter of a cranial structure destitute of the grey material denominated 'brain' by so-called scientists," a rather snappy comeback for a seventeen-year-old with no more than a primary-school education.

6

Fifty Years in Bed: Reluctant Mediums

We come now to some examples of people who seem to show mediumistic tendencies but who reject the role of "medium". One is a woman we interviewed. In her twenties she started hearing a voice in her head. It was telling her "technical stuff," which made some sense to her because she had a technical background. Afraid that she was going crazy, she ignored it until it went away, instead of cultivating it.

What is especially interesting about her case is that she is a member of a Spiritualist church. She even attends groups that study channeled materials, like the Seth books, but she does not want to be a medium herself. Somewhat inconsistently perhaps, she said that she might attend a weekend workshop that helps people develop their intuitive abilities, including healing and mediumship. At any rate, this is a good example of the principle that American and other Western societies cast doubt on the wisdom and even the sanity of people involved in spirit communication. This view affects even Spiritualists.

Mollie J. Fancher (American, born 1848). There has been perhaps no more intriguing "nonmedium" in American history than Molly Fancher. As an article in *The World* put it in 1898, "Spiritualists have asserted that she is one of them. She does not believe in spiritualism. She is an earnest Christian. She does not try to explain her gifts…(or) like to talk of them."[48]

Although it may be difficult to separate fact from fiction, Mary (Mollie) J. Fancher, born in Attleboro, Massachussetts in 1848, appears to have been as much of a medical wonder as a mediumistic one. About to graduate from Brooklyn Heights Seminary, she had to drop out due to "nervous indigestion" with symptoms of weakness and fainting. Horseback riding was prescribed to improve her health, but she was thrown by a horse and hit her head, resulting in severe headaches and double vision.[49] At age 16, poor Mollie's dress caught as she was trying to climb onto a street car, and she was dragged a considerable distance. She would spend the last fifty years of her life in bed, dying in 1915.

Fancher suffered among other things from a spinal injury, causing numbness. A year after the streetcar accident she was thought to be dying on two occasions, went in and out of trance, and her right lung stopped functioning. Her physician pronounced her dead at one point, but her aunt, with whom she lived, insisted that she was not. Mollie went into alternate periods of spasms and trance, and was under constant attention for two months. According to her, "My spasms and trances were essential to my living."

She threw up everything and rejected all remedies put in her mouth. One newspaper claimed that "She ate nothing except the juice of a grape. Occasionally she would hold a banana in her mouth." [50] Her doctor thought that she was insane and administered a variety of tortures, including blisters and shock treatments. She went deaf in her left ear and sometimes went blind. Later she stated, "The loss of my power of hearing was followed by the loss of the sense of feeling. I lost…touch, then…smell, then…taste, and then the power of speech."

"About the month of May, 1866, my second sight…began to develop."[51] She became conscious of the locations of things in the room and could see the position of the hands on a concealed watch, read hidden letters, and tell what people had in their hands and pockets. Her aunt said that Mollie could tell that a thunder storm was coming hours ahead, knew when the fire bells would ring up to five minutes ahead, and knew who was ringing the door bell. As we shall see later in Part Five, traumatic accidents and illnesses often trigger the unfolding a of medium's spiritual/psychic abilities or awareness.

The last week of May, 1866, she went into trance for a week and awoke with no memory of it. A day later she went into another trance that lasted for nine years. Although she would remember nothing from that one either, she managed to spend the nine years writing 6,500 letters and embroidering. The latter had to be done above her head, with her right arm held rigidly in back of her head. At the end of the nine years, her arm relaxed, her limbs untwisted (her leg and foot bones would spasm and go out of joint), and she came out of the trance. Mollie was surprised to see her diary and her embroidery and how different people looked.[52]

After that there were more spasms and trances, usually at 10:00 or 11:00 p.m., and she would sometimes remember having out-of-body experiences and traveling clairvoyance. Some of these "psychic flight" experiences contained information that could be verified with friends. Although she refused to act as a spirit medium for others, she said, "I frequently speak of having seen my mother and other friends around me who are dead....My consciousness of these things is to me, as real as the experiences of my life upon this earth."[53]

One skeptical treatment of spirit mediumship views it as a type of multiple personality (which might be a reasonable hypothesis, except that it doesn't deal with the issue of paranormal information provided by mediums). Interestingly, Mollie herself said that there seemed to be "other Molly Fanchers who are said to be parts of the one Mollie Fancher known to the world."[54]

Indeed there were five total personalities who appeared, named by a friend of hers as Sunbeam (her usual personality), Idol, Rosebud, Pearl and Ruby. An example of how they were independent is that Idol would unravel Sunbeam's crochet work. Since she was not a Spiritualist, Mollie did not interpret any of these "personalities" as "spirit guides" or "controls" for her trance mediumship. None of her five personalities remembered what had happened during the nine-year trance.

Of course publicity about her unusual life led to tests of clairvoyance and claims of fraud by debunkers. She was known for predicting the Brooklyn Theatre fire, after which P. T. Barnum and others tried to get her to go on public exhibition. However, she declined all financial offers and never made money from her apparent paranormal abilities.[55] Perhaps the best tribute to Mollie Fancher lies in the title of an article about her that appeared in *The Literary Digest* after her death: "Fifty Years of Spiritual Victory."[56]

7

"Mine Own Harp:"
A Literary Enigma

Pearl L. Curran (American author of channeled literature, born 1883). Judged by the fruits of her labor (literary works allegedly brought through from a spirit named "Patience Worth"), Pearl Curran deserves to be called the most important "nonmedium" in U.S. history. Born in Mound City, Illinois, she was a mediocre student in school and never attended high school, but she liked music and took voice lessons, which she paid for by doing retail and clerical work in Chicago. From age 18–24 she taught voice in Potosi, Missouri and elsewhere before marrying John Curran. In those years she never thought about or tried writing.[57]

Partly due to her religious affiliation, a confirmed Episcopalian, Pearl never wanted to be considered a medium. Her uncle, the only Spiritualist in the family, was a medium, but she didn't know it until she was 13. "When I was in Chicago, at 18, I played the piano in his church about a month and a half. I didn't like the crowd that came, and the whole thing was repulsive to me....I was raised to think spiritualist seances taboo. Neither my father or mother were of a religious turn."[58]

From childhood until age 30, Pearl claimed to have had no paranormal experiences whatsoever, no "invisible companions", and not even an introspective nature. "It is odd, but I never gave names to my dolls or pets." Her stepdaughter said, "I never heard anything in her life which could prepare her for the Patience Worth writings. They are now 'my religion' and I think it incredible that my step-mother...should be capable of them. The very idea makes me laugh." As to whether her stepmother might somehow be hoaxing, she stated, "She is the soul of truth. I used to think her too darned truthful."[59]

Her husband, John, said that she "was prejudiced against ouija boards and (considered) everything of a Spiritualistic appearance repulsive." According to psychic researcher Walter Franklin Prince, it was generally agreed that Pearl Curran was honest and apparently incapable of producing the literary works she channeled from Patience Worth.[60]

Curran's first experimentation with a ouija board began in 1913 with Emily G. Hutchings' hands also on the board. According to a witness, this started "much as an amusement." Curran's father and Hutchings' mother seemed to come through with messages, and Curran was reluctantly persuaded to continue.[61]

On July 8, 1913 the ouija board "seemed to be possessed with unusual strength at this sitting and started immediately as follows, 'Many moons ago I lived. Again I come—Patience Worth is my name....'" Although Patience was reluctant to give information about herself, she seems to have been born in England, possibly Dorset, in the seventeenth century, to have migrated to America and soon after to have been killed by Indians."[62]

The fascination of the long body of communications to come could be divided into two categories: content and method. Both lead one to the ultimate question: how could Pearl Curran possibly have done this? Facile comments that it is just a case of multiple personality, or that the literature may not be that good after all, do justice neither to the phenomenon itself nor to the complex investigations that followed.

One interesting thing about the content is that it contained odd words and phrases from Patience that Pearl probably would not have known, such as "a mug of beaslings," "beaslings" being a dialect word referring to the last milk of the cow. One analyst stated, "She dictates (some) words to be found only in Milton's time. Many such words have no meaning to her until hunted out by Mr. Yost [one of the investigators] in dialect dictionaries and old books."[63]

One professor of English literature found "the language wonderful" in her novel *Telka*, the words a combination of dialects and time periods used "in their exact original sense" and consistent, with no tell-tale modernisms. Prince pointed out however that in some other works there were a few neologisms (modern coinages), including a few words spoken by Pearl Curran's maid.[64]

Overall Patience Worth used modern English first, "then lapsed into dialect as a means of asserting her individuality and showing that she is another (person) than Mrs. Curran," Prince said. Although "her conversational speech has a substratum in the region of her birth," she uses "elements from different times and places." Some of her vocabulary is hard to find, obsolete, not found at all, or coined. She did not use dialect however in the novel *Hope Trueblood*.[65]

Many of her novels and poems received high critical praise from literary experts. William Marion Reedy said that "*The Sorry Tale* (meaning "a tale of sorrow," a novel about Jesus) and *Hope Trueblood* are works of genuine literary art—the former the most wonderful piece of historical fiction I have ever read." Braithwaite's *Anthology of Magazine Poetry for 1917* included 5 of Patience Worth's poems, 3 from Amy Lowell, 3 from Vachel Lindsay, and 6 from Sarah Teasdale, among other poetic heavyweights.[66] Some literary experts would say in private that it was great literature but declined to be quoted due to the controversial nature of the source (a ouija board).

No doubt there is a great deal of subjectivity involved in judging the literary quality of such material. However, most research on channeled material in general finds that the great bulk of published works that have been supposedly channeled are not very remarkable, and yet there is a small amount that seems to be of high quality and of great significance. We submit that the Patience Worth material is among the latter, and it is too bad that so little of it is readily available today. Here are a few interesting excerpts.

When Patience Worth was asked (through Pearl Curran of course) how the world would regard her utterances, she said, "A pot of wisdom should boil to nothing ere a doubter deemeth it broth worth tasting." Indeed, if this were not the case, there ought to be more of her work still in print.[67]

When asked why there should be evil, Patience replied, "There be not o 'evil; it abideth not. 'Tis dreams awry." This sounds very much like New Age philosophy today on the illusion of being separated from God and on the importance of creative visualization. "How is a man to know God?" She answered, "Alawk, thy heart is packed afull o' Him, brother."[68]

In an interesting passage about scientists from 1919 she seems to anticipate modern chaos theory more than a half century later. "Man's law is precision, God's is chaotic....To man,...complications are chaos, thereby is man deceived....Then to God, man is precisively chaotic; to man, God is the disruption of precision."[69] This might be compared to the idea that reductionist science attempts to construct precise laws under controlled conditions; but outside of the laboratory, interactive reality is much more complex, giving at least the impression of chaos.

When asked about the concept of "cosmic flow," she said, "Nay, they mouth o'er much which be spelled GOD." Later she didn't like the concept of "cosmic consciousness" and called it "swill".[70] Right at the point I (Charles) read this in the library in Lily Dale, New York, a misplaced book by Billy Graham fell off the shelf with no one near it. It belonged on another shelf between Alan Cohen and John Gray. I considered this an amusing synchronicity, as if to say that the traditionally religious Graham, whose views seemed similar to Worth's on these two points, took priority over the modern self-help books of the other two authors, both of which I had read.

In one of her poems Patience says, "Let me believe in the instant, And I need not fear the hour." Now she sounds more New Age again, like "Live in the now moment." There seems to be no support for established religion in, "Build ye four walls and call it God's country?" Another favorite about spirituality: "Man is God without His understanding, seeking the Source of his own creation; he questioneth and becometh confused, for he would drink the Infinite with a Finite cup."[71]

It is difficult to convey an appreciation for her novels with excerpts. However, *The Sorry Tale* is an impressive work for readers who can stick with its length (640 pages) and complexity, since it gives an account of Jesus' life that is full of description and additional unknown events that give the impression that they were written by someone who actually experienced them. *Hope Trueblood*, about an orphan girl, reads like a work by one of the great English novelists and would probably be the easiest and most entertaining for a general audience.

Next there is the question of how this body of material came through Pearl Curran. This aspect truly compounds the mystery, because even if Pearl Curran were a literary genius, it is difficult to imagine her being able to compose in this manner and at this rate. W.T. Allison, a prominent Canadian writer and professor of English literature at the University of Manitoba, called Curran (Worth) "the outstanding phenomenon of our age." Upon seeing her produce fifteen poems in seventy-five minutes, he wrote, "All were poured out with a speed that Tennyson or Brown could never have hoped to equal, and some of the fifteen lyrics were so good that either of those great poets might be proud to have written them."[72]

In one evening she composed 32 brief poems and 7 other utterances, a total of 1360 words, on subjects given by others, all done extemporaneously. Edgar Lee Masters, the noted American poet, said that it was impossible, "It simply can't be done." In other words, poetry generally takes time for crafting and editing.[73]

Although the information came at first through the ouija board in 1913, "Little by little the letters began to come directly into Mrs. Curran's mind, so that the use of the pointer gradually became a mere automatism, and by 1918 the record shows that it simply circled aimlessly." Other people like Emily Hutchings had sat at the board with her, but it soon became clear that she was the medium. She also increasingly got "vivid mental pictures" at the same time. She gave out letters orally one at a time (as one would when seeing what letters were pointed to on the ouija board). This "became so rapid that nobody not accustomed to long practice could possibly follow and separate them into words, even in his mind."[74]

In 1919 Curran happened to look into the eyes of someone sitting there, and letters kept coming into her mind even without looking at the board, after which time she "cultivated the habit more and more of looking away from the board." Later that year she got whole words without needing to spell them out.[75]

The speed of her delivery increased over time as well, up to a rate of 120 letters per minute. She could even answer questions at the same time, or do other things like answer the doorbell. When asked why spelling was used (until later), Patience said that it was to get the message through before Pearl knew what it would be, to prevent her from mixing in her own ideas on the matter. Sometimes two different compositions were intermingled at once, which increased the amount of pressure that Pearl would feel at the top of her head as something was about to come through.[76]

Another interesting aspect of this communication is that it was sometimes accompanied by clairaudience (sounds) and clairvoyance (images) in Curran's mind. She was able to describe these visions at the same time as she was dictating a poem, and they sometimes included her. Pearl said, while "watching the tiny panorama unfold before me, I have often seen myself, small as one of the characters, standing as an onlooker, or walking among the people in the play." If she was curious about what was happening, the little figure of herself would walk around and take part, tasting a fruit for example.[77] This sounds a bit like a lucid dream, in which the dreamer knows it's a dream and feels in control of the action.

Clearly she was not in trance. "I was keenly conscious of everything about me." Also, the medium and the spirit appeared to blend, something that is difficult to explain from either a mediumship or a multiple-personality perspective. "While I am writing there seems to be no definite place where my consciousness ceases, and that of Patience comes in."[78]

In spite of the fact that Pearl Curran did not want to be known as a medium, people did come and ask her about spirits. Patience essentially said that there is a connection between Heaven and earth, our loved ones do come around, and it is allowed for us to try to become aware of them. Spirits do help us, but it is a mistake to rely on them too much, she said.[79]

On two or three occasions Patience brought through messages from other spirits, acting as a "control" for Pearl. Patience also seemed to be able to read the minds of the sitters on many occasions, but Prince, the psychic investigator, did not consider the body of information collected about the sitters to be sufficient to provide good evidence for these claims of telepathy.

Finally, what might account for this phenomenon? From a normal science perspective there is a tendency to label it dissociation and multiple personality (now medically called "dissociative disorder"). An article appeared in the *Psychological Review* in 1919 by Charles E. Cory, who wrote that "Mrs. Curran is an intelligent woman, but her mind is much inferior to that of Patience Worth,…a subconscious self far outstripping…the primary consciousness. This is an indisputable fact, and it is a significant one for psychology."[80]

Cory assumed that it was a case of dissociation and called for more study of her based on psychoanalysis and hypnosis. Pearl Curran refused to be hypnotized for fear that she might lose contact with Patience Worth. Cory never dealt with the issue of all the evidential aspects (the demonstration of paranormal knowledge and abilities). He called the idea that there was a seventeenth-century spirit involved an "illusion" and just assumed that Curran had somehow acquired all of the knowledge involved by some normal, forgotten means (what we call "cryptomnesia", although neither he nor Prince used the word).[81]

Prince concluded as follows, "Either our concept of what we call the subconscious must be radically altered, so as to include potencies of which we hitherto have had no knowledge, or else some cause operating through but not originating in the subconscious of Mrs. Curran must be acknowledged."[82] This seems to be a fair statement, considering the array of wonders his investigation uncovered.

Of course there is always the hoax hypothesis to consider. But keep in mind not only the apparent good character of Pearl Curran, but also her apparent lack of ability to simulate such a feat given her background. Casper S. Yost, another investigator, noted that none of her visitors were ever charged a penny for seeing her, and that the Currans incurred significant costs for a secretary to keep records and to reply to correspondence. Of course there were royalties from the literary publications, but these amounted to less than the expenses.[83]

Although there still seems to be a remote possibility that Pearl Curran's physical brain was capable of such feats on its own, we are lead to consider the spiritual hypothesis. If there is such a spirit as Patience Worth, why did she pick Pearl Curran as her medium or channel? Patience said, "I hae (have) said it be a trick o' throbbin (vibrations or throbbing coming through). The wench be atuned unto the throb o' me....Follied un (one) she be, but, I say me, pithed o' (made up in the core of) the thing that be like unto a siller (silver) string." She called Pearl "mine ain (own) harp, a whit awry—but mine ain harp, withal."[84]

Nowadays, we might consider other paranormal hypotheses, other than spirit mediumship or possession (which could be considered a type of mediumship in which the spirit takes over to one degree or another). One might be a type of superESP, in which there is no limit to how our mind can gather information from anywhere, anytime. How this awareness of information would then be converted into composition skill at a rapid rate by Curran's brain is still difficult to explain.

What about past lives? Maybe Pearl Curran had a past life as Patience Worth. Sometimes past lives are considered an explanation for people who seem capable of speaking languages or dialects they have never studied, but this level of carryover from a past life is way beyond the usual claims.

Tuning into the one mind or cosmic consciousness would be another possibility, something akin to superESP in fact. This is also one type of explanation that spirit mediums sometimes use for what they do, especially those outside of the Spiritualist tradition.

For all of Pearl Curran's insistence that she was not a medium or even a Spiritualist, it is ironic that when she died of pneumonia in 1937, the funeral was conducted by a Spiritualist minister.

I (Charles) have one final comment on this favorite case of mine. One day I picked up a copy of *The Sorry Tale: A Story of the Time of Christ* (published in 1917) in a library in Lily Dale. As with her other books, the author is listed as Patience Worth ("communicated through Mrs. John H. Curran"). Lo and behold, it was a personally autographed copy, dated December 29, 1925, signed "Mrs. John H. Curran, *'Patience Worth'*." The skeptic in me wondered why it was signed Mrs. Curran first, followed by quotation marks around "Patience Worth", as if Worth were merely her pen name.

But then I put my hand on the autograph and thought about Patience Worth and Pearl Curran, as if I could connect with them by some sort of psychometry. I started to feel some energy in my hand, and I felt the thought (just my imagination no doubt), "You'll learn more by readin' the book than by warmin' your hand on my signature." Just the kind of feisty thing Patience would say.

8

The Cigar-Smoking Dog: Present-Day Mediums.

As interesting as it is to comb the biographies of mediums in library research, interviews with present-day mediums bring us closer and allow us to ask our own questions of them. Here are some of our favorite cases, with a few additions from artist/photographer Bill McDowell who interviewed some of the same people.

Raymond Torrey (American medium, born 1909). Ray, the singing medium, is a resident of the Spiritualist community in Lily Dale, New York. Although he had no significant psychic experiences in childhood, from age 15 he seemed to be very psychic at work, being able to find things. As a kid he lived in Silver Creek, only twenty miles from Lily Dale, but his Baptist mother told him to stay away from Lily Dale and its mediums "unless you got troubles." "When you die you go into the ground until the Lord takes you away," she said, in opposition to the idea of contacting spirits.

In his early thirties, Ray was influenced by his very psychic wife to visit a medium in Lily Dale. This encounter "opened everything up" for Ray, after which he started reading about mediumship. He noticed that his intuition would help him on his truck-driving job, telling him what places would have a pickup for him.

Soon Ray was singing in choirs, attending Spiritualist circles and giving messages in Spiritualist churches around Buffalo and Jamestown. When his wife came to do mediumship in Lily Dale in the 1940s, Ray was often asked to sing.

One night in a circle in Jamestown he was "taken over" (in trance) by a Native American spirit guide named Black Hawk from South Dakota.[85] Ray felt that he was growing taller (Black Hawk was reportedly 7' 6" tall). People later told Ray that the spirit guide had spoken through him and given them his name, and had made Ray stomp around on the floor.

That night Ray woke up in bed and got an image in his mind of a fire and teepee and twelve Indians in the driveway. But then he went to the window and saw the same scene outside, including an image of himself sitting out there in the center. Then the wind blew the live ashes down the driveway. One by one the Indians and then the teepee disappeared, and it just looked like his driveway again.

This was early in Ray's mediumship career, and it was as if he were being initiated or as if he had "graduated". From then on he became more and more able to sense things. Just before that he had been a three-pack-a-day cigarette smoker, but the next day he quit completely.

I (Charlie) confess that before I got to know Ray, I saw him as a nice old man but didn't take him very seriously. He would (and still does at age 90) walk slowly up the aisle, supported by his cane, in the outdoor message services at the Stump and at the Forest Temple, singing a hymn like "In the Garden." Everybody would smile and love to hear him talk.

One day as I sat there wondering if his spirit messages were that good, I saw a grumpy looking man in the audience (congregation) sitting there with his arms folded. The thought occurred to me, "Now there's a man who really needs a message…, But *I'm* sure not going to give him one when it's my turn."

Well, Ray came to him, and I thought, "Oh, brother, what a choice." But Ray said to him, "You really like the sound of trumpets, don't you?" For some unknown reason that was just what the man needed. He brightened right up and said, "Yes," in an enthusiastic voice. The transformation was like a miracle. I think of that message every time I have the tendency to get judgmental about somebody else's mediumship. And Ray may not even have known why he mentioned trumpets. Mediums often have no clue why they say the things they do, pointing out that the messages are not for them.

Lynne Wiltsie (contemporary American medium). Lynne is also a resident of Lily Dale. Although she was 40 when she first came to Lily Dale for a reading, her investigations into Spiritualism as an adult started to make sense out of her childhood experiences, such as with astral projection or traveling OBEs (lucid dreams of flying).

Throughout her life in a military family, she had experienced many religious organizations: Lutheran, Methodist, and later on Unity. After her introduction to Spiritualists, one class lead to another and in a few years she was active in church and eventually doing professional mediumship.

Lynne's most important spirit guide is Black Bear (an Iroquois Indian represented symbolically by the animal). Once she was thinking about painting a room (she considers it his room), and she had in mind yellow. But Black Bear kept telling her to paint it blue. She went to the store and found a can of pre-mixed "mist yellow" paint on sale. When she got home, she said, "I'm painting this room yellow." Black Bear said, "blue." She opened the can, and it was…blue.[86]

Looking through the interview notes for this chapter, I (Charles) saw something about Black Bear I wanted to ask Lynne about. Then I spotted her one day at the Lily Dale post office, but I didn't get to talk to her. Two days later I prepared to paint the trim in the bedroom in Penelope's cottage. She had bought a good brand, "Behr" (pronouned "bear"), with a picture of a bear on the can, looking very much like the bear picture on Lynne Wiltsie's sign in front of her house. The paint was supposed to be white. I opened it, and it was…blue. Penelope decided to have me use the blue paint, after I told her the Wiltsie story, on the theory that if spirit wanted it to be blue, she would get used to the oddity of white walls with blue trim. It may not be a highly evidential case, but I thought that it was an amusing synchronicity.

Confirmations. Many of the mediums we interviewed will have their stories told in bits and pieces throughout other chapters. However, one of the most interesting "bits" to sample right away would be the confirmations mediums get that their messages or readings are meaningful. This is especially important for mediums in Western societies, where intuition is suspect and takes a back seat to science.

Gretchen Lazarony of Lily Dale has had a number of very interesting confirmations. Once she saw (clairvoyantly) a dog with a lit cigar in its mouth. She wondered if she dared tell such an absurd thing to the woman who had come for a reading. When she did tell her, the woman explained that she had lived at the end of a milk-truck delivery route. When the driver got to her place he would turn the truck around and throw his cigar out. Her dog would run over, pick it up, and run around with it in his mouth, appearing to be smoking the cigar. Gretchen's moral for the story: never interpret. One might also say, don't edit, because bizarre details may have some significance, symbolic or otherwise, for the sitter.

The medium in this next case will be anonymous, just because the unpleasant nature of the confirmation should not be left as the only association with this excellent medium. Once she told a woman who had come for a reading, "Please don't let your niece go to school tomorrow…. You've got to call your sister tonight and stop it."

The woman did call her sister and said, don't let your four girls go to school. The medium had identified the particular girl by initial, which turned out to be the initial of her nickname. Sadly the sister let her girls go to school anyway, and the one little girl with the particular-initial nickname was picked up after school and murdered.

Police found out about the medium's statements and interrogated her about possible involvement in the crime, since she seemed to have known about it beforehand. When they found out that she had never known the people before and had not been to the state in which the murder was committed, they changed their attitude. Then they asked for her help. By that time it had been a very trying experience for her; she had felt intimidated.

Although mediumship can be a very interesting and rewarding experience for the medium, especially when there are confirmations, this last case is certainly a good example of the problems that can arise when the message is unpleasant, whether it turns out to appear accurate or not. As we shall see later, mediums develop rules for dealing with such matters.

9

"The Ask-Rice Woman:"
A Chinese Medium

Since spirit mediumship is a virtually universal phenomenon, it is useful to have an example from another culture. The following is an abbreviated version of a much more extensive treatment in one chapter of (Charlie's) book *Chinese Ghosts and ESP: A Study of Paranormal Beliefs and Experiences.*[87]

First of all, spirit mediumship is much more important in traditional Chinese society than in Western societies. People consult mediums as a part of ancestor worship. One's ancestors can be very helpful in matters of health and wealth, if they are properly honored with incense at the family altar, and if they receive the things they need on the other side through the burning of paper effigies.

An example of such an effigy would be a symbolic paper-and-wood model of a Mercedes automobile complete with tape deck and a lucky-number license plate. In turn you might ask them to help you win the lottery to be allowed into low-cost government housing. If you don't treat them right, you can become ill and unsuccessful.

Consequently, a trip to the medium (the *mun mai poh*, "ask-rice woman") is a serious matter, and not just an opportunity to "chat with one's aunty," as I was accused of doing when I went to one for observation purposes. I observed one medium over five sessions trying to contact ten different spirits. In about half of the readings she was amazing. Sometimes she was not, especially when she worked such long hours and became ill.

Some details were so specifically accurate that I was stunned, such as when she had my deceased aunt describing how my mother used to get itchy skin on her arms and hands. The medium rubbed her own forearms just the way my mother did. Overall I would say that it is evident that she was way above chance in getting things right.

40

I will now give excerpts from one of her better readings. I brought a Chinese man in his early twenties, let's call him Peter (pseudonym). Peter wanted to contact the spirit of the young bride of his friend in Colorado. She had died in Colorado in a car accident. Peter was staying with his parents in Hong Kong, having returned recently from the States. The following quotations from the reading are translated from the Cantonese language (the medium did not speak English).

Peter gave her just the name of his friend's wife. She said, "I've found someone twenty-six years old, a boy." Wrong one. But then she started to click.

"She didn't die in China or in Hong Kong. She died in America." He had not told her where she had died, but this might have been a plausible guess, if she thought that Peter had spent time in the U.S. because he knew me. "She didn't die at home or in the hospital. She died in a car accident." Right. Speaking as the spirit, the medium said, "I like you (Peter) very much. I did not like my husband." Peter did not know if that was true. At any rate, the medium had not been told that the woman had a husband or that she was unrelated to Peter.

"When I died, my brain was smashed. Did you know that?" Peter answered, "Yes, I know." Peter told me later that he had seen the accident report. Her head had been nearly severed at the neck from the blow.

Then she said incorrectly that her husband had a house and girlfriend in the U.S. He did get a house in Canada after her death, and some would argue that this is not a miss, since "America" is often used by Hong Kong Chinese to include Canada as well. He did have a girlfriend, we found out later, but Peter didn't know how close they were.

Peter said to the spirit, "My best friend (her husband) said that you saved him in the accident." The spirit replied, "Yes, I held him. If not he would have died." It is unclear what actually happened from the little that Peter's friend told him.

There was other inconsequential conversation. Peter thinks that she said (incorrectly) that I had taught the spirit in college (perhaps a logical guess about our relationships). Peter was very impressed overall, and so was I in spite of a few apparently incorrect statements.

In general the Chinese who went to this medium judged her based on whether her statements seemed in character with the spirit. One woman was dissatisfied on the grounds that "My grandfather would never say that." At the time I tended to see the medium's work as some kind of ESP. If she seemed to do way better than chance guessing, I was impressed. This happened in 1980. It would be thirteen years later before I would take more seriously the possibility that a medium was actually contacting the spirits of the dead.

PART II

PENELOPE'S JOURNEY

10

A Mystical Childhood

It is interesting for me to look back at the spiritual experiences in my life that have led to the development of my intuition in general and my mediumship in particular. Actually I have always known that I was a spiritual being. I credit that to my grandmother (mother's mother) Irene Smiley Cosner, whom we called Mommo.

Very early in life I began to learn about the power of two or more people gathered together with the common purpose of prayer and healing. My sister was born weighing only two pounds, six ounces. Mommo called her our "miracle baby" and arranged for two or more people to pray beside her in the hospital for weeks. In addition to praying, the prayer partners changed the 78-rpm records of classical music and kept the metronome going to replicate a mother's heartbeat.

Mommo also told me to pray for my sister everyday and listen to hear her secret because she was new from God. She said God was everywhere, and we could always know everything because God was everything, if we would "be still and know God". She spoke of how we chose our parents, and of how the baby's soul had chosen me for a sister. She listened to me when I spoke of other lives and who I had been in those times. We would walk down the street and identify the "old souls" we passed. She also taught me to bless others every time I heard a siren or saw an ambulance, and to smile a blessing at each person I saw. That habit has stayed with me to this day.

Mommo was already seventy when I was born. As I recall my childhood it seems to me that I spent a lot of time with older women like her. My earliest memories of being nurtured are of looking up into my grandmother's hazel eyes. Mommo and the women who worked in her household gave me my image of a loving, spiritual environment. I would dream at night of growing up strong, capable, nurturing and black like Mommo's helpers. I still feel nostalgic and flooded with love when I hear or sing American spiritual hymns like we did then.

I remember learning to read by age three because I wanted to get the small, colored scrolls with a Bible verse as my cousins did when they came to Mommo's house. I remember six of my cousins doting on me like I was special and later my doting on my younger cousins. The extended family of more than ten attentive cousins in town created my ideal of how to live. I often find myself recreating that ideal of spiritual family at church or in the small Spiritualist community of Lily Dale, New York.

I credit Mommo for my strong intuitive ability and spiritual development. Sometimes we would play psychic games. Mommo would have me sit still and hold a key, with the intention of being one with the key. She said we were all one. Then she would hide the key, and I was to try to see what the key would see. After I had the image, I would walk around the house until I could match the views (from high or low) that the key and I saw. Then I could locate it. This early training serves me well today. People will call for a telephone reading, and I am able to "connect" with them no matter what their location.

I also had an NDE, near death experience, around age three that I consider most influential in my psychic development. Probably due to the NDE, I learned to leave my body through the crown chakra when I went to bed. I was glad to go to bed so that I could travel through light of many colors. I had the sensation of being tiny like a pea with the multi-colored tunnel of lights all around me. There was also a humming sound and a feeling of vibration. Imagine being inside a balloon or conch shell and having it tapped, then experiencing the humming vibration from the inside. I traveled toward a bright white light, but I don't recall ever reaching it. Instead I was just nothing yet everything; I was the "hum". It was all there was.

In the morning I'd wake up and be back inside my body. Occasionally I'd remember being with guides and teachers who taught me and loved me on these trips. I would know whole poems or other things beyond my capacity (even now). Mommo was interested in what I had learned from my journey, and we would sometimes discuss these other times and places with her friend Glenn Clark, a minister. In Delaware Ohio, I also attended Camp Farthest Out with her, and I loved sitting on Rev. Clark's lap while he sang songs and lectured. I was young enough to think we were at "Camp Father Stout". Reverend Clark's belly had the best jiggle when he laughed! I learned to connect spirituality and joyfulness.

Mommo always seemed to know who was calling before she answered the telephone, and this was normal to me. Mommo also knew when someone had passed into spirit and would tell my grandfather that a patient was about to die or had just passed.

She and her friends would also pray, meditate and give messages. Sometimes I was invited to take off my shoes and stand on the leather-topped coffee table to give messages. I felt special because what I had to say was considered important enough to break the rules about standing on furniture!

Sometimes I picked flowers with my grandfather, Dr. E.H. Cosner, known to me as Daddo. He would take bouquets to his patients when he made house calls. He said our love and healing stayed with the flowers and left a healing presence in their rooms. I began to learn of healing touch through his example as an osteopathic and homeopathic doctor.

At our own house across the street I remember sitting on our stairs and thinking that if God was everywhere then he/she was the air. If I had just broken a rule, I tried not to breathe because then he would be inside of me and know about it! If I breathed out, I wondered if Mom would then breathe in God and know what I did. I went across the street to Mommo and Daddo's, and we talked about my dilemma. They said God was also me as well as in my breath, so I couldn't be too "bad".

At a recent family reunion my cousin said that she remembered how I would sit on the stairs for long periods of time and talk to myself in the mirror. (I wonder if that is like mirror gazing as a way of contacting the spirit world.) She said that I had an adult vocabulary; in fact my aunt said I never acted or sounded young. ("Adult attitude" has been found in children who remember past lives.)

What I remember is having conversations with myself and others, whom I would now call spirit people. At the time they were as real to me as my family. There was also a special spirit person whom I called my Turquoise Master. I didn't need a mirror to see him. He appeared to me in a long turquoise-colored robe when we were alone. When others were around I would perceive him only as a turquoise ball of light. Only I could see him, and we talked throughout the day, virtually every day. We used thought "words"; this communication seemed normal to me.

I can recall my Mother wanting me to pray, and I would answer that I had been praying all day. Every thought was a prayer, why should I do it out loud and again? She made prayers into songs, and that was not something I always did, so I loved to sing prayers with her. She had no interest in my guides, messages or past lives, but until the day before she died we sang prayers and hymns together.

Because this is a book about Mediumship, my nuclear family is not often mentioned. I did not receive any positive feedback or encouragement from them for my physic development. In fact my mother would punish me for talking to spirit, speaking about things that were going to happen or talking about other lifetimes. My sister has never seemed interested.

As a child my most loved person was always my "Daddy Jack". At age 88 he is still a wonder to me. He visits us at Lily Dale and says I was always a strange one, "and now there is a whole town of characters like you who talk to dead people." He still says that he does not understand even though he has had a reading from others. He believes in doing to others as you want done to you, and he exemplified devotion in caring for my mother for 27 years after her brain aneurysm. He says that he has no need for religion or the unseen; his "church" is in nature: golfing, playing tennis, sailing and skiing. It suits him well since he can still do all of those things at his age!

Obviously, however, it was through my grandparents' influence, not my parents', that I developed intuitively. However, I believe that the difficulties I encountered with my mother led me to seek solutions through philosophical inquiry and comparing religions. Later, it led me into counseling and the Twelve Steps. After I healed, it led me toward my training and work as a psychotherapist. My mother was an outstanding community leader, but she had many emotional problems. It made my childhood difficult, but it also jump started my spiritual growth and transformation.

Looking back there were at least five deaths of family and neighbors in my first five years, yet I don't recall going to a funeral or having someone spoken about after they died. I would see them as spirits and talk with them: my baby sister (not the "miracle baby" who survived), my father's parents, and two neighbor girls. One death troubled me greatly. It was a girl who lived next door to Mommo. I recall telling Mommo that there were no colors (no aura) around the little girl, and I was worried. She told me that the child was a "blue baby", but I argued that I didn't see blue. Soon after the girl died, and I remember sharing my remorse with Mommo and wondering if I had caused the death. Of course it is not unusual for young children to think that their thoughts cause events. I was fortunate to have a teacher like Mommo to clarify my misperceptions.

I was fortunate to have someone who was a mystic to share my other experiences with. Recently I read a book called *The Indigo Children* by Carroll and Tober.[88] I recognized that these children were basically like me as a child. They can see auras, speak about past lives, and they question the reason and source for rules. I do not think that that these children were rare before 1980 as implied by the book, but I am glad that the authors help parents to recognize them as gifted children rather than as weird or pathological.

11

The Shutdown

My life changed radically at age nine when my family moved from Ohio to Pennsylvania. My father was offered a better opportunity for advancement, and we moved from living across the street from my grandparents to a house in Erie, Pennsylvania. I lost my extended family of relatives and especially my grandparents who were metaphysicians. It was during this time that I "shut down" what psychic gifts I had. I had learned by age four that it was not smart to talk of such things, except with my grandparents. Without their support I no longer astral traveled at night, and I stopped seeing my Turquoise Master and other spirit people.

I was still interested in spiritual and philosophical subjects however. Some experiences from this time have no doubt influenced my spiritual development as a healer and minister. At age 13 I was to recite the Nicaean Creed before the church elders in order to join the church. I had memorized it, and thought long about what parts were correct and what was misguided. My mother was superintendent of the church school, so I was eager to please; plus my peers were watching. I stood and recited the Creed with my corrections: I said that Jesus was God's son but not his only son. I thought he did not descend into hell because there was no hell. I didn't think he would judge the quick and the dead, he would just love us. No doubt some of these ideas were reflective of my reading of the Unity church magazine *Daily Word.* To my horror, an elder who looked imposing in his morning coat, stood up and accused me of blasphemy.

Fortunately the minister, Dr. A. Ray Cartlidge walked over and placed his hands on my quaking shoulders. He said he was glad to have a thinking member in his congregation and that he could recall another young teen who had challenged the church elders. I learned from this that it was safe to have one's own spiritual perspective. I also learned to respect others' beliefs.

The Presbyterian Church offered me other teachers as well. Miss Emmaline Reed, who had served as a missionary in China and India, would always talk with me about reincarnation and other beliefs that I would bring to her. I learned from her to appreciate service to all God's children and to want to teach.

In Michigan, at Camp Miniwanca, a British gentleman whom we called Kodaya would share his philosophy from his life in India. He would also listen respectfully to my ideas about the nature of our being and of the universe. At age 15 I thought that God was energy manifest as light vibration (like my experience of vibration and lights). I believed that when we died our energy merged with all other energy. So when we chose to be born again it was like taking a ladle and dishing out energy that had a little of each person who had ever lived in it.

He helped me to discover how or why I could sometimes meditate or go to sleep and come back with information. He and I talked about how there was an encyclopedia (he called it universal records) of all knowledge that has been or will be known, all truth, and it is available to all of us. Kodaya encouraged me as I studied Hinduism, transcendentalism and existentialism, etc. So did my grandmother. I only saw her once or twice a year, but she sent me books by Emmett Fox, Brother Lawrence and Kahlil Gibran. The last I loved and memorized.

Mommo also sent a book called *As a Man Thinketh*.[89] With so much solitary study as a teenager, I mixed that book's concepts up with my over-responsible oldest child's attitude, the Presbyterian sense of predestination, and the Unity concepts that I interpreted as my soul being responsible for what happened to me and therefore creating my reality. I didn't sort that mix of BS (belief systems) and emotion out until I later met a Unity minister, Jack Boland, in my mid-thirties. I look back now and choose to see how those books and my early experiences developed my compassion and strengthened my commitment to help others.

12

Rebellion and Reemergence

By college I began to smoke, drink and protest against all authority. This included participating in civil rights and antiwar demonstrations. I was not the only person of my generation who did this of course. I spent two of my first four semesters at college on disciplinary probation for breaking rules that did not make sense to me, like being required to attend chapel and to dress in a skirt in order to eat in the dining hall. I would only abide by rules if the authority figures would reason with me and explain the "why" of them, and if I was convinced they were right. This quality had also caused disciplinary challenges with my parents when I was between the age of 13 and 18. I demanded to be treated as an equal and to be given choices. When I heard the explanation "because I said so" or "that is the rule because I am your parent," I would rebel against the arbitrary injustice of it.

I married young and had 3 daughters before I was 30 years old. Certainly becoming a parent at age 21 expanded me spiritually. I practiced what I read from thinkers like Kahlil Gilbran, Eric Fromn, Eric Butterworth, and Maria Montessori. Giving the children the respect and independence I wished that I had been given, I taught them to meditate and other things that I had learned from Mommo. This chapter is about my spiritual development that led to my work as a medium, so I am not writing much about my children who are now grown. However, I always considered parenting my most important role and my soul's primary spiritual task.

Dr. Lewis Avery was my most important spiritual teacher during this time. When I was in my twenties I was working as a teacher, and I had internalized the stress of my work and the challenges of a difficult marriage (we had different aspirations and behavioral style). Back pain led me to Doc Avery. He adjusted my back, and I became curious about what was so special about his healing energy. Finally I told him that I wanted to know what he knew, and he offered me a book called *The I Am Presence* by King.[90]

I stayed up most of the night reading it. My temples vibrated, and I sensed spirit presences in the room. I saw spheres of light begin to cross the room. I knelt down on my knees and was embraced by spiritual love. One sphere of light I recognized as my Turquoise Master from long ago. Another was pink, another deep blue. They lightly touched my forehead (third eye) with a blessing and then disappeared. I went to see Doc the next day, not with back pain but with the feeling I had come home.

During the five years I studied with him, he taught me to communicate without words. This was the first formal development of my psychic senses that I had received from a teacher. Until then it was just a natural gift. Doc scolded me when I told him that I had learned to manipulate the energy of traffic lights and change them to green so I didn't need to stop. He taught me the responsibility for my actions that comes with spiritual growth. He helped me to learn equanimity.

The verdict is still out when I think about him telling me that he would know I had attained some mastery when I could watch my parents be squashed by a Mack truck and remain equanimous. Intellectually I understood his point that the surviving spirit would be fine, but I thought it would be harmful to suppress emotional energy. He thought he had moved beyond emotional reactions. I began to learn how our beliefs and values influence our feelings. I learned to chant, create affirmations and use "I AM" decrees.

Once I had a serious fall from an extension ladder and responded by leaving my body but not coming back in feeling centered. Doc healed and supported me as I again would come and go from my body, much like I had as a child. Doc viewed the astral plane as dangerous and wanted me to go to the etheric, then to the mystic plane. I was OK with astral travel at night, but I did not have good control or conscious choice, it just happened. Sometimes after the fall I would just suddenly be up in the corner of the room watching others and myself. The "watcher" or witness could observe my body and mind (thoughts and feelings). Yet I could also observe myself observing. I was lucky to have Doc as a psychic teacher; a psychiatrist probably would have treated me for dissociation and delusions!

As I was experiencing unhappiness in marriage, I began to use the chants and decrees to dull the pain. I started to drink wine at night "in order to sleep." I was using spirits instead of Spirit. So I had a secret from Doc (drinking wine), and with time that taught me how God can always work with the truth, but we get as sick as our secrets. Our souls yearn to be known, yet I was trying to hide a part of myself from him.

Doc's group were vegetarians, they didn't smoke or drink, and in fact he and his wife chose to raise their energy to a higher consciousness rather than to have sex. I once suggested that idea, and my husband met with Doc and me to discuss it. My husband said that that when Doc got me as pure and spiritual as the Virgin Mary he would consider the idea!

I began to see that I wanted mastery and to ascend rather than to deal with life problems and embrace being fully human here on earth. I continued seeing Doc as my physician, but I began to seek other teachers and paths because I could see how I had created a detour instead of a path to love here on earth. I think that if my life path had been easier I would not have become such a spiritual seeker.

13

West Meets East

In the late 1970s we decided to move back to the land. Within two years I had "burnt out" trying to care for three children, develop and run a preschool, and build a passive solar house from the ground up. Always creative, I dealt with my adrenal exhaustion and the news that I had a cyst on my left ovary by going to the Combined Therapy Program at the Himalayan Institute in Honesdale, PA. When I arrived in the cold rain of November, Swami Rama himself happened to be by the door. He said, "Young woman, you have not been taking care of yourself," and then he told me about the next ten days as he escorted me to my room. I had a physical by one of the doctors and began a ten-day program of biofeedback, nutrition, meditation homeopathy, yogic breathing, hatha yoga, and cleansing. Daily meditation became the most important practice to developing my mediumship as an adult.

I was doing biofeedback and becoming very frustrated with the monitor when Swami Rama arrived, put the sensors on each of his fingers and proceeded to make each finger read a different temperature that I named! When I was in his auric field my health and capacity increased dramatically. Another day I was uncomfortable when he raised his voice at a young intern. He unobtrusively placed my fingers on his wrist (pulse), and I could sense that his physical state was perfectly calm. He later explained that whereas I could read the slightest nuance of expression from a person, that guy would only have ears to hear if someone sounded angry.

I began to learn how much our mind and body interact and how to have the freedom to act in the world while remaining centered. In the science-of-breath lab I learned that when I was concentrating on something like a math problem I would exhale and forget to inhale. This was a major part of the adrenal exhaustion. Learning to choose how I breathe is another foundation of my mediumship.

One day Swami Rama came over to the table where I was having lunch and suggested I take my tray to my room. He followed me there and said, "Young woman, your stomach does not have teeth. You talk instead of chew. Please sit and chew each bite 35 times so your body can make use of the nutrients." I began to make the connection between food and the well being, peacefulness I need to sense spirit.

At night Swami Rama would give lectures on the various branches of yoga. He would often stop and draw a comparative quote from the Bible for those of us who were students in the Western tradition. The links of commonality that he drew between traditions reminded me of Mommo talking about the many paths up the same spiritual mountain called life. He had a marvelous sense of humor, and I often thought that Jesus would have laughed and taught as he did.

At a later visit I asked him if he thought I should consider becoming an initiate. By the end of the conversation I knew that my soul had chosen to be born in the West this time, eating foods of the West, and I would take the Eastern concepts of meditation, holistic health and well-being and use them in my Western life. I now think that the fact that I asked him, rather than said I needed to become a student, was key to his responses. I told him that I observed that many initiates seemed to idealize him as I had done with my dad when I was a kid. He appeared to agree that many Western students were seeking the ideal family (I never directly asked him this; he had nodded which I interpreted as agreement).

I have studied yoga psychology for years, beginning with my time at the Himalayan Institute. Although my spiritual journey took other paths I admired Swami Rama, and I hope to study with his successor, Pandit Tigunait, Ph.D.

14

The Journey

I view 1982 to 1994 as my time to grow through workshops. I had left teaching. My children's needs had changed, and I accepted a position as interior designer. I also did some freelance architectural design. During this time I attended workshops instead of buying cars, clothes, or luxuries. There was a banquet of spiritual food in workshops that took the place of my time with TV, friends and neighbors, hobbies and vacations.

I attended Unity churches, Spiritualist churches, The School of Healing and Prophesy, several 12-step programs and hundreds of workshops and classes. As a medium I believe that spirit works with the gifts, strengths and experiences we have. It seems to me that spirit moves in close to me and uses my nervous system and impresses me with thought forms. Spirit can only work with the "program" that is there. (More to the point, I can only receive within the context of my highest vibrational consciousness).

I think that Charlie is gifted at "translating" from spirits of a different culture. I believe that is because he can understand many languages, and years ago he taught Latin and Greek. In my case I appear to attract discarnate spirits and spirits still on earth (you are as much a spirit now as you will ever be, as our friend John White says in Lily Dale), who want to connect more joyfully with their spiritual selves. This can be through discovering their soul's purpose, creating balance in life or exploring various spiritual traditions. I can help people who have challenges with self-esteem, emotional trauma, addictions or co-dependency. Why? I am an experiential encyclopedia of modalities, therapies and resources!

A partial list of resources that spirit can use includes the following: in the last 20 years I have studied Transcendental and Vipassana meditation, as well as other meditation forms. I have taken classes in nutrition, hatha yoga, tai chi, and various forms of breath work. I participated in programs using the

Twelve Steps[91] and *The Course in Miracles*.[92] These still guide my daily life. I studied with more than a dozen mediums and five Native American teachers. I became certified in mediumship, Reiki, spiritual healing and therapeutic touch. I took classes about the chakras, yoga psychology, kinesiology, dowsing, using music and crystals for healing, and electrical acupressure evaluation.

This "learning journey" began in 1982 when I met Jack Boland, the teacher who most influenced my life. Being with him was coming home. How I came to him is a story unto itself. On a snowy November night, two years after my first visit to the Himalayan Institute, I was troubled by a conflict at home. I jumped into my diesel-fueled car and headed toward town. A mile from home the hood flew up, and I discovered that in the heat of emotion I had not unplugged the heat lamp that kept the fuel from freezing! I stood in the slush and snow and pulled in the long cord.

Back in the car I completely surrendered. For the first time in my life I did not have a plan to solve a problem, and I just let go. I recognized that I could not think of a solution to the issue at home and that no human power could help me. Cold and wet I said "HELP" out loud. From the back seat I clearly heard the words, "Go to the mall and buy a book." I turned around, but no one was there. This was my first mediumistic experience of "direct voice" (although I did not know the term for it). I heard the same words a second time and wondered about my sanity! This time the distinct words were coming from the right of me.

I started to drive and wondered what book to buy, but no answer came. I arrived at the mall a few minutes before closing and intuitively chose one entrance over the others. As I entered, my friend Amy was walking toward me holding up a book, and she said, "Why haven't you told me about this book?" I asked, "What book?" She showed me the cover, said something about "God", I thought, and pointed to the store. I went there and picked up a copy, and convinced them to let me buy it even though they had closed their register. I think that the synchronicity was sent by God, but the author was Og, Og Mandino. The book was called *The Greatest Salesman on Earth*.[93]

I read the entire book that night. The next morning as I entered the local Unity church I heard a man ask, "Who would like to go to Warren, Michigan next weekend and hear Og Mandino?" Of course I answered that I would. Mandino was the featured presenter at The Church of Today, Jack Boland's church. For the next decade Jack was my teacher.

In 1985 I went for counseling with Jack for marital problems and to deal with the fact I was drinking wine "in order to go to sleep." He stood up and asked me to shake hands on the deal that "Never again on the face of this earth will I have wine or another alcoholic drink." Jack told me that Unity was a way of life but the Pavillon was where people should go when their life wasn't working.

The Pavillon of Gilles DesJardins, in Canada, had a 30-day program based on the Twelve Steps to a spiritual experience. Jack was the spiritual director, and many of his church staff spent a month there. In 1985 I and most of my family also went. Both Liliane and Gilles Desjardins have been essential to my psycho-spiritual growth. Their excellent program is still growing in North Carolina, and I encourage you to visit their Website *www.pavillon.org*.

15

Trance Channeling

In the summer of 1987 I had many spiritual experiences. One happened at a Course in Miracles week-long workshop at Unity on the Mountain in Hamilton, Ontario. Alan Cohen was the facilitator. While there I had an extraordinary healing experience. I sat on the healing bench as a healer named Paul put his hands on my shoulders. I became aware of energy, colors and breath that seemed to just flow through me. It flowed in, around and through my body in a large infinity-shaped pattern. It was as if I were being breathed rather than being the breather. Then energy began to flow through my spine and out the top of my head, and I was in a place/space that was only colors. It was much like when I was a young child leaving my body.

Looking back, how would I explain the state of being? Ecstasy? Love? Oneness? Awe? Joy or bliss? No words capture it. Then I was not aware of anything, There was neither oneness or nothingness, existence or non-existence. In my experience in that state there is not an observer, there was just being…yet I could just call it a pause of not being too! After two hours of sitting on a healing bench, I "came back" to consciousness. I was surprised so much time had passed, grateful that the healer just sat there beside me, somehow knowing not to interrupt me, yet knowing to not leave me by myself. For the next several months I had a light, joyful sense of being. I would sit down to meditate, and energy would move through me. It would have been impossible to not dance and twirl that summer! I now think that that this was a spontaneous kundalini-rising experience. Kudalini is the divine energy that flows through us and the universe. It is described as a coiled serpent that rises up through the energy centers (chakras) of the body.

In July I went to Cleveland, Ohio for a weekend workshop with Shirley MacLaine. Yes, I went out on a limb. I was interested in learning about how she, a Westerner, taught about the Eastern concept of chakras. I was very impressed by her use of humor, especially her good-natured reaction to all the jokes about her in the media at that time. I also learned a lot about having a unique style to one's presentation of self and how to lead large groups of people through visualizations. I believe that this chakra work, my kundalini experience, and possibly the energy of the Harmonic Convergence led to my trance channeling. It was believed at the time that the alignment of the stars and planets was unusual and would allow for a change of consciousness on Earth, a true "New Age". I do not know if that was magical thinking or real, but I did do my first and last trance channeling at that time.

A friend decided to have a celebration on the night of the Harmonic Convergence. Fifty people gathered at a retreat center in New York State. People had been invited to lead a Native American ceremony. I was pleased to go because I had a past-life recollection of being a Native American man, yet had never been to an actual Native American ceremony. The group was gathered, and the leader was more than a half-hour late (we later learned there were car problems). Virginia asked me to lead the group in a meditation or visualization while we waited. I remember being inspired to make a sign on the third eye (forehead) of each person and murmuring a blessing.... Then I became aware, conscious of myself more than an hour later.

I had had a complete "blackout". That term is usually used in connection with alcohol use, but I had not consumed any alcohol in more than two years, and I had never experienced a blackout when I did drink something. Nevertheless I did not recall any of the ceremony I led. Today I know that this was trance channeling, and the channel can move, talk and still be in trance. I was told that I had lined up the people from youngest to oldest. Then I led the entire group through a native dance. Although in a trance I danced and moved around the fire. I also had people (including myself) bow down to the directions (east, south, west and north) as I explained the strengths and symbolism of each direction as well as other spiritual meanings of the dance.

After more than an hour I became aware that I was a black raven flying around the fire about 6 feet in the air. At that moment of awareness I also knew that I wasn't a bird and came immediately back into my body. I felt disoriented and unsteady on my feet. Two friends came over and helped support me.

People started coming over and thanking me, asking to study native culture with me, and sharing what a meaningful experience it was for them. I looked at my friends and wondered what kind of thing had happened. I was horrified to know that I didn't know what anyone was talking about and to see how dark it was outside. I had missed the entire experience. When we talked about it after the group had left, I wondered if it was an aspect of myself from a past life or some spirit from another dimension that had led the ceremony. How would I ever know? I had no idea because I did not remember or learn anything!

It also violated my sense of personal responsibility. I believe that I should be discriminating and make conscious choices about my words and actions. I believe in individual responsibility for our words and mediumship so I made a decision never to do that again, and I haven't. If I could receive instructions so I could make a conscious choice to channel I would change me mind. As a result of this experience I sought out Native American teachers and ceremonies.

16

The Mystic Path to Mediumship

Throughout the 1980s I had used Louise Hay's book *You Can Heal Your Life*[94] and her metaphysical causes of illness and healing affirmations to heal each area of my life. I also used Shakti Gawain's[95] visualization processes to transform my life. Through the daily study of the Course in Miracles I had become tired of doing and wanted "to be". I had begun to pray for the concept of grace and knowing that my will and God's will were one.

Then in 1988 I became ill with viral encephalitis, and instead of learning through the path of the metaphysician I began to learn the path of the mystic. I did not know that this was a spiritual developmental stage at the time. I think that we humans are always search for meaning, and this is the explanation I gave for the experience after the fact. Now I view mysticism as living a life of prayer that results in intuitive knowledge and the experience of God consciousness. The mystic allows life to be exactly as it is and knows it is good, whereas the metaphysician creates life as she/he would envision it. Both are needed.

At the time all I knew is that my affirmations and denials no longer worked. Could my soul have chosen this, or was this the result of choices I had made? I was "receiving" (being cared for), and I may have wanted to be less busy, but I had not meant that I would not be able to work, drive or even have the capacity to feed myself! It was my first time of experiencing complete dependency on others. I credit my (then) husband with most of my recovery. After the crisis I was left with chronic fatigue syndrome, fibromyalgia, Hashimoto's disease (low thyroid), and chemical and food sensitivity.

As I temporarily lost cognitive ability I also reopened my psychic senses. While recovering, I spent the summer mostly in bed on our screened porch overlooking a valley. I spent a lot of time becoming one with the blue heron that flew over the valley. I could view the house and valley from a different perspective and be free of my physical limitations.

During this time I also experienced the return of my Turquoise Master and had the opportunity to learn from him again. There was also a female presence whom I sensed as nurturing. I did not see her like a person or apparition, I saw a tube of light that was pink. I smelled roses and had the feeling of being loved and cherished. The peace was exquisite. With both spirits I would ask questions and "know" answers in my thoughts. The spiritual experiences were healing, but the emotional, physical and financial aspects were very difficult.

I lost my job, yet I was spending a lot on doctors and complementary medicine. I went into therapy to uncover and heal hidden pain and to learn to accept grief and losses. As I encountered other-than-conscious fear, grief, and anger, I could see that these states weakened my compromised immune system. I wasted time and energy wondering, "How had this happened, or what had I done wrong?".

Whatever the reason for my illness, through it came the most important lesson that Jack Boland ever taught me, "What happens doesn't matter, it is how you handle it that matters." Instead of analyzing the past, the lessons were present moment ones: being humble and teachable, surrendering to trust and divine will (when I couldn't imagine this was the divine plan for my life). I also learned to move to acceptance even though this was not my picture of my life, and to give up that idea of "karma" and accept grace. I began to learn acceptance and loving life exactly on its terms. I watched Jack experience an inner joy, in spite of illness and discomfort with his bone cancer symptoms and chemotherapy. I modeled Jack and practiced inner joy. This was a seven-year mystic journey.

I knew that I was ill, and I was also having unusual psychic experiences and no one to discuss them with. I understood the power of a group for healing. I prayed that I could find like-minded people and healing nearby. (Jack's church was six hours away in Michigan, and I did not feel well enough to travel that far).

About this time I met a medium named John White at a get-together at the "Unity Church House" in Chautauqua, NY. I looked over at him and said, "You know something that I need to know". The only other time I had that feeling was years before with Dr. Avery. John said that he was a medium at Lily Dale, less than a half-hour away. I had never been to a medium. At that point I did not call the intuitive work I had done with my grandmother, or the trance channeling, mediumship. I booked an appointment with him, and that reading began my formal development as a medium.

I thought that John was really strange when he greeted me with the news that my deceased grandfather had been sitting there waiting for me since 2:00 AM. My appointment was for 2:00 PM. But he described Daddo and went on to talk about me doing mediumship with the flair of evangelist Kathryn Kuhlman. I did not know of her, but I soon signed up for one of his beginning mediumship classes and for a past life regression with him. Both were dynamic and healing.

At my first class I saw visual images of a monkey, a palm tree, coconuts, etc., and the person I gave this message to made sense of it according to the "psychic dictionary" that John was teaching us to develop. My next message came as a mental picture of an older man sitting on a front porch of a white house. He was smoking a pipe, and I recognized the smell as being the Sir Walter Raleigh brand. Once the person acknowledged who this was I heard (knew) thought words from him. The spirit was very talkative. This is an example of clairvoyance (seeing), clairsentience (sensing the smell) and then clairaudience (hearing).

After the exercise was over the spirit kept on talking (in my thoughts), and I finally raised my hand and told John that the spirit wouldn't shut up. It was an important lesson that he taught: it was my body and my spirit, so I had dominion and control. I told the spirit to stop talking and to leave, and he did. I now teach that important lesson in every mediumship class. In my opinion there are too many people willing to hand over their power to others. While formally learning mediumship it took me about five years to learn how to control the phenomenon. But I think I was slow in learning to take my power back in everyday life also!

After my class with John in 1988 I signed up for a Spiritual Insight Training weekend at The School of Healing and Prophesy in Lily Dale. I knew I needed to heal from illness, and I longed to spend time with kindred souls. In 1989 I took their second level class, then completed the two-year ministerial program.

An important point in "The School" was that we used techniques from neuro-linguistic-programming, NLP, to model each facilitator. We worked on the premise that if one person could do something, then each of us could if we adapted their process to ourselves. This involved listening for their beliefs and past experiences. We would also watch their physiology and see if they were accessing information using visual, auditory or kinesthetic senses. We watched the sequence of their process and replicated it.

After keeping my mouth closed most of my life about visions and intuitions, it was a "coming home" to go to these classes. For the first time since being with my grandmother, I could allow myself to be myself without fear of ridicule for my "second sight". They were also teaching me how to control the experiences.

For example, one day I sat with a young man and described his grandfather. The grandfather had been a farmer, and he wanted the man and his father to plant a particular crop that spring. Then I noticed the guy looking at my arm. I looked down, and I became conscious of rubbing my right forearm, which was covered with an awful-looking rash. The man was visibly upset and said that his grandfather's arm looked like that before he passed into spirit. I had been unaware of the rash or of the itching. (The rash faded completely within the hour.) While some other students were learning to access information kinesthetically, one of my instructors said I had a PhD in kinesthetics, and he began to help me gain control over the experiences.

One weekend I went to southern Pennsylvania to give a group of seven readings. I was exhausted and felt rather ill afterwards because of experiencing the pain that spirits felt before death. As I started to read for one woman I had an excruciating pain above my left ear, and the woman revealed that her fiancé had committed suicide with a gunshot to that spot. An hour later I read for another woman and brought through her mother who died of renal failure. I literally went to the floor on my knees with pain in my back. Later that day I had difficulty with breathing as I identified a father who died in a fire. This was the first year that I was accepting money for intuitive work, and I was ready to never do readings again.

The following weekend the instructors at the School helped me to sort it out and to develop other options for spirit communication. I said a firm "no" to any future kinesthetic pain. I tried their suggestions. I asked to see a visual picture, and that worked well for me especially if it was something that I would have noticed when they were living; like a limp, false teeth, needing a cane, or using an oxygen tank. I learned that I could also just 'know" what happened, or I could get a light sensation on some area of my body, and as I named it have it pass away. Now I can prepare for a strong personal boundary when I know I may be contacting spirits. Even so, I am still learning and can be still be unprepared and have physical reactions.

During that time my friend David called on the telephone and asked if I would pray with him. In prayer he asked that Spirit help me sense something about the whereabouts of his son's friend. I closed my eyes and felt severe pain in my head. David asked where the boy was, and I automatically became one with the boy and described the view. I knew I was on the banks of the bay between Cherry Street and Frontier Park, looking over at Presque Isle in Erie, PA. I could see the moon reflecting on the water at a 2:00 p.m. position. I was troubled because I couldn't sense how the boy was, only the head pain. David contacted the parents, and within an hour the police found the body based on the description.

Some mediums do work to locate missing people. I do not choose to do so anymore because I felt the boy's suffocating depression before his suicide, and my body had to recover from the physical reaction. I have asked Spirit to give me information that can serve to prevent tragedy and death. I do not what to know about situations that I cannot prevent or heal.

17

Angel Impressions

In the early 1990s I gave a reading in Massachusetts that I remember because of how honored I felt to be able to be of service. I was seeing a doctor who used traditional medicine and homeopathy, plus his staff offered acupuncture, nutrition and psycho-neuro-immunology. I went for a visualization session for myself, not expecting to offer someone a reading of course. But as soon as I sat down in the office I was receiving information from spirit for the psychologist. She did not look pregnant, but I was hearing about a baby.

I was the client paying for the hour, and it seemed a violation of boundaries to give a message, so I simply said, "I am psychic, and I am aware of a message for you. Please ask me after the session if you would like to receive it". That was brave of me because I usually do not volunteer information, or receive information, until the person requests it of me.

What was different this time was that I heard that Gabriel, *the angel*, was the source, and I felt compelled to offer the information. I had never thought much about angels. I knew that Dr. Avery called upon them. I thought that they might be a different species of beings after I read about them in a magazine in the 1970s. The article said the Soviet cosmonauts had seen angels. The angels had stayed around for several days, and scientists risked talking about it.

After the session the psychologist asked for her message. I delivered it, not mentioning the source (Gabriel) because that sounded pretentious. I told her that wise men from the east were making major decisions. It was presently November, but by Christmas a child would be born, and that next Valentine's Day was an important day for love to come into her life. She thanked me with tears in her eyes and said that she had miscarried recently. I told a friend about the message because I felt so honored by the experience of sensing an angel, but the message itself did not make any sense to me.

The psychologist called me the following March and told me that she and her husband had just brought a baby boy home. After the fall of Communism, they received from Eastern Europe, on Valentine's Day, a baby boy who had been born at Christmas. They had named him Gabriel without knowing the source of the message! This was *my* confirmation that the message was really from the angel. I was thrilled later to be invited to meet the child.

On August 19, 1991, (*my* birthday), I met Gabriel, the angel, "in person". This time I saw him as well as heard him. I lived in Pennsylvania, but I had gone to the healing temple in Lily Dale, NY, because I had not had success in healing severe back pain. I sat in the front row near the healing benches, but with the pain it took me so long to get up that other people would make their way to the healers before I could stand. I finally surrendered my desire and frustration.

Then, standing at the front on the right side of the temple was a large being. He was smiling, and I felt peaceful and without pain. We talked with thoughts as I had done with my Turquoise Master. I kept closing and rubbing my eyes to see whether he was real or would disappear. I looked around at others to determine if they saw him. I couldn't tell, but he was still there and laughing at me when I looked at him again. He said that his name was Gabriel. He was so big, I asked him how tall he was. He said that he was 8'6". I saw him as translucent, dressed in a long robe, glowing with a golden bronze light. I asked, "Are you real?" He laughed, winked and said yes.

Now I wish I had asked a lot more! Instead I was awestruck, peaceful and full of mirth like him. I did ask him about my back. He told me to go to a physical therapist. I was so surprised, I wanted him to just fix it! He obviously heard my reaction, and he laughed. Then he said I would be meeting her (a PT); it was all arranged. I sat in his presence for awhile and then slowly got up to leave. When I had walked to the back of the temple, I turned to see if he was still there. He laughed at me and raised his hand in what I interpreted as a blessing and a good-bye.

Because it was my birthday I was meeting others for lunch. A doctor from France and his partner were there. She spoke French and only a little English, but during lunch I learned that she was a physical therapist and used the Feldenkreis method. She came to my home for a four-day visit and worked with me. My back was healed and has remained so. I learned that my needs can be met by others if I let them know what I need. I don't require supernatural healing, though I still find it unusual that an angel would suggest a physical therapist! I have been asked questions about Gabriel. No, I did not notice wings, and I have not been honored with his presence in the past ten years.

18

Shamanic Lessons

In the early 1990s I went through the disintegration of my marriage and later a divorce. As I look back on it, it was a shamanic journey of embracing my shadow self and perhaps in some way a healing for the planet. I have come to think that there is a societal consciousness. We each take on a piece of healing the world when we embrace and release illness/dysfunction. Or when we let go of relationships, roles, jobs, or residences that are no longer filled with light and joy. As we heal, the planet is healed.

I still loved my husband, but our marriage had the same challenges, without resolution, for 24 years. I was not only bored with the lesson but also knew I required peace, not strife, at home. The stress was also very detrimental to my health. I had a holisitic doctor who finally said that he didn't see how to help me to recover. I continued to use the nutrients, thyroid medicine and homeopathy he suggested. In addition to psychotherapy, I took supplements such as black cohosh and Bach flower essences to help me to deal with the shadow parts of myself and others. I thought that this was important because when we heal, the planet is healed. Also, there are two sides to every human belief and feeling: for example, attraction-aversion, love-fear. (However it is possible to transcend duality).

With illness I was not able to work very often, so I had plenty of time. Jesse Stoff, MD, was my doctor. In his book *Chronic Fatigue, the Hidden Epidemic*,[96] he suggested that his patients find something creative that would allow them to be so submerged in the activity they would forget time (and health problems). I began creating collages of wood or art papers. Then I added feathers, shells, crystals, weaving and stitching to my art. Soon people were giving me animal parts: turtle shells, deer antlers, wings and feathers of road kill. That was disconcerting because I was a vegetarian at the time, but soon I saw the ceremonial art of Cynthia Gale of Earth Prayers Gallery and began to create my own.

In the fall my husband and I were at a healer's course with Roslyn Bruyere when we took a walk to discuss our marriage. In the morning class I had prayed for an answer about the viability of our marriage. As we walked under a tree beside Chautauqua Lake a black bird dropped a skeleton of a fish, and it landed at my feet. The flesh was gone; it was picked clean. Fish and water relate to the second chakra and relationships. It was a sign to me that we had given and received what we could, and there was no nurturance left. But I wasn't yet willing to let go.

In the spring we had been in counseling for months when I was going to take a trip to teach yoga psychology and give readings in the Washington, DC area. The day I left I prayed for guidance. I didn't want to end the marriage, but I knew that the conflict was taking its toll, so again I asked for a sign. I heard a thud and opened my eyes to see two robins lying on the deck. They had flown into the glass doors and were lying facing opposite directions. The female was dead.

By summer I finally filed for a divorce, and living in the same house was too difficult. I went to Lily Dale. Once there I was asked to lead the 8:30 a.m. meditation at the healing Temple. I hadn't slept well, and at 6:00 a.m. I meditated and rested against a tree by the lake. I had prayed, saying, "I don't even know what to pray for." I was doing what had to be done but felt so much grief. When I opened my eyes a swan was standing within six feet of me. Swans represent grace to me. I felt more peaceful, and I walked over to lead the meditation. At lunchtime I went back by the tree to eat a sandwich, and I discovered 24 white swan feathers where I had sat earlier. I cried as I experienced the grace. I picked up one for each of the 24 years married and said forgiveness prayers. I found a young tree and began to carve a feathered ceremonial stick. All summer I would woodburn, and each feather was a call for love to the situation and a prayer: to release, to forgive, for healing of us, others, the planet.

I spent the summer at Lily Dale. As I drove back home in the late summer I came over the crest of a hill at 55 mph and locked eyes with a huge buck standing in the center of the road. After hitting him, I got out of the car and sat about 12 feet from him until he passed. As I raised my head and opened my eyes I felt his large rack of antlers on my head, along with the buck's power and sense of territorial boundaries. I had never before felt such strength. In the past I had tried to avoid conflict, but now I perceived that my place was back at my house. Later that day I was sitting on the deck, and two dozen turkeys flew out of the tall grass twenty feet from me. They are the give-away bird and also represent thanksgiving and abundance. I knew that phase of my life was complete.

19

Travels with Charlie

Charlie and I first met at a Spiritualist church in 1995 and had some interesting experiences In Erie as described later by Charlie in Part Three. When I first traveled to Gettysburg with Charlie he offered to show me the battlefield. I had never been there or ever even read about the Civil War. I always thought it sounded gruesome, and all I knew was that it had torn families apart and so many men had died. I had had enough of war when I had heard news about Vietnam on television.

We set off for the battlefield the first morning, and although I had slept well the night before, I got very drowsy as we entered the military park. Charlie woke me up as he parked by Little Round Top. Walking up hill I told Charlie that I was aware of a spirit presence who wanted to talk and to write to "Sarah". I felt a male spirit close behind me. Charlie could feel heat with his hand a few inches behind my back, though it was in the shade. I was in a light trance and had some trouble remembering it all later, but Charlie observed carefully what was happening.

On the way up the hill I began to take on the feelings and thoughts of the spirit. It became difficult to walk due to pains in my left hip and right ankle. I was aware enough to know I should be capable of walking without a severe limp, but I could not. Looking over the trees and rocks from Little Round Top I could see the scene the way it was this July (1995) and how it had been in July of 1863. The trees were different, there were men in uniform, pools of blood, and more heat and noise instead of silence. It looked like both scenes or dimensions occupied the same space. The spirit began to talk to me about what they were fighting for and how honored he was to serve his country. I felt distress at the sights; then he let me look through his eyes, and I felt so proud of the men.

On a second rip to Little Round Top the spirit came again. We asked more questions. The spirit said that he had not died at Gettysburg; he just wanted to use my senses and visit it again. This time he talked to me about how his mother had a religious influence on him. He went on to describe other historic battles, especially those executed by Alexander the Great. I had the opportunity to truly walk in another person's shoes, and it changed my perception of the Civil War. I felt patriotic because the spirit radiated the power of true sacrifice for the principle of freedom. Charlie took detailed notes on all of this as I channeled the spirit's ideas.

We have been on Little Round Top several times since, but I never encountered (or was "possessed by") this spirit again. It was evident to Charlie that the spirit was Joshua Chamberlain the union officer. Charlie then called his friend Mark Nesbitt, author of several books including a series on *Ghosts of Gettysburg*. Coincidentally Mark was in the process of writing a book on Joshua Chamberlain. Mark said that Sarah, the name I heard the spirit talk about contacting, was the name of Chamberlain's mother and of his sister.

When Charlie told Mark about the pains in my left hip and right ankle, Mark replied, "She said that? She said that?" Those were the two places Chamberlain was injured in the battle of Gettysburg, a point not even mentioned in the film *Gettysburg* (which we saw later). There were several other points from my experience that matched Mark's knowledge of the history. For example, Chamberlain's mother had tried to get him to enter the seminary, and I had heard spirit talking about his mother's religious influence.

Charlie points out that a skeptic or debunker would suggest that I might have read or heard about these things long ago and forgotten them on a conscious level (cryptomnesia, hidden memory). Charlie thinks that this is possible though unlikely. What convinces him even more is my subjective experience (in which he has confidence because he knows I'm not a hoaxer) and the fact that he felt heat near my back.

Six years later, in 2001, something else happened to give us pause. Charlie received an e-mail from a woman who had seen Mark and Charlie on a television program about Gettysburg ghosts. Charlie has received many such e-mails and letters over the years because the program has aired dozens of times on national cable TV.

What was unusual about this contact was that the woman told Charlie that she had been on the battlefield recently (in the vicinity of Little Round Top) and felt that the spirit of Joshua Chamberlain was trying to "take her over" (possess her). It frightened her, and unlike me, she fought it off. This was the *only* time anyone had told Charlie about such an experience on the battlefield (that is, one involving possession or mediumship rather than just a ghost or apparition), except of course for me. What are the odds that both of these experiences would involve the same officer and the same place?

Certainly this woman had had no opportunity to hear about my case, which we had told only a few people. Subsequently, however, Charlie referred her to me, and I did talk to her about it on the telephone. She was relieved to discover that I had had a very similar experience, because she had been frightened, and my verification helped normalize it for her. She had also done some research and found that Chamberlain had revisited the battlefield many times during his later life.

Before meeting Charlie I never thought or cared much about ghosts. Now I joke that I've never seen a ghost but I've been one (Joshua Chamberlain). There are at least two other experiences in my travels with Charlie involving "ghosts" I should tell you about. Several times we have stopped at old inns in the hope (at least in Charlie's hope) that they will be haunted.

Once we stayed in a bed-and-breakfast in Gettysburg that is supposed to be haunted. Within a forty-five minute period the following things happened in our room. As we lay in bed, Charlie heard someone walking through our room, as if it were right through the bed. Since this is impossible, he checked to see if there was anybody in the attic above us (there was not). I had the mental feeling that there were spirits present having a conversation, although I could see no one. The lights dimmed and brightened again a few times. Then there was an electrical storm, and the air conditioner, which was running, gave off sparks.

I am not a ghost hunter, although I have been called in to perform as a psychic or medium in a few haunting-case investigations. Nevertheless, on one of our travels Charlie and I engaged the waiters in a conversation about the supposed haunting experiences people had had in an old inn in Virginia. They said, for example, that glasses had moved by themselves in their hanging rack over the bar.

As we sat waiting for our dinner, Charlie made the comment to me, "I don't think we'll be visited by anybody tonight." Just as he was completing these famous last words, I saw a wreath on the wall about ten feet from us lift straight out from the wall by about a foot, then fall. I saw it directly, and Charlie saw it out of the corner of his eye. Later he explained that this "out and down" motion is common in poltergeist and physical haunting effects. We both had a good laugh.

However, I also picked up mediumistically some other information in this case. When I visited the bathroom I had the impression of a surgeon. I asked him about this and heard that he had operated on people in the back half of the house where I was. My eyes were also drawn outside to a large old tree. He said men rested near there before and after the surgery. Later we questioned the staff, and they said it was a Civil War Hospital.

20

Mediumship in the Classroom

Charlie and I work together in much of his sociology course at Gettysburg College entitled "Science, Knowledge and the New Age". Part of this course is about scientific and institutional approaches to topics like spirit mediumship. We wondered if students would be willing to set aside their judgments and attempt the experiences of meditation, healing, and mediumship. We ask them to "check your belief systems on this invisible shelf by the door and pick them up again on the way out." This has truly been a rewarding experience. Our aim is to stimulate open thinking, but in fact some remarkable things have happened as well. Some students seem to be natural mediums; others are amazed when they get highly evidential intuitive messages.

I have discovered that the biggest skeptics are the people who are most impressed when I bring through an undeniable proof of spirit survival. For example this spring I was demonstrating message work while sitting in a circle with a dozen students. I became aware of an older gentleman in spirit who had been a highly respected and authoritative professional when living on earth. The student, who previously did not believe in communicating with spirits, agreed it was his grandfather after I described him and told the student that he was the namesake of his grandfather. Then I asked if he had any questions. He said, "Is there anyone else there?" I answered, "He says that he is with a teenage boy who was in your family." The student was startled. "Your grandfather says that he has been with your cousin every moment since he died of leukemia." I just "knew" the facts and said them. At that point I also saw an image of the grandfather with his arm around the cousin.

The cousin had in fact died of leukemia, and the student attributed special meaning to the comment about them being together every moment due to the fact that the cousin was buried on top of the grandfather. The following day the student called to say that he, his mother and his aunt were grateful to know that the cousin was well and with grandfather. This healing of grief is why I willingly continue this work.

There have been several other students who have shared their messages from class with other family members and have continued the conversation with us. One was amazed by the specific description of her deceased father's habit of visiting a certain club with an unusual name; this detail brought tears to her eyes and a feeling that he must be present.

I told another student once about seven sisters who used to sit together and quilt. He knew this must be his mother and aunts. I also picked up the name Lucinda (an uncommon one) that I was afraid to tell him, thinking it must be my imagination, only to find out later that it was the name of one of the sisters.

This past year we decided to offer our perspectives on mediumship to the Alumni College, a wonderful institution at Gettysburg College in which returning alumni can take two or three-hour mini-classes in a variety of subjects. We had not been burnt at the stake yet for daring to examine subjects like mediumship in regular classes at the college, but we began to wonder if we had bitten off more than we could chew as we watched some prominent older alumni and a high-ranking college official enter the classroom.

We were relieved to encounter an interested, enthusiastic response, partly due to the respectful atmosphere in the room no doubt. As it turned out I was able to bring a message to a prominent retired professor that seemed to mean a great deal to him. I described to his satisfaction his grandfather who had been so important to his academic upbringing, and his parents (who had been taken suddenly in a car accident at a fairly young age).

21

Public Demonstrations of Mediumship

I have found the "public" work, giving two or three-minute messages from the platform to be the least satisfying and most challenging aspect of mediumship. I think this is because I view my work as healing work, and the platform's intention is to prove the continuity of life beyond death, quickly, to as many people as possible. Few recipients feel free to respond in public beyond a yes/no answer to the message or to the spirit messenger. It also involves the medium's charisma and showmanship to hold the interest of the congregation in this day of quick sound bites and dazzling entertainment.

In our interviews we learned that some mediums contact the spirits and get the message ahead of time. Others receive and deliver the message during the time they are in front of the group. The three teachers that I have had from England say that they usually develop a contact with one or more spirits before they work. They usually identify the spirits and then describe them, asking the members of the congregation to claim them. However, it easily takes 15 to 30 minutes to do platform work in this fashion.

At Lily Dale it is an implicit norm that you come to at least two or three different members of the congregation in five or six minutes. Before the service I meditate or take a nap so that my mind is still enough to sense the presence of spirits. I get nervous with public speaking, let alone when I haven't a clue what I am going to say! So I have developed a system based on modeling some of the traditional Lily Dale mediums. When in Rome do as the Romans do.

One day in 1996 as I walked to the service, a medium told me that her guides find the people's relatives and line them up with the strongest communicator first. I decided on the spot that that was as good a system to model as any. I decided to ask Moses to go gather up the relatives. I figured that he had

had good experience leading people when he was in the desert with the Israel-ites. I then asked Joshua (Chamberlain) to line them up, or "get the troops in order" as it were.

That efficiently dealt with any doubts of mine that the spirit relatives would be there. Because I know that we are all one mind, I don't care if this is "real" or a figment of my imagination. Nor does it matter to me if it is the Moses of the Bible or the Joshua of the Gettysburg battle. I recognize they may have something better to do, or that "guides" are just a belief of Ameri-can Spiritualists. The only "guide(s)" I have ever clearly seen are my Tur-quoise Master and the angel Gabriel. I wish I could see a guide when I work.

At the public services I say a prayer asking for healing, love, truth, wisdom, understanding and joy of the highest while I wait to be called to serve. I also surround myself in light and ask loved ones in spirit, teachers, guides and angels to join with us. The process for me is that I am called upon, I walk to the front of the group, say hello, then ask a person if I can come to them. I do not know how I choose the person. It simply seems as if an item of their clothes or something about them attracts my attention. I know that some mediums say they see a light or other sign over the person. I just figure that there is a message for everyone or that that my other-than-conscious self directs my attention to the right person. Is it any wonder I question my capacity? It is strictly intuitive, not at all rational.

After the sitter has said yes to getting a message, I listen for and describe a spirit. Male, female? Young, old? Relationship? How did they die? Other facts or places that would identify them. If time does not seem too rushed I often state three facts, then ask, "Do you understand?" or "Do you know who this is"? There is only time for a yes or no. Then I ask the spirit for a message. In my mind, I ask the spirit, "What do you want to say?" and then I say it. If the spirit only wants to be recognized and say "I love you," I will often ask for a message using my psychic senses. Old-time spiritualists will instruct mediums to give "a greeting not a reading." However, I have found that many people do not have a strong need to communicate with spirit loved ones or friends, but they do have a strong desire for a message about their own lives, no mat-ter how brief it is. I view this as a change from the 1880s when our cottage was built and Spiritualism thrived. People had more contact with their extended families then, and many people had lost young children plus rela-tives/friends in the Civil War.

I am often surprised at how concisely Spirit packs information into several minutes. I have been the most comfortable when at our church message service I can talk with the spirit and each sitter for about five minutes. But unfortunately it is common to walk to the front and hear the chairperson ask you for "just three quick ones". For me that can create tension and is not conducive to the finest of seeing, hearing and sensing. I use my belief systems to cope with nervousness or self-consciousness. I view myself as simply the messenger, not the creator of the message. I am a tool, like a telephone, for the message to be transmitted through. I have certainly devoted time, money and practice to fine tuning the instrument. However the messages are for others; they are for service, love and healing between spirit and the receiver. They are rarely my business. In fact I think that I go into a slightly altered state not only to access the information but also so that I won't recall what is not my business.

Here are some examples of my public messages. Just the day before writing this I gave three messages, then as I started to leave the chairperson asked me to give one more. I noticed a man near the back left with a turquoise shirt on and asked if I could give him a message. I rationally thought that I called on him because I was wearing a new turquoise dress, and his similar-colored shirt caught my eye. I briefly closed my eyes and surprisingly recognized the spirit! It was Antonio, the grandfather of a man I had given a message to in a previous year. The sitter (person in the congregation) was too far away for me to see his features clearly, but I told the man I must know him because I had his grandfather Antonio with me. The spirit was as easy to identify as if I had been in the presence of an old acquaintance. Perhaps easier because he stepped in so close that he seemed to mind-meld with my nervous system, and I got goose bumps. The man said yes, I did know him, and Antonio was his grandfather. It is not common for me, but it is fun when I identify the person by knowing their spirit relatives!

At the end of another service this week the chairperson asked me to "Give just one more quick one." I noticed a woman on the end of a front row. In haste I said, "May I come to you, the woman on the edge?" The crowd burst into laughter, then I heard what I had said. I recovered enough to identify her grandmother who had been intuitive and spoke in churches. Grandmother said that she practiced "elocution" with marbles in her mouth. She gave me a song about "whenever I feel afraid I whistle a happy tune." She told the woman to just do whatever she was afraid of, fake it till she made it, and she would be right there with her. I walked away with the group laughing. That night the woman said that she herself got up and gave messages after her message. The encouragement was needed because it was only her second time doing public mediumship and the first time with so many people! I had not known that she was a student medium.

22

Private Readings

The best part of mediumship for me is private readings. I have the opportunity to establish rapport with another person, and to experience a dialogue between spirit people and others. I most often do this work on the telephone as in the first of the three examples below.

A woman whom I had never met called one day for a half-hour reading. Just as we were about to hang up, I was aware of "Aunt Ruth" in spirit. The woman said yes, her Aunt Ruth had died last year. I told her that Aunt Ruth wanted to tell her about a ruby ring that she wanted her to have. The spirit of Aunt Ruth also said that the woman's mother now had Aunt Ruth's chest of drawers on the second floor of her home. Aunt Ruth told her to pull out the drawers and look for a false back panel to the second drawer, behind which there would be a secret compartment containing the ruby ring.

I was delighted when the woman called back that night with a confirmation. She and her family had not even known that such a ring existed. She was delighted with the ring, her mother was thrilled to have evidence of her deceased sister Ruth, and I was pleased to receive a physical confirmation.

Shortly thereafter I gave a reading (in person) for a dear friend, and *her* Aunt Ruth (a different person) came through. My friend Sue and I remember how she kept interrupting us, but we can't recall her having anything significant to say. That serves to remind me that most readings are not zinger stories!

On another occasion I gave some readings in Massachusetts while visiting my daughter. As I talked with a young woman, I described a man in spirit, then said, "He says that you two have a "Sticky Wicket". She cried and said that sometimes when her dad came home from work, he would comment on the situation there by saying, "That sounds like a sticky wicket". Then they would go to the corner bar called the Sticky Wicket and talk about her mother who suffered from schizophrenia.

After the reading I learned that she also had unresolved issues with him. There was never a memorial service for her dad because of her mom's illness. I suggested we create one. The following day she brought together some friends. She talked about her dad and showed pictures of him from age one to the time of his death. When she saw how innocent he looked as a child, she cried and forgave him. We ended with a memorial prayer. The healing of grief and gaining closure are very important in my work, even more important than the evidentially of the message.

Here is another story about healing grief. I was invited to a home in Maryland to give psychic readings. These are usually fun events, and the people leave with a cassette tape instead of Tupperware. In general, my experience of these reading parties is that they are more about psychic messages than about mediumship. The following reading from that party is an exception.

At the beginning of a half-hour session with one woman, I was aware of "hearing" (suddenly singing two songs inside my head) "Take a Message to Michael" and "Michael, Row the Boat Ashore." When I asked (in my mind), "So what does that mean?" I saw in my mind's eye limp Raggedy Ann and Andy dolls, followed by 21 or 22 cupcakes (I couldn't tell exactly how many). I shared these impressions with the woman, along with the fact that a young man was very grateful for her help with his parents' grieving. He expressed his love for her and his wish that she would take her life off "hold", live her dreams and be happy.

The woman then shared with me that her brother, whose first and middle names were Andrew Michael, had been killed along with his girlfriend in a car accident by a drunk driver exactly one year ago to the day. Their death was on the night before his twenty-second birthday. The experience of hearing from her brother allowed her to let go of the mixed feelings she had about being happy and wanting to get married amidst the sorrow of her and her parents' loss. I was honored to witness and help deliver a gift of love and freedom that day.

23

A Client's Point of View

I have shared some of my stories. But I view my work as being about healing. I see it as a process of service. We haven't yet looked at the healing process from the view of the client. I have asked a client, who later became a dear friend of mine, to write about her process. These are the word of Lynda Terry who is now a meditation teacher. I would make only one comment. I met Lynda twelve years ago at the first psychic fair that I went to. I would not now mention such a deep issue as abuse in a first reading or at a public place. Spirit was able to heal despite my naivete. Spirit gave me a lot of healing work to do as a pastoral counselor between 1990 and 1994. In 1995 I decided to get a MSW at Temple University and be state licensed to work as a counselor. I wanted to be sure that I knew and could use what "professionals" would do. The following are Lynda's own words:

> I first met Penelope Emmons on August 11, 1990. I remember the date precisely because I always have looked on that meeting as a major turning point in my life. I had gone to a New Age fair in Erie, Pa. with my 19-year-old daughter, who had never had a reading and wanted to try it. My own experience with readings was limited—I'd been to Lily Dale a couple of times and to a woman in the Erie area twice. Neither of us had ever seen or heard of Penelope. I actually did not intend to get a reading that day, being more interested in buying books and jewelry. But when my daughter came to find me, all excited about her reading with Penelope, I impulsively decided, "Oh why not? It will be fun to see if she 'reads' that she just read my daughter before me!"
>
> When I sat down at Penelope's table after paying my money, I did not have any particular reaction, but within five minutes, I forgot all about whether she would make the mother-daughter connection. Within 10 minutes I was sobbing because of information about childhood sexual abuse that she had accessed, and which led to a healing realization for me. And by the time the short reading finished, I knew two things: one, that

my life was going to change dramatically because of what had been set in motion by our meeting, and two, that she and I would meet again, as we had some sort of spiritual work to do together.

I did not share these feelings with Penelope; I just took her card, thanked her, and walked away in a daze. Within a week of the reading, I took steps to change several aspects of my lifestyle based on information she had given me. These steps resulted in my physical health, which had been deteriorating for some months, to begin improving. Within three months of the reading, I located a meditation teacher and persuaded him to come to Erie to teach me to meditate. I had been wanting to learn meditation to help with my health, emotional difficulties and the effects of a high-stress lifestyle as single parent and corporate manager. In the reading, Penelope received guidance that I begin meditating as soon as possible, even though I had said nothing about my interest in the practice to her.

All during this three-month period, Penelope would come into my thoughts frequently. I would think about calling her, then decide, "no, it's too soon for another reading and besides, what would I say: 'hello, I don't know why I am calling except that I feel I'm supposed to know you?' Yeah, right!" Actually I did end up saying something like that to her. The fourth night of my five-day meditation course, I walked into the house where it was being held—and there she was! It turns out she was friends with the man who owned the house, who was a friend of mine—but none of us knew that the other knew the other, so to speak!

Not sure if she would remember me, I reintroduced myself as I sat down on the couch beside her, told her she'd been on my mind a lot since the reading and that I felt she and I were to do some sort of work together. She did not seem surprised, but just smiled, reached over and patted my hand. The next week I called her and set up an appointment to come see her—and we were launched on a journey that began as reader and client, quickly evolved into teacher and student, then friend and friend. Those initial readings/sessions gave me the resources, confidence and enthusiasm to go deeper in my own spiritual journey and life changes. I learned a great deal from both the wisdom she accessed through the readings and the life wisdom she shared with me from her own journeying. A bond developed between us that changed the dynamic of the relationship, and we began to spend time together as friends. We discovered that I had wisdom and experience that was of value to Penelope also. She was just starting out with doing readings "officially," when I met her, and found it difficult to view her gift and service as something to be promoted and marketed. Since my background was in marketing communications and public relations, and since I was an enthusiastic advocate of her skill as a medium/intuitive, I was happy to offer her suggestions for how to attract clients, etc. I also referred many friends, family and colleagues to her.

Over the years, Penelope's readings and guidance predicted and influenced many events and decisions in my life. Not that I always listened to or followed the information offered—my Leo personality has no trouble feeling free to ignore what doesn't feel right or what I'm not ready to hear/face! But so much of what she has offered has been remarkably on target and helpful that I greatly respect and value the guidance that she provides. I trust her, I trust her sources, I trust her motives and intent. From the very first reading she always made it clear that my free will controlled my choices, not her, and I've always acted from that basis.

Some of the things Penelope has told me don't seem to make sense or fit at the time she tells me them, but weeks, months, even years later, I will remember them or listen to one of the tapes of a reading again, and have that aha! moment of seeing that her words bore fruit. My first reading provided two good examples of this. One thing she told me was that she saw me changing. She said it was like I had put up walls around me, defenses to protect me, which had made me very brittle and hard, in a sense. She said, "what I see is like the brittle edges are being broken off, allowing you to become softer, lighter." This is exactly what began to happen over the first months after I began meditating. I became less angry, less impatient, more open and loving. In fact, one night, after about two months of daily meditation, my young son said to me, "Mom, you don't yell at us as much anymore—you're a lot nicer!" My family and friends will attest that this change has been a radical, real and permanent one—and that the way she described it fits quite accurately.

The other curious thing Penelope told me in that first reading was that she saw me with someone who she said looked like a wise old owl, and that once he came into my life I would feel more secure and freer, and she saw us living in a wonderful house. When I asked how soon this person would appear, she would only say soon. So when it didn't happen after a year or two, I decided it was one of those pieces of a reading that didn't quite fit or didn't apply. Yet, the man I met 6 years later and who became my husband does kind of look like a wise old owl—and we do live in a wonderful house—so who is to say what "soon" means?

Penelope figures prominently in the story of how I came to meet my "wise old owl" husband in another way as well. She predicted him coming into my life as the third of three relationships I would have, which happened; she described his appearance, age and professional background accurately; she predicted the month we would meet, and the month "it would be settled," which was the month we married. A year earlier she had urged me to take a full time job I was offered because "it would lead to something better and to me doing spiritual work with students, etc." It was by taking that job that I met the woman friend who introduced me to my husband, that I discovered the spiritual path I now follow, that I became a meditation teacher and do much of my meditation group work with college students.

Most recently, Penelope worked with me to get to the metaphysical roots of a physical condition that had developed, with the result that the condition spontaneously resolved itself the very next day. This situation is a good example of how it is with Penelope and me now. While we began as reader and client, the friendship now dominates our relationship so that the give and take and normal conversation between friends can lead spontaneously into readings. In this instance, we were at a Memorial Day weekend picnic in the country, talking on the front porch. The conversation got around to my physical problem and before either of us knew it, she was in reading mode and leading me through an intuitive imagery/regression exercise that led me to the realization that healed me.

When things like this happen, I am reminded of the truly amazing gifts she has been given and feel great gratitude and humility that she came into my life. But I also know her as a human being with frailties and contradictions like everyone else. Her gifts, however, also make her remarkably loving, generous, and empathic. In the early years of our friendship, I once asked her how she does what she does. "No one's ever asked me that before," she said in surprise. Not in a way that meant, how dare you ask, but in a tone that was more like "hmm—how DO I do this?" So she tried to explain it to me and in that conversation, I felt that I had been allowed to peek into a marvelous and mysterious world. Yes, I know—we all have the potential within us to be more intuitive, to tap into these capabilities. But some of us were sent to be way-showers for the rest, to light the fuse for others' transformations. That's how I see Penelope. She would be the first to tell you she is uncomfortable with that perception of her, but I would argue it's not such a big deal. I also see myself as someone sent to be a change catalyst for others, but the gifts I've been given and the way they manifest are unique to me. We both struggle with how to do our work in a culture and society that can be fearful, suspicious and resistant.

Penelope once told me about her trip to an Ayurvedic clinic for a consult about her meditation practice. Many doctors in the clinic wanted to have a look at her, it seemed. At the end, one of them sat down to explain to her what the situation was, but he started by saying, "do you know that you are a reishi (an Indian term meaning a gifted sage or spiritual teacher)?" As I remember her describing her reaction, it was twofold: one, she was relieved to have someone understand why she was the way she was—to "get" it; and two, she was horrified by the thought that people might think she was a guru of some sort. In all the years I've known Penelope, this ambivalence about her destiny and how she is perceived has been there. When she's working as a reader, she's fully alive and present, and there is no question that this is the work she was born to do. But part of the time, she just wants to feel and think and perceive like a "regular" person. Her experiences of what lies beyond the five senses most of us would pay a lot to share; yet she pays a price for her gifts that those of us who don't share them can't even begin to imagine.

Nearly everything wonderful about my life now, I can trace back to something Penelope led me to. She led me to some not so easy things too—but for the purpose of healing them, releasing them, moving on or going deeper. One of the most astounding experiences of my life took place when I went to Penelope to do some spiritual work about relationships. After a two-year period, the first in my life, of being happy with myself without a man, I began to feel I was ready to try a relationship again. When I told her this on the phone one day, she said she couldn't see anyone in my energy field for the foreseeable future, and that there appeared to be something blocking the possibility. I said "well then let's do the work to remove the block." When I went to work with her, she spent a great deal of time trying to get me to get out of my head and into pure feeling. Finally, she sat beside me on the couch, put one hand on my back and one on my chest, at the heart center area, and just waited. Within seconds, I felt this shifting in my chest like a logjam of ice breaking up, then a powerful sense of release and opening, then great emotion and tears as waves of love came forth in me. From that point, I had no trouble accessing the block and working with her to clear it away. Two months later, a wonderful man came into my life.

PART III
CHARLIE'S JOURNEY

24

"He Was Supposed to Study Spirit Mediums, Not Become One."

As a sociologist and anthropologist I am "allowed" to observe and analyze the experiences of spirit mediums. This is participant observation, an acceptable method in social science. However, many sociologists would say that I have overstepped my bounds by actually attempting to do mediumship myself. Somebody is bound to say, "He was supposed to study spirit mediums, not become one." Some anthropologists would say that I have "gone native."

There is a danger of "going native" in any participant observation study. However, I have deliberately become deeply involved in the process of mediumship so that I might best understand what is going on in "the mind of the medium." This is what is sometimes called "participatory science." It is a little bit like the mad scientist drinking the chemicals that turn him into Mr. Hyde or make him invisible. It is, to some scientists, going way too far.

After all, haven't I lost my objectivity? This is not the place for a lengthy debate on the "myth of objectivity" from a sociology of science perspective. The important point to make is that I feel that I have one foot in a rational skepticism, and the other foot in the phenomenon. There is no special reason why you should believe me. Any scientist, social or natural, has some set of perspectives (biases). But it is important for you to know where I got mine, and why I like them.

25

"It Can't Be; Therefore It Isn't."

The best cure for B.S. ("B.S." stands for Belief Systems; I learned that from Penelope) is curiosity. I have had a curiosity addiction for as long as I can remember. And my curiosity is the best guarantee that this book does not contain some convenient, comfortable fantasy. I want to *know* about spirit mediumship, not just believe in it. Just how much it is *possible* for us to know about it, socially and otherwise, is of course another question.

Although I did no mediumship of my own before 1993, the roots of my curiosity about the paranormal go way back. As virtually an only child until age 18, I spent a lot of my time in solitary thinking. An excellent student from about ninth grade, I cared a lot about learning but not much about grades (for example, I would have been valedictorian of my high school class if I had been paying attention enough to know that my health-class notebook was required, not optional).

On a typical Saturday I would spend hours at the Erie Public Library wandering all through the mostly nonfiction shelves like a kid in a candy store, reading bits of this and that, and come home with as many books as I could carry. A little knowledge was a dangerous thing, and based largely on a misreading of my idol Aldous Huxley, I turned my teenage rebellion into devout atheism. I found out many years later that Huxley was critical of traditional religion but very spiritual.

I remained secure in my materialistic, atheistic view of a scientific, cause-and-effect universe from eighth grade until my sophomore year at Gannon College (in Erie, Pennsylvania), when I took a course in psychology from Prof. John Fleming. The course contained a section on parapsychology (the study of psychic phenomena). As I saw it, there was no rational explanation for ESP and psychokinesis (PK, influencing things with the mind).

Dr. Fleming presented some fascinating and troubling accounts of research findings that conflicted with my perspective. My curiosity left me no real option. I couldn't accept the "normal science" attitude that psychic phenomena "can't happen, so they don't." I had to investigate.

The way I chose to investigate was to do my own PK study. I rolled three dice at a time for a total of over 200,000 trials the next summer, just for fun. (I told you I had a curiosity addiction.) I "tried" to get (thought about) a five on each upward face. The results were an excess of 1 1/2 to 2 percent more fives than there should have been by chance. This may not sound like a big deal, but the chances are billions to one against it for that many rolls.

Of course, I could have cheated, but I'm quite sure that I didn't. It's not like me, and I kept very careful records. Besides, this was to find out for myself, not to convince the rest of the world. What's the point of cheating at solitaire? Prof. Fleming pointed out that my dice could have been biased (they were regular drug-store dice, not perfectly balanced). Therefore, a psychology major, as part of his undergraduate thesis, took my dice and rolled them in a laboratory with a mechanical device and without my presence. The fives came out slightly *less* than chance this time, suggesting a slight bias *against* rather than *for* fives in the dice, if anything.

This was not a publishable finding because of a lack of adequate controls, but it certainly suggested something interesting to me. I have been hooked on such questions of the paranormal ever since. Also, I moved up from atheist to agnostic.

26

Synchronicities along the Path

It is odd, but for the longest time I never thought that I had any special psychic ability, although the dice experiment started me wondering at age 19 (and I have had other PK experiences with watches etc. beginning in my 30s, which we can skip). There were some other strange occurrences, however, that began even before that. Probably the first is the story of the number "420".

Beginning in high school I noticed that the number 420 was coming up frequently in my life. For example, our house number was 420, and so was my locker number at school, and the house number of one of my best friends. At the time I knew nothing of the concept of "synchronicity", which Carl G. Jung the famous psychologist used to refer to "meaningful coincidences."

Two things distinguish synchronicities from "mere coincidences." First, a synchronicity happens too often to be explained reasonably as "just a coincidence." Second, there may be some apparent reason for the occurrence, some symbolic message for example, that contains meaning or significance for the life of the person involved.

One problem with the concept of synchronicity in everyday life is that it is difficult or impossible to establish a probability framework within which to judge just how far beyond reasonable chance occurrence the events are. At least we know that there are 1000 different three-digit numbers, of which 420 is only one. But it would be a staggering job to record all of the three-digit numbers I was exposed to, and then see if 420 was overrepresented.

However, subjectively it really did seem that I was getting an extraordinarily high dose of 420s in high school, and then again at other times in my life over the next 40 years. And yes, these 420s have seemed to occur in meaningful contexts rather than just randomly, for example as check numbers when the item is very expensive, or house numbers of especially significant people in my life.

At age 24 (in 1966 or 1967) I was teaching Latin and Greek at Gannon College (my alma mater) when my old psychology professor, Dr. Fleming, invited J.B. Rhine, the founder of American parapsychology, to give a talk at a banquet. Dr. Rhine had seen the data from my dice experiment and found patterns typical of a classic PK effect.

Excited about meeting Dr. Rhine, I decided on my way to the banquet to ask him what he thought about my 420 phenomenon. When I arrived at the Professional Building in Erie, I looked for a sign to indicate where exactly the banquet was being held. The sign indicated that it was on the fourth floor...room 420.

Dr. Rhine said that the old numerologists would have tried to link it to my birthday. "When were you born?" he asked. I had never thought about it; November 20, 1942. Not a perfect fit, but enough to make me think. I was certainly not then, nor am I now a follower of numerology or astrology. But what do I know?

Over the years there were other fits of 420. I was very good friends with a group of students from the Philippines who lived at 420 Woodlawn in Bloomington, Indiana, one summer. I paid cash for a new car one time and noticed that the check number was 420. Penelope and I bought a very special, custom-made set of dishes from a potter, without knowing the precise cost. When the bill for all the pieces was totaled it came to exactly $420.00, 6% tax included. These are only a few of the more memorable ones.

Then I noticed that 420 rubbed off on a few other people. One day I was describing this puzzle to a college class. Afterwards a student came up and told me that she and her boyfriend had the same number. Every day at 4:20 p.m. they would look at their watches to see if they were doing something significant at that time.

My son Lee thought that the 420 story was interesting and noticed it happening to him. He told his high-school friends about it one day as they were driving out to see a friend on the outskirts of Gettysburg. They didn't know the house number, and when they arrived they discovered that it was 420. Lee named his amateur video-producing company "420 Productions" and chose the number as part of his car license plate, until it became too much of a joke. "420" has become popular in the youth culture because it is supposedly a police code number for a marijuana violation.

Jung was fascinated by Rhine's work with ESP and considered it a form of synchronicity, since it seemed like a beyond-chance occurrence with no apparent causal explanation. However, I did not see my 420 synchronicities as having any connection with psychic abilities of my own up through my 20s.

My next significant adventures with the paranormal came from observing ESP in someone else. This woman helped me try out an ESP test I was about to use in my class. Out of a few hundred record albums, with which she was only slightly familiar, I chose four by a random procedure, kept them in another room, and asked her to draw pictures of the covers. In a subsequent test I had her draw the pictures precognitively ("knowing beforehand"), before I even knew exactly how I was going to select them (by coin flip and dice throw).

In both cases, after drawing her pictures, then seeing the albums, she was able to tell which album covers were which (that is, to put them in ABCD order). And her drawings were uncanny. For example, for the Beatles "Abbey Road" she had four stick figures walking across the road, just as on the cover. For "The Frank Sinatra Story" she had a man's head with a hat on just like Frank's.

On another occasion she was able to guess what two-digit number I was thinking. For example, "23." Right. I asked her to try again. "71." Right. Again? "18." Right. I knew that the chances of getting three two-digit numbers in a row correct were one in a million (1/100 cubed). I was so stunned that I could not continue. I was almost frightened. Today I am surprised that I did not continue with more numbers. This was the first time we had tried this number game, and I think we did it only one other time, with mediocre results. She did give other amazing examples of her ESP at other times as well. Her ESP was not infallible; no one's is.

Of course this result was not obtained in a strict laboratory setting and would not convince a debunker who "knows" that there is no such thing as ESP. But this is the story of how I became open to the study of the "paranormal," and how it led to this study of mediumship.

27

Ghosts and UFOs: Daring to Study the Paranormal

In 1980 I went on sabbatical leave and conducted my first formal study of a paranormal topic, which resulted in the book *Chinese Ghosts and ESP: A Study of Paranormal Beliefs and Experiences*. Essentially it was a sociological, anthropological and parapsychological study that demonstrated that ghost experiences in Hong Kong and China were basically the same there as in the West. There was a chapter in that book that examined spirit mediumship and its connection to ancestor worship (see Chapter 9). Although it was a good sociological study, I still felt a little defensive about the parapsychological part, which is not OK for a sociologist to do. "Not OK" means not acceptable in normal science, and therefore not likely to attract any grant money.

For my next sabbatical (1987) I got more respectable and did a "normal" study of the political situation in Hong Kong leading up to the return of Hong Kong from the United Kingdom to the People's Republic of China in 1997. This resulted in the book *Hong Kong Prepares for 1997*.

However, by 1994 I was back into another supposedly paranormal topic: UFOs. But by this time I was much less defensive. I had come to see the whole problem of paranormal studies as a case for the sociology of science. In other words, such topics as ghosts and UFOs are not inherently "flakey," although they tend to be sensationalized in mass media. In fact they represent significant puzzles at the forefront of our knowledge, but since they do not fit into our "normal" explanations of the universe, anyone who investigates them openly is likely to be either ignored or condemned by the institution of mainstream science.

This is the main point of my 1997 book *At the Threshold: UFOs, Science and the New Age*: there is plenty of interesting evidence for the UFO phenomenon, enough to establish ufology as a worthwhile subject. The reasons for the scientific taboos against UFO research are social rather than scientifically logical. By now I was convinced that it was both interesting and important to investigate questions that violated rigid conceptions of the universe, from both a social and a natural science perspective.

28

Watch Out!:
Messages from Mom?

In 1993 something happened that revived my interest in spirit mediums that had been dormant since my study of Chinese ghosts and ancestor worship had led me to try to contact my aunt through a Chinese medium in 1980. My mother died. Of course the emotional impact of that loss might explain my interest in mediumship and have clouded any rational judgment I might have had about it. That's what I thought at first too.

The first indication that my mother might be communicating with me from the other side came a couple of months after her death. My father and I were looking at a book on roses that someone had donated to a public library in memory of Mom. As Dad and I sat there turning the pages together, I had the notion that Mom was up to my left looking down on the book with us. Try as it might, my rational mind could not find anything to base this impression upon. I felt that I knew, but I didn't know how I knew.

As we left the library, I wondered if I should tell Dad. He might think that I was foolish. I told him anyway. He didn't laugh at me. He took it seriously, although he hadn't had any feeling about her being there.

I don't remember the first time it happened, but shortly thereafter I began to hear Mom's voice, always in my left ear (internally, not like a voice outside of me). I thought at the time that I must be making it up, but when the sensation of an actual recognizable voice eventually faded away (I still get frequent impressions of her thoughts but very seldom the voice now), I found that I could not make it happen or "imagine it" that way.

Another reason the rational part of my mind has for possibly accepting this intuition is that many of the things that the voice told me turned out to be evidential (that is, provided me with verifiable information that I did not know). One of the earliest ones occurred when I asked my dad where the birthday candles were in his house. He thought that they might be in the kitchen cabinets but had no idea where exactly. In my mind I asked Mom where they were. I heard, "Not up there; down in the drawers." I looked toward a drawer on the left, but she said, "Not that one; the one in the middle." I opened up the drawer in the middle and found them.

Certainly one such example is not all that impressive, but it has happened many times, and still happens, with seemingly much better and quicker results than by chance. One time I entered a very large grocery store for the first time, looking for bottles of soft drinks. I was very tired and did not feel like exploring. I thought, "O.K., Mom, where's the Pepsi?" I immediately got a mental impression of direction and number of rows. I went straight to it and picked up the bottles. It made me smile.

This was just "practical magic" perhaps, but it also felt like one more confirmation of a link to Mom. I realize that a parapsychologist would say that it might be clairvoyance rather than a connection with the surviving consciousness of my mother. A debunker might call it a lucky guess on my part, and I would agree if I had not experienced a great many situations like this.

One very common occurrence was getting help ushering flying insects out of the house. Many times I asked Mom (in my mind) to get a bee or fly to go toward a window I had opened. It was fascinating to wonder if my great luck in getting them out quickly was really just luck.

Probably what started me doing this was the time I saw an ant wandering through my bedroom. It climbed on top of my alarm clock and lingered there in rather strange fashion. I got the notion to communicate mentally with the ant to get it to come to the right front of the clock. I was thinking, "Mom, can you get the ant to do that?" I was astonished when it did. After lingering there for a while, the ant left the clock and went a few feet away.

I decided to test the phenomenon again, asking Mom to bring the ant back to the exact same spot on the clock. I got a sense of awe when it did just that, for no apparent motivation. There was apparently nothing there to attract the ant. This seems quite bizarre, but actually there are societies, including China, in which insects are thought to contain or represent human spirits.[97]

I think my favorite "Mom" experience is one that happened to me while I was running through the old neighborhood around Dad's house, the "420" house in Erie where I stayed while on sabbatical leave in 1994–5. Over a period of one year I ran that route more than a hundred times. I regularly "tuned in" on Mom while running. That time I heard her voice in my left ear as usual, this time saying, "Watch out." About two seconds later a little girl on a tricycle unexpectedly made a u-turn right back toward me. I had enough time to get out of the way, but it made me smile.

For most people that would be enough of a synchronicity to be considered "evidential". However, I tend to be so skeptical that I need more evidence than that to show me that something remarkable is going on. I tend to get double synchronicities. About ten seconds later, after I had turned onto another street, I heard her voice again say, "Watch out." About two seconds later a teenage boy did the same type of u-turn maneuver back toward me. Again it was easy to get out of the way. I interpreted the whole thing as a clear signal to me that I was really getting a communication from spirit.

Thinking more about it, I realized that I was never in any real danger. Both bikes were going slow and came to a stop in plenty of time for me to get out of the way. There was clearly no connection between the two children. One had not seen the other apparently, and there was no intent to do anything either to annoy me or amuse me or whatever. They were really paying me no mind.

Nothing similar to these two identical u-turn maneuvers happened to me during that entire year outside that 10-second span, nor any other time in my recent life that I can recall. One incident of my seeming to hear the voice could have been my own precognitive clairvoyance (which is already far-fetched from a scientific point of view). But having two of them so close together adds the element of a very strange synchronicity, something that mere ESP cannot account for. If it was not a message from Mom, what was it?

Over a year later, when I was back living in Gettysburg but had come up to visit Dad, I went out for another run. By then I had been pretty well convinced that I was communicating with Mom, but my rational brain never lets go of its skepticism (for which I am grateful). This was at a time when I still heard realistic voices in my head rather than just thoughts. I asked Mom in my mind, "Do people survive as spirits after they die?" Think about what an absurd blend of intuition and reason that is, asking a spirit whether there is any such thing as spirits.

The answer came back, "No. We're all dead over here." Then I heard laughter in the background (I wasn't getting any mental pictures to go with it). As funny as this sounds to me now, I was not amused at the time. I could tell that it was not my mother's voice. Then I realized that it was my Aunt Mary's voice, which was quite a surprise, because I had seldom if ever heard her "spirit" voice before. Aunt Mary is one of my mother's twelve brothers and sisters, all of whom predeceased her. Aunt Mary was a real joker, and it sounded just like something she might say.

A bit annoyed, I said, "I want to talk to my mom." Aunt Mary replied, "She's in the other room, playing the harp." More laughter, which I interpreted as coming from other members of the Noyes clan (my mother's maiden name). A bit later my mother did make an appearance, and we had a discussion about mediumship etc. It felt real on an intuitive level.

When I thought about this exchange rationally later on, I wondered at the complexity of it all. Could and would I have made up such a thing in my head? It was certainly unexpected and apparently unmotivated. However, I could not discount the possibility that it was an elaborate dialogue between my rational and intuitive minds to dramatize the issue of survival of the spirit.

I should mention that I did have one other lesser set of spirit communications in those days. The deceased father of a friend apparently appeared to me in a vision once when I was in bed. In the dark, both with eyes open and eyes closed, I saw his head in reverse black-and-white, like a photographic negative, coming steadily closer to me for a few seconds.

Since I had never met the man or even seen his picture before, I asked his living daughter to show me a picture of him later on. When she did, I was disappointed; it seemed not to be him. However, then I saw another photo from a different time in his life, and I recognized him by his hair and facial features. Later, on at least two occasions, he seemed to be giving me evidential messages about road conditions when I was driving, things that occurred a few minutes afterwards.

29

"Yearbook Pictures:"
The Psychic Fair

Now I should tell you about my first significant connections with Spiritualists. It was my sister Celeste who first introduced me to Lily Dale when she was teaching voice at nearby Fredonia State University. This was before our mother died. But after Mom died, it was her death and my spirit messages from her, beginning in 1993, that really got me interested.

Due to my book *Chinese Ghosts and ESP*, radio stations have often invited me on talk shows, especially at Halloween. I also appear on two televised videos about *Ghosts of Gettysburg* and on a "Sightings" TV show about the same subject along with my friend Mark Nesbitt, author of the *Ghosts of Gettysburg* books. Around Halloween in 1994, I was asked to be on a local talk radio show in Erie.

A week or so prior to the broadcast, the host told me that she wondered if a friend of hers was trying to contact her from the other side. She never revealed what exactly gave her the idea that he was, but she told me this. One day when she arrived home she started thinking about him and about some yearbook pictures they had been dealing with. It was odd, because she hadn't thought about him for a long time. When she got inside the house and looked at the newspaper, there he was in the obituaries. He had been killed in a car accident.

"Well," I said, "I see they're having a psychic fair at the Spiritualist church this Saturday. Why don't you go get a reading there and see if you can contact him that way?" She totally rejected the idea and informed me that she was a Catholic, and that it would be a mortal sin to contact a spirit medium. I thought that was a bit extreme, but I didn't want to tell her how to interpret her religion.

I had wanted to go to the psychic fair myself, based on an ad in the paper. It was great fun, and I got a reading from Kitty Osborne, who ended up being one of my teachers in mediumship classes after I was inspired to join the church based on the fair.

Kitty's reading was excellent. It all seemed to apply very well to me, except for the very last thing she said. "I'm seeing something about a young man who died in a car accident, and it has something to do with yearbook pictures."

I said, "That doesn't seem to fit for me, but I think I know who it's for." I was stunned, but I was so wrapped up in getting a reading for myself that I didn't think to ask her for more information about this tag-on message. I wanted to kick myself later.

When I got home, as soon as I walked in I got the notion that the man's name was Bill (pseudonym for another common name) Ebersome. I looked though the Erie phone directory and found no listings with the name Ebersome. Then I called the talk show host and told her about the message at the fair: young man in a car accident, yearbook pictures. Her reaction was, "You're making this up, right?" I can't say that I blamed her. It sounded too good to be true. What medium is going to guess something like that? It was much more to the point than, "You're about to take a trip." I don't think I have ever heard a spirit message about yearbook pictures before or since.

In spite of her negative reaction, I asked her sheepishly if his name was Bill Ebersome. "Ebersome?", she said, "Where did you get that?" I was wrong. "O.K., but what's his first name?", I asked. "Bill," she replied.

That perked me up. At least I had gotten his first name right, which is a start, even though it was a common name. Then I wondered if I had heard "Ebersome" wrongly; maybe he was saying that he loved her "ever so much" or something.

That was in the fall of 1994. It was the beginning of my interest in getting messages for other people instead of just for myself. I took several mediumship classes and gave messages and longer readings for people in Spiritualist churches, especially the First Spiritualist Church of Erie. One thing I noticed was that messages for myself came mostly in auditory fashion (clairaudience), the voice of my mother in my mind, which faded over the years into thoughts mostly without sound. But when I received messages from other people, they were mostly mental pictures (clairvoyance), although I felt that my mother was acting as my spirit guide, feeding me the information when I asked her for help.

30

Yesterdays: Meeting Penelope

Before long I met Penelope at my church, once when I was the speaker, and once when she was. A mutual friend of ours told me that she needed to introduce me to her (for some reason she could not identify). All three of us had gone to McDowell High School, but Penelope was four years younger than I, and we were not there at the same time.

A few weeks after our second meeting I was driving along 18th Street in Erie when I heard an advertisement for a place called "Yesterdays", where you could dance to oldies. I said to myself, that sounds like fun. Then I noticed that I was driving right by the place as the commercial played on the radio. How funny. Erie is the third largest city in Pennsylvania, population about 200,000. Not a tiny place. An interesting coincidence.

The next day, on some apparently unmotivated whim, I called Penelope just to say hi. She had given me her card and had asked me to give her a call some time. When I did, she seemed to need somebody to talk to, and I offered to drive over. "O.K."

At Penelope's house we had quite a chat. I could see that she was a bit upset, so I suggested that we go somewhere to take her mind off things. Then I told her that "yesterday" I had been driving past "Yesterdays" when I heard their ad on the radio. Would she like to go there? As it turned out, she had been there with two women friends and had wanted to go back. She had even asked one of her male friends if he would like to go there to dance, and he had declined. From her perspective, I had been sent from the universe, not only as somebody to talk to (which she had asked for just before I called), but also as a dance partner.

Of course we ended up married a little over two years later. But there is one more "Yesterdays" story. On a later trip to Yesterdays to dance, Penelope asked in her mind for a sign from the universe as to whether she should be going out with me. Very soon a man dressed in biker gear paid the waiter to bring us drinks ("whatever they're drinking," which turned out to be colas) as a tribute to "true love." I scratched my head in wonderment over a biker buying us drinks, and Penelope figured that she had her sign.

31

In Search of the Medium's Mind: Confirmations

Although I was still finishing up my book about UFO researchers (*At the Threshold: UFOs, Science and the New Age*), I had decided by 1995 that I wanted to do a sociological study of spirit mediums. Penelope and I spent a little time in Lily Dale that summer and got to work in earnest in the summer of 1996. Now I want to recap some of my experiences in doing that research in chronological order.

It seems as if I were being guided by a kind of cosmic lesson plan. The social scientist in me realizes that that sounds a bit flakey, but I can document it. 1996 seems to have been the year of the confirmation. Remember that I was not just a sociologist observing as an outsider. I was also (and still am) a student medium, partly for its own sake and partly to get a better understanding of "the mind of the medium" as a participatory scientist.

I needed to discover if I could really act in the role of a medium, and to discover what that felt like. And in fact I got confirmations galore in 1996 when I needed them, more dramatically than in later years when I was supposedly more experienced. From my participant observation notes I see that I received 10 *significant* confirmations from 40 message services in summer 1996 (in which I delivered a total of about 80 messages). In summer 1997 I received 10 from 46 services (a total of about 92 messages). In 1998 it was 4 from 29 (about 58 messages).

To clarify these data a little, let me point out that in most public message services the mediums get very minimal feedback, usually only a few head nods or very brief comments. About half the time it is difficult to tell if the person receiving the message has gotten anything out of it to speak of. Often the feedback is negative, such as "No, I can't think of a Delores in spirit." It is important to say that I certainly don't think that even the best mediums appear to be anything close to perfect.

On some occasions the congregation (audience) member makes a public declaration in the service like, "You're right on," but this is not likely to happen more than once or twice in a one-hour session. Many or most of the "significant" confirmations happen when someone approaches the medium right after the service or even another day to say how meaningful and/or evidential the message was.

Among my 10 significant confirmations in 1996, 6 were given right in the service itself, but 2 of these gave me additional supportive information after the service as well. With our methodology it is impossible to tell how many other "very good messages" went unrecognized or unreported, either our messages or those of other mediums. The same goes for unreported "stinkers" (apparently poor messages).

I am making no comparisons among mediums in terms of how accurate they appear to be, or in terms of how many confirmations they get. Also, by one interpretation, "There are no wrong messages, only wrong interpretations." On the other extreme a debunker would doubt even the confirmations, saying that many of them are probably "force-fit" by the sitters who want to believe. I will say that I have noticed that Penelope not only gets a great many confirmations later on, but she also inspires a lot of visible positive response in most of the people right as they get her messages.

Remember that the purpose of this book is to see things from the mediums' perspective rather than to focus on testing them. From my perspective as a student medium, the following examples from my confirmations in 1996 went beyond a few nods of the head; they were "significant" in leading me to believe that I might actually be doing mediumship and in getting me to understand what it felt like.

The first one that really intrigued me was a message I gave at the Stump ("Inspiration Stump" in Leolyn Woods at Lily Dale) on June 22, 1996. I told a young woman that I saw her (had a mental image of her) inside a house with boarded-up windows, and that that was not so good, because it's hard to see out of a house with no windows. I said that I thought it symbolized some sticky situation that she should get away from, that was keeping her from seeing or experiencing things. I can't tell from my notes whether my interpretation was actually part of the message. By my standards now I think that I would have left out the interpretation, feeling that it was not really part of the message.

I can still remember the woman looking at me expressionless as I gave her the message. Sometimes my rational mind wonders how I get the courage to stand up and say such absurdities. The only answer is that I try to keep a good intent. "I am not trying to be a fraud. I want to be helpful and interesting. I trust that it will happen the way it is supposed to. And I'm curious about this, so I try it." But there is still a little voice in the back of my mind saying, "You're a fool, Charles Emmons."

Later on the woman came up to me and told me that she was about to house-sit a place in the Caribbean. The owners told her to board up the windows of the house as a protection against hurricanes. However, she was concerned that she would not be able to see anything. Now I call that a "significant" confirmation, for something a lot more specific than "I see travel in your future." I thought to myself, "How did you do that?" I really had no clue, nor had I expected to be so right. I felt like a bystander in the process.

Two days later I gave a woman a message in the Assembly Hall at what we call the "indoor Stump", when bad weather threatens. I said that I had "a concern about a man" and that it was not for me to know or say. I went on with something about a stream in the country and sitting under a shade tree, watching water going over the stones etc., deciding what she really wanted. I also said that her ways of approaching the matter so far were not appropriate, but that she would discover new ones.

Again I had no idea if this woman was getting anything out of what I was saying. After the service, however, she told me that I was right on (although she didn't explain how exactly). She had had a couple of private readings, but they had not gotten to the concern that she had come with. I had hit it, she said. What was significant about this confirmation was that I had apparently said something that had resonated with her needs. Many mediums would say that that was much more important than the specifics of my message. Nor did it matter that I had little idea what I was talking about.

Five days later, June 29, I got an even more important example of the same lesson. This time I was at the Forest Temple outdoor service. There was time for just one more message, and I was called on to give it. I felt that I had a message for a real no-nonsense looking guy wearing a tank top and sitting in the front row. I thought to myself, "Do I really want to give this?"

I began by saying to the congregation, "As a student medium one of the things I have to learn is to give what I have and not edit so much." Then I looked at the man and asked, "Did you know that you have a guardian angel?" I had never been inspired to give anything supposedly from an angel of any kind before, and maybe not since. He said, "No," in an interested voice.

"Well," I said, "There's a guy here who claims to be your guardian angel. And he says that you have forgotten something or left something behind." As this was going on I was getting a mental picture of some kind of round object off to the side, but I had no idea what it was, so I didn't mention it.

After a brief pause, the woman sitting beside this man clapped her hand over her open mouth in an expression of shock. Meanwhile he still looked puzzled. I said, "Maybe *she* knows what it is."

He cast a quick glance at her, then got a dawning of recognition on his face and exclaimed, "Oh!" I quickly added, "He says it's not as bad as you might think."

I was really curious what this was all about. Walking away after the service, the fellow explained that he had used to wear a medallion formerly worn by his deceased father. One day the chain had broken, and he had put it in a drawer, intending to get it fixed sometime.

He wanted to get in touch with his father in the spirit world. His mother had also died, and he really wanted to know if they were all right. He had intended to bring the medallion to Lily Dale, thinking that it might help him connect with his father, but he had forgotten and hadn't noticed its absence until my message.

Once in Lily Dale he was amazed how people, including the woman he had come with, were getting messages. But he hadn't gotten one yet. Now he had to go back to Rochester (interestingly the chairperson of the service was Judith Rochester), and this was the last message service he had time to attend. In his last service, he got the very last message given.

It is no exaggeration to say that he was very impressed and very pleased. He wanted proof of his parents' survival, and to him the statement, "You forgot something…left something behind," was enough to tell him that the spirit world was aware of his intent to bring the medallion. And saying that "It's not as bad as you might think" meant that it was O.K; they got the message anyway.

If the purpose of mediumship is healing, this was a successful message. And I had no idea what I was talking about. Maybe if I had been a better medium, I could have recognized the round object as a medallion. I don't think that a parapsychologist or a debunker would be very impressed with this case as proof of anything, but the man without the medallion was excited. And the student medium felt useful.

A little over an hour later I was giving messages at the stump. I didn't get any "significant" confirmations this time, although one woman did a lot of nodding of her head as if she knew what I was talking about. As I went back to sit down, the woman chairing the meeting gave a disclaimer about how student mediums need support because they're just learning. However, it's odd to give this *after* student mediums give their messages. The last thing she said was, "It's very difficult. That's all I'll say." My fragile ego took that to mean that she would refrain from saying how poorly I had done. This is a good illustration of how easy it is to doubt one's own mediumship. No matter how well you may have done an hour earlier, who knows if you'll ever be able to do this slippery thing again?

Just as I was sitting on the front porch of the cottage we were renting, writing down my notes from this last session and stewing about what the chairperson had said, three women walked by with a little girl who said "Hi." Then her mother saw me and said, "We saw you at the Inspirational Stump…You were very good." "Thanks, It was fun," I replied. Then the girl said, "I remember. You (gave a message to) the little girl." Nice social support, right when I needed it.

32

Something's Really Happening Here

Two weeks later (July 13, 1996, at the Forest Temple) I received the message that had a bigger impact on me than any other (not counting two messages I never actually gave on August 22, 1996, to be explained later). This is a good example of the problem of picking the right person for the message.

It is also another case of my getting a message ahead of time, although I think that some details were added in the process of delivering it. I had a picture in my mind of what the woman receiving the message should look like. And when I got there I picked out the most likely looking young woman with light hair. However, somebody gave her a different message before I had my turn. Since ideally you should not give one person more than one message per service, I then wondered what I should do. But then another woman came in after that who looked even more like my mental picture of the correct recipient. One lesson for me in this incident, then, was to trust that "spirit" will guide you to the right action if you have the right intent. I realize that that requires a leap of faith; I don't do faith very well.

When I was called up front, I said to her, "I have a friend of yours from high school here. He died in an accident." She started crying already, which shook me up. I was concerned about my responsibility; good grief, what if this is all baloney?

"It happened between one and two years after graduation," I went on. Right again. As it turned out, everything I said seemed to be right.

"He says that he was in the band, but you weren't." Right. "But you were somehow connected with the band, and you traveled together, in a bus or something." Yes.

"He doesn't want to interfere, but he misses the reunions etc. Guys would never admit they loved somebody, but he liked you a lot." Lots more crying at this point.

Then I got something about a little 6-year-old girl. I had the impression, although I didn't know how, that this part of the message was not from him. I felt that it was piggy-backing on the other message. The woman could not place who the little girl was.

I was stunned and intrigued by all this. After the service I sought her out to tell her two more details that I had left out. First, I said, "He didn't know you as well in the last couple of years as he did earlier." "That's right," she replied, "I moved away."

Also, "I saw a blue or green emblem or something. Were those your school colors?" No, she said. Black and gold were. But blue and green were the colors of the band uniforms. That threw me. Why did the band have different colors from the school colors? Although it had not been part of the message, I had just assumed that this would be the high school band.

As I came to find out, the band was a rock band, not the school band. Everything in the actual message was correct. She traveled with the band in a little bus they had (not a school bus).

One more thing, she said, "I think I know who the little girl was. I babysat a little girl a lot. When the family moved out west she died of carbon monoxide poisoning (at about age 6)." She cried again.

That was the last day I gave messages before returning to Gettysburg, but we were back in Lily Dale on August 19, 1996. I received significant confirmations the first two days back. One of them on August 20 was interesting. I was tempted to edit out what I was getting because the very last message from another medium was about pipes. I gave it anyway, asking a woman if she knew that she had leaky pipes in the basement, parallel to the floor. The reply was yes, some furnace pipes were leaking, and they had left home so that they could be worked on while they were gone.

That happened in the auditorium, where the Forest Temple service had been moved due to threatening weather, but an hour later the Stump service was held outside. At the Stump I began to give a message to one man totally cold, without any previous impressions. I said something about "coming activities" and got a murky view of an image that meant "uncle". Not very good. I told the congregation that this is what happens; you don't know if you will get anything.

Then I asked (mentally) why. To my surprise I saw a very clear small green light with my eyes open. I wondered if it could be some kind of after-image on my retina, but when I closed my eyes it disappeared, and it reappeared when I opened them again. It seemed to be out there in the distance. It looked real, and there didn't seem to be any possible way for a green light to be over there, up fairly high in the trees. Then the light disappeared.

I asked the man if he knew of any upcoming activities in which he was an important planner. He said yes; he had a business. I asked again (mentally) for information, and I saw the green light again, as if it were out there in the middle of the Leolyn Woods. I told the man that it was a go-ahead and that his uncle (in spirit) was giving him encouragement. This experience doesn't qualify as a confirmation (by my standards), but it was very significant to me, because I rarely see things externally, just internally in my mind's eye when doing mediumship.

It is uncommon for mediums to get significant *disconfirmations*, partly because of general social norms against being unsupportive, and partly because people think that the message might turn out to make sense later on. However, on August 21 I received a friendly but strongly negative response to a message I gave at the Stump. I told a woman that I saw a collie dog in the middle of a big grain field. It was someplace in the Midwest, maybe Wisconsin. It was a very clear image with a very nostalgic pull. In spite of my enthusiasm, the woman said that she had never had *any* kind of a dog, and that she had never even traveled to that part of the country.

The next morning in the small meditation group at the Healing Temple, there was the same woman sitting two seats away from me. After the meditation I asked her if she had thought of any relevant meaning my message might have. It is very unusual for me to press a point like this, but I had been so certain that I was getting something very real and emotional. In fact I had gotten that message before arriving at the Stump and had even been drawn to go into the Pet Cemetery first. I had had the notion that I was communicating with the spirit of a dog. And I didn't think that I was picking up on some future dog. It felt as if it were a past event.

Well, the woman said no; she thought that it was a total miss. We stopped talking about it, and we walked out the door of the temple together. At the end of the walk, a man who had been in the meditation group, two seats more beyond her in the circle, came back toward us from down the road. He had left the building before I asked the woman about the message, and now he was returning.

The man said to us, "I've been told that when there's a synchronicity or coincidence, you're not supposed to ignore them. You gave her a message at the 5:30 stump about a collie dog. My wife was sitting behind her, and she wondered if it (the message) was for her. We had a collie who ran in the field on a 70-acre farm in upper Ohio. She was wondering if she should speak up...(wondering) if you were getting it through her."

Speaking of synchronicities, it struck me that the three of us were all at the meditation, among about 10 people, when there had been perhaps 100 at the Stump, and a few hundred altogether visiting Lily Dale. Of course the message was not all that remarkable, and I said "Midwest, maybe Wisconsin" when it was upper Ohio. However, it sounds as if it might be an example of what parapsychologists call "displacement", getting an ESP message that is not quite focused on the right person or object.

I should think that displacement happens not infrequently when there are so many people packed into the seats at a public message service. What adds to the interest in this particular case is that Penelope was at the Stump that day, and when she saw me get a disconfirmation, she told me right when I returned to my seat that she thought I had delivered the message to the wrong person.

Not only that, but in the Forest Temple service an hour earlier I had given a message to someone who wasn't paying attention as it turned out. Someone else behind her was nodding her head thinking that I was talking to her. Afterwards the other woman and a friend sitting with her came up to me and insisted that my message about "hanging in there" was really theirs. I wondered if I had received a lesson in displacement, not once but twice in the same day.

August 22, the same day that I went to the morning meditation and found out about the possible displacement of my dog message, was the last day I did mediumship in Lily Dale in 1996. At the 1:00 p.m. Stump the very same day, I had my single most significant experience telling me that something "real" is at the core of spirit mediumship, even though it did not solve the mystery of exactly what it is or how it works. Although I have had many more experiences, this is the one that my skeptical, rational mind reluctantly accepts as strong evidence that there is really something going on here.

From your perspective, there is no reason why this tale should convince you. I could be lying or exaggerating (I'm not). It convinces me because it happened to *me*. But it didn't happen to you, so you'll just have to wait and get your own zinger experience!

Ironically I never actually gave either of the two messages involved. Aware of the problem of future distortions in the memories of past events, I write this from the detailed notes I took immediately after the event.

Especially when I first began giving spirit messages and readings, I would worry that I would not be able to come up with anything when I went up in front of a group to do "platform" mediumship. Therefore, I used to meditate and ask for information ahead of time, even before going to the event, let alone before standing up at the event. It seemed like cheating, because I had generally been taught to plug in right at the time of giving the message (although it is evident that other mediums often get things right before they come up front).

I was lying down in bed just before coming to the outdoor Stump service at 1:00 p.m. I got an image of a tall, thin man with moustache and glasses standing in a particular place in the audience. I saw (in dream imagery) a gang of his relatives cheering him and holding placards, saying that he was a success. But he had a wrinkled brow and would not accept that he was a success. He could know a little about this now; there was a door partly opened and with a light blue light, but the door would open the rest of the way later.

Another message I received while lying down was to be for the youngest girl there who was not a baby, but I did not get an actual picture of what she would look like or where she would be in the seats. I was supposed to tell her mother that the little girl was very talented in music and very creative. However, the only problem would be if her training were too restrictive; then they should back off. She was a "dawdly-doer", very active and curious.

Then I got up and went off to the Stump, a service held in the middle of a glorious, old-growth forest. There was a big crowd, approaching 300. Out of all those people it was obvious who the tall, thin man in the moustache was. He was standing right where he was supposed to be, as in my mental vision I had had while lying down in our room. Before I was called on to come up and give messages, another medium came to him and gave him virtually the identical message (except that she didn't mention the door part). She had the crowd of relatives, and told him about not accepting that he was a "success" and everything. I was stunned.

I have noticed that I often get synchronicities in twos. I think it's because I am so skeptical that I need a double-whammy to make an impression. It's a little like a cosmic wake-up call. "Pay attention, Charlie, something is really happening here."

Now for part two. Although I had not seen an image of the little girl, it was obvious from the statement "the littlest girl who is not a baby" who that was in the crowd. I spotted her with her mother. There was no other girl that little who was not a baby. I was still ready to give *her* a message. But, again, another medium before me went to the mother and told her almost precisely what I was going to say about the little girl. There was only one significant difference. Whereas I was going to say talented in "music", the other medium said "dance". Of course the two are closely related.

After the service, I went up to the little girl's mother and told her that I had been about to give her essentially the same message. The woman said that I was the fourth medium to tell her that message, and that indeed her daughter was very musical.

I had that eerie feeling that something very mystical was going on. The rational (but fair, I think) part of my mind was trying to imagine the odds of picking the right person out of 300, knowing what they look like and where one of them would be, and doing it twice, then compounding that by hearing virtually the identical, fairly specific messages given to those people that I had thought of precognitively (before the event). I knew that the odds had to be astronomically against it.

Of course this does not eliminate some kind of ESP explanation. I might just have been using precognition on a future event, but that is pretty amazing in itself. It is difficult to imagine any completely definitive proof of spirit communication that rules out ESP.

I have heard some mediums talk about tuning in to other mediums' messages in a message service, but I never do. That is not entirely true; sometimes I think about rather specific isolated details that happen to be said by another medium, but these are rather few and might be just coincidence most of the time. But these two full-blown examples that happened to me, both in the same service, were way beyond mere coincidence I should think.

Then a perfect end to my summer in Lily Dale came after my last message service (the 4:00 p.m. one on August 22, 1996), when a man asked me for a private reading. Nobody had ever asked me that before. I thanked him and said that I did not do private readings and could not give readings on the grounds in any case. It had been my year for confirmation that mediumship frequently does happen (whatever it is exactly) and that I could really do it (often enough to challenge the skeptic in me).

33

Doubts "Du Jour": Forever Skeptical

One nice thing about my skepticism is that it gets discouraged but has eternal life. It always makes a comeback. It impresses me, as I read over what I have just written, that the better confirmations I received in 1996 should have been enough to last a lifetime. I also had more confirmations in church services between the 1996 and 1997 Lily Dale seasons that I will not go into right now. However, I seemed to get a new spiritual and sociological lesson plan for 1997 that included new questions about mediumship and about my role in it.

As we have pointed out before, it is typical for mediums to have doubts about what they are doing in this skeptical, "rational" culture. Our friend Martie Hughes, who is also a medium, told me in 1997 that I was having the typical "doubt du jour" syndrome. Once I had stewed about one doubt for a while, I'd come up with a new doubt for the next day. For a while I worried about whether I was giving the message to the right person, whereas previously I had just taken it for granted.

Another doubt I had was whether I or anybody should be giving messages when they often seemed not to make sense. Suppose that 10 or 15% of messages (or longer readings) are quite amazing. That's wonderful. And suppose that most of the rest are fairly good, clearly better than chance-level guessing (although that is very difficult to measure with detailed, qualitative messages). Even under this optimistic scenario, there must be 20% or more, let's say, that are "not very good." I worried that the "bad" ones might be considered unethical or harmful. My way of coping with this doubt has been to say that my intent is good, and that people should use their own rational common sense about anything they get in a reading.

Although I had already been tentatively "convinced" in 1996 that mediumship was real, both in others and in myself, my skepticism was still crouching in the back of my mind, ready to spring. I listened in 1997 to messages at the Stump and at the Forest Temple, often harboring unkind thoughts about how some of them, including my own, sounded like a…(fill in your own unkind expression here). These doubts were punctuated by miniature miracles that shook me out of my judgmental funk, like the time medium Ray Torrey transformed a man with the simple comment, "You really like the sound of trumpets," as described in Chapter 8.

In 1997 we were also hearing a lot of things in interviews, classes and conversations about the right and wrong ways to do mediumship. We had wanted this study to focus on the mental processes of mediumship and how mediums made sense of this in their view of the world. But here we were getting our noses rubbed in politics and rigid rules, something we had wanted to steer clear of.

On a personal level I had enjoyed the blissful feeling and fun of giving messages in a supportive environment, like the one I had experienced in Spiritualist services in Erie. Although I found the debates over proper method that circulated elsewhere a bit annoying (and sociologically interesting), at least I could give messages at the public services in Lily Dale without much interference. I received some minor social control from chairpersons, like a reminder to identify spirits and not to just give a message, but student mediums like me were treated well.

One night, however, on the same day we had heard a medium tell us all about how most mediums did not have proper training, I was told by the chairperson at an evening fund-raising event that I could not give messages without a letter from my church saying that I was a good medium. This surprised me, because I thought that I had established a good reputation based on all of the public services I had worked.

I had no desire to challenge this and was about to leave when a woman came up to me and thanked me for a message I had given her about two hours earlier at another service. This confirmation was especially interesting because she had seemed to reject the message at the time it was given. I had told her about a spirit guide offering to help her with the wisdom of Native American cultures with an emphasis on Mexico, and that it would be even better if she would go there. She immediately said that she had no plans to go there.

However, that night she explained to me that another medium had told her to go to Mexico, and in fact she had been there several times already and had liked several parts of it. She just had not yet studied its ancient wisdom. As in my examples for 1996, it seemed as if my fragile ego were getting a spiritual boost when I really needed it.

Another doubt I began to focus on involved minor confirmations that sounded like poor evidence or stretches. I told one man that I had an impression of a woman in a print dress and full apron, and said little more than that. He stopped me after the service and said that I had described his mother well, and he made some other (I thought) rather obscure connection to something else I had said.

In a similar example I told a young woman that her grandmother said that it was O.K. to give kids options, but they need some rules. And I saw things popping out of drawers. Afterwards the woman's mother said to me, "You really captured my mother-in-law." She wanted me to give her a private reading (which I couldn't do of course).

Although I was courteous and grateful to people like this, it also made me wonder how discerning people are about what they hear from mediums. It is possible, I guess, that I gave some little details or body language that triggered recognition in the sitters. And perhaps the important thing is that they felt good about the experience. Maybe it was healing and inspiring. Picky me wanted it to be "true" and evidential as well.

On the somewhat positive side, in 1997 I began to get stronger feelings of recognition when I was confident of being right about a message. This happened to a lesser degree in 1996 too, and it was not always right, as in the case of the collie dog, which might have been right but displaced. One that was disconfirmed in 1997 was a message for a young woman that she was an athlete and intending to give up basketball for serious volleyball. That made no sense to her. I told her that I would be a "shopping-bag medium" and asked her to take that with her. Maybe it would mean something later.

The one I was the most excited about before giving it happened on July 5, 1997 at the Forest temple. I saw a man in his 50s or early 60s and just knew that there was a famous hockey player in his family. I saw a clairvoyant movie in my mind of a hockey player skating up fast and stopping on a dime with a spray of ice shavings. I told him that he had a strong hockey connection.

He lit up and said that his grandson played for Team Canada at the junior level and was a draft pick for the National Hockey League. I then said that he would end up playing for the Montreal Canadiens. That did not seem likely at the time, since he was drafted by a different organization. I am still curious to discover if that will ever happen.

On July 29 I felt very confident about another sports-related message. I got an impression of the Notre Dame fight song being played very loud over a man's head. When I told him that, he shouted, "Yes!" and shot his fist up in the air. He was a big fan. My impression was that both the hockey and the Notre Dame messages might have been "merely psychic" and not necessarily messages from the spirit world (if there's really a difference). They could also be sheer coincidence, because they were not very detailed, although I was more interested in them because of how certain I felt.

On July 23 I told a young African-American woman that an older uncle was there in spirit who had lived in the Baltimore/Washington area and had met Duke Ellington. He wanted to tell her that she was a "Sophisticated Lady." She said that that was possible; her grandmother had eight brothers. But what meant the most to her was that she has a poster of the musical show about Duke Ellington called "Sophisticated Lady" in her room. Two years later, in July of 1999, I received a healing from her in the Healing Temple. She reminded me that I had given her that message, and she always remembered it. On a personal level, that is the kind of confirmation that makes mediums joyful about their work.

I had one other very interesting confirmation experience in 1997 that took place in a mediumship class. We were to have a partner we had never met. I sat across from a white woman and immediately got an impression of a black man. I doubted what I was getting and wondered if her personal attitudes would be in opposition to hearing that she had a black relative. I told her anyway. He wore an old stovepipe hat, had a big beard, and lived in the deep South near the Mississippi River. I heard the word "multiracial". A bit later I felt Jackson, Mississippi, 1878, thinking also that it was in the middle and western part of the state, not that far from the river.

My partner responded that her daughter has often been asked if she is black. The family figures that there must be some black ancestry, and her husband is from the South. They also have a picture of her great grandfather, and he has a full beard. She asked me if that could be him. I asked and got the answer, "That's not me. It's my descendent (or son?)."

Then it was my partner's turn to read me. She had never done it before in her life. She told me that I was a history professor. "Not bad," I said. "I'm a sociology professor." It turned out that she had a sociology degree too.

She also told me, "I have Aunt Ethel here." She said that she knew me when I was two, and my partner said that she could see her under a grape arbor by a barn. This was really intriguing, because I had just recently been thinking about my Aunt Ethel in connection with an old picture I had seen. I have no real memory of her, but what was said could have been true. And "Ethel" is not a very common name to guess. A Spiritualist would also comment that this shows that anyone can do mediumship, although many like to argue that it takes years of training to develop properly.

I would like to tell one more amusing confirmation story from 1997, although it's really Penelope's confirmation. But I was a witness. We were sitting at the Fire Dept. picnic dinner on August 2 when a man walked up to our table. He had told her after a recent message service that she had given him a very meaningful message. However, he hadn't recognized the part about "a man who came to him with a lot of love with the letter W." But by now it had dawned on him that his father's name was Walter. He had just called him Dad. Sometimes evidential material takes a while to sink in.

34

Synchronicities and Guidance

I often say that the synchronicity rate is about three times as great in Lily Dale as elsewhere. And I wonder how much of it could be the place with all of its energies from 150 years of mediumship, and how much it could be just the fact that I can get away from my usual routine there.

I have a theory that if there is spiritual guidance in the world, some of it could come through synchronicities gently set up through micro manipulations so as not to be so obvious. This is based partly on the idea of chaos theory in which tiny changes in initial conditions result in large effects down the line, throwing off our nice, neat theories about how things are predictably organized.

One little example of this perhaps happened one day in 1997 when I was walking toward the National Spiritualist Association of Churches (NSAC) building in Lily Dale. I felt a little twinge of intuition tell me that I should go *right* around the auditorium instead of left as I might usually do. By the corner of the auditorium a woman talked to me briefly about seeing a groundhog run under the building. This delayed me just long enough to run into our friend Connie Griffith who told me that an important interview had been arranged for us with one of the visiting speakers at 3:00 p.m.

If I had not seen her, I would probably have been holed up in the NSAC archives until 5:00 p.m. and missed the interview appointment. What would it have taken to set that up? First placing the thought in my mind to go a different route, and second getting the groundhog to put in a timely appearance, and maybe a third adjustment to get the woman there who commented on the groundhog.

One other example of a synchronicity for 1997 involves the playing of the song "Ashokan Farewell" by the keyboard player in the Healing Temple. This was a theme played in the Ken Burns PBS series on the Civil War. I associate it with my residence being in Gettysburg. I put in my notes for August 2 that the song was played four out of the last fives times I had been there just at the time I was sitting up at a healing bench. This is a very unusual outcome, considering that there must be at least 20 different songs commonly played during the healing period at the services. I checked to make sure that they were not playing it deliberately for me. They were not, but I think that by 1998 or 1999 the chairperson of the service was trying to make it happen.

Some of my personal guidance comes not through synchronicities but through spiritual communication with my parents during a meditative state or while I am taking a light nap (my mother died in May 1993 and my father in November 1996). On my last day in Lily Dale in 1997 I heard the following. I was expecting too much from my mediumship. I had received big confirmations especially in the previous year, and now I was learning that the phenomenon cannot always be repeated or replicated. The sets of procedural norms that mediums set up cannot always produce results. Even the best mediums cannot always do the incredible.

I was also being eased toward the realization that my mediumship was mainly to help me understand the process and the world view of the medium. My main goal is to write about the subject, not to become a famous medium like James Van Praagh. I woke up and looked at the clock. It was 4:20. Honest. I wrote it down.

35

The Psychic Teeth:
Apports and ADCs?

I should relate some things that happened in Gettysburg about this time, not all in 1997. Probably the oddest one is the case of the psychic teeth. I'm still looking for a normal explanation of this one. One day I found four large molars in the sink among the silverware. My mind worked overtime, accusing other people of putting them there or accidentally dropping them out of a container or something. I even hypothesized that a workman who put a filtration unit in the basement had picked up some plastic teeth down there, part of a necklace perhaps left by a former tenant. The water filtration company had to make ten trips before it could fix our drinking-water system, and Penelope thought that symbolically it was like "pulling teeth."

My plastic necklace theory was based on the fact that there were neat round holes drilled in the teeth. When I took them to my dentist, he said that they were *real* molars, perhaps from a teenage girl. The oddest thing was that they had not only holes but file marks, perhaps indicating that they had been used to demonstrate tooth structure at a dental school, the dentist thought.

I boiled the possible explanations down to two very unsatisfactory ones. For those who like normal explanations, I suggest that some mysterious person walked in off the street and dropped them in our sink for no rational reason. My paranormal explanation is that they represent an "apport" which is a material object materialized from the spirit world (apports are relatively rare as psychic phenomena go but have been reported in the parapsychological literature). It turns out that one of Penelope's grandfathers was a doctor who also worked with teeth sometimes. She often gets the sensation that he communicates with her mentally. Perhaps he left them as a joke about how the filtration repair was like "pulling teeth."

After we moved to our own house, I found two items one day side by side on top of a wicker chest. One was a 1924 buffalo nickel in very fine condition; the other a very old style paper clip (maybe a calling-card clip). I can believe that these were objects from the items I saved from my father's house after he died. However, they would have been very securely contained inside boxes that are in drawers. Again the household was interrogated, resulting in no satisfactory explanation. If this is another apport, the best I can do for a symbolic explanation would be my father saying, "Don't get clipped (cheated), and don't take any wooden nickels."

In that same room, which is my home office, I have experienced what seem to be olfactory apparitions from my father. On several occasions I have smelled my father's "personal smell", mostly in my office but also in Penelope's office. Penelope thought she might be smelling it too (in her office), and my son Lee was very sure that he was smelling it at the same time I was (in my office).

Once I smelled my father's aftershave, the very distinctive "Pinaud" brand. It was in my office again, and this time I could localize where it smelled the strongest, right at a chair that had belonged to him. I hasten to add that I have a very poor sense of smell, but this was quite strong and distinctive. I was not thinking about him at the time, and I did not have any of that brand in the house up to that time. Smelling a man's aftershave is a very common type of after-death communication (ADC) according to research by the Guggenheims.[98]

Probably the most significant ADC to me happened on my birthday in 1997. I walked into my office early that morning to find a string of green pepper lights on. They are part of a display of popular culture artifacts on top of my filing cabinets. I had been rearranging things there the previous day and can be absolutely certain that the lights were not plugged in when I left the night before. I am "Mr. Cautious" and always make sure that all my lights are off; I very rarely plug those in in any case. For someone else to plug them in would require climbing around behind a sectional sofa.

For somebody else to have done that would seem highly unmotivated (perhaps not as bad as dropping teeth in a stranger's sink), and the only other people with keys are security and housekeeping (someone comes in to empty my wastebasket in the middle of the night). A debunker would prefer one of these highly unlikely possibilities (or some other undiscovered normal cause).

To me it represented my parents using lights like candles on a cake to say, "Happy birthday, Charlie."

36

Further Adventures in Lily Dale

Some confirmations take longer to sink in than others. In the summer of 1998 I finally realized part of the symbolism that should have been obvious to me earlier. A couple of years earlier I had taken a weekend class in healing and mediumship. While I was part of a group healing on a man who was sitting in a chair, I had the experience of seeing him as if he were a young boy of 7 or 8. This makes no rational sense, because he did not really look any different physically. And I felt that he needed some tender, loving care because of something that had happened then, but it was none of my business to know what.

After the healing I told him all this. He said that I was right on and asked me for more information. I said that I saw him at that age playing outside, rolling a tire, and then something disturbing happened back at the house, and people had to go get him to tell him. He did not respond to my details until the next day. Meanwhile I told Penelope about it after the session, and she said to me (without knowing anything about the man), "He lost his father, didn't he?" Somehow that felt right, but I didn't know. The next day he told our group that he was 7, almost 8, when he was out playing and people came to tell him that his father had just died when a car collapsed on him back at the house.

What took me two years to realize? Probably the part of the message about rolling the tire was a reference to the car, but I hadn't picked up the significance of it. At the time I had only wondered if he was actually rolling something while he played outside. Of course the real significance of the message was that the childhood trauma was what needed to be healed in our healing session.

I had some very good confirmations in 1998, but not very many. In one I told a girl that she had had a court jester doll that went up and down on a stick when she was little, and she had. In my church in Erie I gave a woman a very detailed description of her and an older boy playing with frogs in a pond near a big red barn when she was a kid, and how the buildings were situated, which she confirmed.

However, I was still bothered about the times I couldn't get it right. Once I was helping out at a fundraiser, and I went up against a stone wall with one woman. Everything I said got a "no" from her, even though I felt that I was getting good stuff. The other mini-readings I gave were fine. One was really quite good apparently, in which I described a man's working with graph paper a lot (which is part of his research in chemical engineering) and some other things about his life. Nevertheless, I focused on the negative.

After the affair I asked the chairwoman what I should have done about my "bad" reading. She said I should have given the woman her ticket back so that somebody else could try. She also was able to guess which of the five people I had trouble with, and said, "That woman was like a stone wall for me too when I tried to read for her. She's like that. Don't worry about it." This comment contrasted with the woman's statement to me that nobody had ever had trouble reading her before. One final irony is that the chairwoman is the same person who told me the year before that I could not volunteer for a different fundraiser without a letter from my church.

I continued to fuss over this "failure" in spite of the explanation from the medium in charge. Reluctantly I volunteered for the same event three weeks later and seemed to do O.K. But this experience had a lingering effect on me for at least another year.

One positive development in 1998 was that I noticed several examples of apparent short-term precognition. For example, I was sitting in a circle one night and got an impression of the name "Bruno". I was startled right after that to hear a woman in the circle say that there was a presence of a dog there, and she thought it might be her dog "Bruno", not a very common name.

Two weeks later, in the same circle, I got a whole series of mental images of scenes in Hong Kong. Shortly after that the leader asked us to imagine a wonderful place we'd like to be. It seemed to me that I had responded to the request ahead of time.

Probably the funniest example happened in an after-dinner discussion at a friend's house. I was impressed with the word "Gefilte fish" and wondered why, but I didn't say anything about it. Maybe ten or fifteen minutes later someone said the word. It was seemingly totally unpredictable based on earlier conversation. Considering the cultural environment, I could live in Lily Dale and not hear that word for ten years, I bet.

The spiritual part of me considered these precognitive flashes to be an indication of psychic sensitivity of my part. The skeptical part of me figures that there is no way to establish a probability frame for this but admits that it's peculiar.

I had some fun synchronicities in 1998. Jung would have counted the precognition as synchronicity too. One I think of is the time archivist Barbara Farraro at the Marion Skidmore Library in Lily Dale told me about two references. They were to Elizabeth Kubler-Ross's example of a woman who supposedly came back in spirit form and left an actual, physical letter behind, and to Raymond Moody's research on mirror-gazing. Although she had a general idea of my research topic, she did not know that I had just the day before looked at both of these examples.

Another "coincidence" had special meaning for me. One morning I was feeling blue and heard (in my mind) that I needed a little faith, not just wall-to-wall synchronicities to make it easy to accept things. I went outside to take one of my "book walks", in which I walk a few miles and read a book at the same time. There was a little patch of grey cloud over my head. A quick mini-shower sent a drop right down at the end of a sentence in the Guggenheims' book *Hello From Heaven*.[99] It read, "Ruth, I'm telling you, your mother's here." My mom's middle name is Ruth. That was close enough for me.

Did you ever wonder whether synchronicities are always good? And if "bad" things happen, do New Age folks just ignore them, or call them something other than "synchronicities"? Penelope and I had our share of bad luck in the summer of 1998, and we're not sure how to frame it. In one sense it seems to fit my pattern of double synchronicities, but does it have some "metaphysical lesson" to it? Or is it just a set of unfortunate occurrences with no meaning?

Our summer was divided into two separate trips to Lily Dale from Gettysburg. The first one was a very productive three weeks in terms of library research and interviews. The second was essentially two weeks of health care. On August 1, the date of our second arrival, Penelope slid on some loose pebbles a couple of hours after we got there, fell down in the street and broke her left foot. At first it appeared that there were two broken bones, but later there proved to be four (2 x 2). Penelope spent the rest of her summer holiday with crutches and/or wheel chair, and of course it put a crimp in our research activities.

After a trip to the emergency room the next day, we went to a restaurant, at which she bit down on a piece of stone or bone in a sandwich and broke two crowns. We thought we had completed two double events, the lesson, if there was one, being to be more careful. Some people tried to make a bigger metaphysical lesson out of it, such as that Penelope was subtly undermining herself or something, which neither of us took to. Penelope says that the lesson is to watch where you are walking and notice the potholes in life.

Then on August 13 (as Walt Kelly used to write in *Pogo*, "Friday the 13th fell on a Thursday that month"), we took a day trip to Erie and had a spark plug blow out of the engine, making the car undrivable (we were told). We ended up renting a car and having our car towed 300 miles to Gettysburg at great expense, which turned out to be unnecessary because the plug could have been just screwed back in.

When that happened I commented, "That's interesting; now the car has two things wrong with it." The other was that the air conditioner had stopped working. If there was a lesson to the car problem, we couldn't figure out what, because we had just spent money to have it tuned up and examined before the trip.

When we were finally ready for bed that night, we got out our bed-time reading. Penelope and I have a custom of reading to each other aloud just before lights out. Perhaps the only genuine synchronicity in all of this is that the reading in our book, a collection of short stories by James Thurber, turned out to be about his problems with cars and car repairs.

One thing I have noticed about the synchronicities or sign-posts in our life in recent years is that we seem to "get what we need when we need it." When the budget begins to get in sad shape, something comes along to help it, like a small windfall of unexpected work to make some extra money. In the case of the car, by the end of the year we found a good used station wagon, just like the one I said I wanted, advertised locally at a reasonable price (I couldn't even find one on the internet), allowing us to make the car without an air conditioner our second car.

By the summer of 1999, the foot, crowns and spark plug were history. Penelope had trouble remembering which foot she had broken, and my memory of the car had to be jogged by looking at my notes. That year we had a new challenge. Penelope bought a cottage at 13 (oh-oh) Second Street in Lily Dale. It needed a fair amount of work, and it turned out not to be finished when we arrived. I won't go into the details of additional expenses incurred by having to redo much of the work.

Our ability to do research was greatly reduced in the first two weeks because of the rush to complete enough of the remodeling by the beginning of the Lily Dale season, when noise has to stop. The Spiritualist part of me saw the next event as an example of how "we get what we need when we need it."

On the first day that I headed toward the archives at the NSAC building to do some more library research, I had another one of those little intuitional twinges that told me to go to the right instead of to the left as I had intended. I then happened to see our friend Ozzie Osborne (the healer, not the rock star) working out in front of his house. I had wanted to ask about the health of his wife Kitty (the woman who had given me the reading at the psychic fair and who ended up being my teacher in mediumship classes in the church I joined). He told me to go up to the house.

In the course of our conversation, Kitty asked me about our research. Then she asked if I had a literary agent. I said no, but I was thinking about trying to get one. Then she showed me pictures of a friend of hers who was a good literary agent. She handed me his card and suggested that I call him. I thanked her and was heading for the door when the phone rang. She said, "Maybe that's him." It was. I got to speak to him on the phone, and he told me what to send him. Although we did not end up working with that agent, the conversation set me on a clear path to get a few chapters written.

Then I continued on to the archives. That day and the next I was able to determine that I had gotten everything I needed that was available from old journals (in addition to books I had read in the past three years). That meant that I was ready to write immediately and that I could finish preliminary chapters that summer instead of the next. I felt that I had been compensated for the time I had to spend helping with the cottage, and that we were getting spiritual help in the writing of the book (my rational mind is screaming that that's crazy).

By now I feel that my main mediumship goal is clear: to write this book. I still do some message work at public services, and I continue to get some good confirmations (but I think you have had enough examples by now). There is one more part to Charlie's journey, however, that I really must tell.

I have always been fascinated by physical phenomena, like the psychokinesis (PK) involved in my dice experiment, and in other uncontrolled events like my apparent affect on self-winding watches and on electronic equipment. The apports I mentioned above (the psychic teeth, and the nickel and paper clip) are physical effects as well. The only clear-cut physical effect I have experienced in a haunting happened when Penelope and I both saw a wreath jump straight out from a wall and then fall to the floor in an allegedly haunted inn (right after I said, "I don't think we'll be visited by any ghosts tonight.").

What I have really wanted to see is physical mediumship, such as table-tipping or levitation. I have considered this to be a possibility, based on all of the research I've seen in parapsychology. However, physical mediumship raises eyebrows because of all of the fraudulent examples that have been uncovered, especially around the turn of the century.

In the early 1960s I saw a table-tipping demonstration at a private party in Erie, PA. I was at the table when it rose straight up at least a half foot. When I left the table and looked underneath for strings or wires, and checked everybody's hands and arms, I could find no hoax. However, I was suspicious because I saw the two people in charge whispering to each other right before we started. Also, I was so skeptical that I found it extremely hard to believe that it was even possible, in spite of having done my dice experiment, which demonstrates a very weak effect at best. I have wanted to speak to the one fellow who did it ever since, now that he is a Roman Catholic priest.

Finally in 1999 I saw it happen again. And this time I am quite sure that what I saw was real. And so is the PhD candidate in chemical engineering who sat across the table from me. It happened in a mediumship class with 35 people in the room. There were five of us at a card table. We placed our hands lightly on the table with our fingers spread apart in order to form a circle of hands touching at thumbs and little fingers.

In this position there was a slight "ouija-board effect." In other words, without knowing who was doing what, the circle of our hands produced a little movement. But of course it only rocked the table a little. Nobody had any contact with the sides or bottom of the table. There was no normal way to make it rise under these conditions. Moreover, there were several students sitting on chairs around us at a short distance, and they were looking under the table to check things out.

And then the medium came over to our table. She said that it was begin-ning to move (which it wasn't, except very slightly side to side as I have said). She put her hands palm down completely on top of the table just a few inches to the right of mine. I had her in complete view and could see that the rest of her body was away from the table. In a few seconds the side of the table to my left rose up about six inches in two or three seconds and stayed there for ten or twenty seconds. Then it sank back down rather quickly, but it rose again about the same amount and at the same rate with the medium's hands on the table. After another ten or twenty seconds she left our table and walked away. It stayed up for a few more seconds and then collapsed. We were unable to get it to rise again without her.

I checked the details of this later with three other people who had been at the table. The next day I had a long discussion about it with the chemical engineer. He analyzed the situation, pointing out that the medium had no way to get any leverage to lift the table in any normal fashion, since the legs were on the very corners of the table, and her hands were completely on top. He agreed with me that the rising of the table seemed like a buoying effect rather than a yanking or pulling. It would have been very obvious if some-body on my left had lifted a knee to push the table up, and it would have been a much less smooth sensation. This table tipping reminded me of the way the table had risen for us in 1964; it felt as if the room had filled with water and floated it up. And when it dropped it just let go, as in this case.

I couldn't believe that the engineer was so calm. He said without any apparent emotion that it was a confirmation that such things can happen, and that our knowledge of the laws of physics is incomplete or insufficient to explain this type of levitation. When I asked him to try to imagine how a debunking scientist would explain what we saw, he said, "A wind came through the room and lifted the table." We would have noticed.

Without precisely controlled observation with instruments, our eye-wit-ness accounts would not be accepted in normal-science circles. But we know what we saw. Ultimately I could be wrong about anything, but this experi-ence was like coming home to that first dice experiment of mine. It wasn't publishable in a physics journal, but it confirmed in me the notion that there was something missing in the standard rational, scientific explanation of the universe.

That standard scientific view is the main barrier that makes it difficult for people in this society, including me, to embrace the role of spirit medium.

Later we will examine more closely how some people have managed to do it anyway.

PART IV
"SO WHAT?"

So far we have tried to entice you with a sampling of interesting experiences from mediums past and present. But this is only the beginning. There are a number of fascinating questions to be raised about all of this. Not the least of which is, "So what?"

This question was Penelope's idea. I (Charlie) had always tacitly assumed that any open and inquisitive person would be fascinated with spirit medium-ship and would experience it if they could. It never occurred to me to ask what the purpose of it was.

This difference between Penelope and me dawned on me gradually. Years ago, when we first met, I was surprised that she was interested in spiritual things but not especially in ghost experiences (apparitions). To me such things as ghosts and spirit mediumship were all challenges to standard science and therefore were intriguing. What if they were real? How would this change our view of the universe?

But Penelope scarcely doubted the existence of the "paranormal", having experienced visions and other wonders since at least age three. The important question to her was, "What are the spiritual lessons here?" My favorite expression of hers on this issue is, "This is not a parlour trick." Hmm, was my scientific curiosity about these things as trivial as a fascination with trick magic? I have some further devious sociological ideas about this to explore later, but first we should hear Penelope's thoughts on the purpose of spirit mediumship and related matters.

37

My (Penelope's) View of the Purposes of Mediumship

First I will define my understanding of mediumship as a Spiritualist, then my belief systems before practicing Spiritualism. From both perspectives I believe that the answer to "So what?" or "Why use mediumship?" is that the purpose of mediumship is for healing. I am often in awe of how mediumship is a vehicle for how we can love and be loved, serve and be served, transform and help others to transform.

Many Spiritualists limit their definition of mediumship to mean a form of communication from a discarnate soul/spirit. So what is a soul or a spirit? In my understanding, if spirit is the consciousness, then the soul is the vehicle that contains the spirit. The soul incarnates on earth with a personality (ego) and individuality (higher/spiritual self).

In mediumship discarnate spirits communicate by the blending of thoughts using the medium's psychic or astral senses. A spirit will often come in the same form (body features) and personality as when you knew them, offering something that you already know as evidence of their presence. So if you knew the spirit as a recovering alcoholic who was in business and died of a heart attack, these facts may come through the medium.

Within Spiritualism this type of spirit identification is emphasized primarily in public religious services. For example, one summer as I was about to give a message to one woman, my attention went to a light, the sole remnant of gas lighting in the auditorium. When I asked (mentally) "So what?" I was aware of a medium (who is now in spirit and who had worked at Lily Dale). I knew instantly that she was related to the sitter, and she was impressing me with the thought of the Wizard of Oz (with multiple meanings).

Public messages are brief, and time did not allow me to explore the thought of Oz, but I did hear connections between the names Dorothy and

Em and her aunt. The sitter acknowledged these names. I had the unusual experience of the spirit also speaking directly to me and saying that I was improperly dressed. I said so to the sitter, and she acknowledged that her aunt had been a Lily Dale medium and that slacks would not have seemed appropriate to her.

Those sitters who are used to giving or receiving messages often reply verbally with confirmations because they know that otherwise it can feel like talking to a disconnected telephone line! Unfortunately, such interactions are a luxury; mostly I just get up and give several messages and sit down. I must just know the meaning was for them, not for me or about my ability.

Sometimes mediums stress bringing through the spirit's name and relationship. I find that emphasis over-rated, but then I am not good at recalling the names of people I was introduced to yesterday! Too often, for my personal style, mediums toss out names, and I think "So what or why?" The American two-to-three minute format per public message does not allow the time to explore who all of these "dead people" are.

However, sometimes I do get names as prominent parts of the message. For example, once I immediately thought of the hymn "Amazing Grace" and knew that Grace was the spirit's name. Sometimes the name is heard like a word whispered just beyond my left ear.

When I came to one woman, first I heard the name Mary. As I mentally said "So what?" to Mary, I heard the name Ellen. Then I heard Mary Ellen said together as one name. I said this information as I was hearing it, which took much less time than typing it. The sitter was helpful, responding that her mother (in spirit) was Mary, her grandmother was Helen, and her own name was Mary Helen. I think that the spirit impressed names onto my mind/thoughts. Because I had not thought of or used the name Helen in years, I did not have the resource of the name Helen to use; thus my misinterpretation of it as "Ellen". I later learned that hearing from Mom touched the sitter's heart, and the message was a boost to her self-esteem and a confirmation to take the career direction she had begun.

In my experience of message work with discarnate spirits (Spiritualist mediumship) it appears that they will often prove their capacity to be with you in daily life. Spirits often impress the medium's mind with situations from their time on earth with you, or with current events and feelings in your life that are probably known only to you. It appears to me that spirits who are loved ones or old friends do not predict, prophesy, or interfere with an individual's free will. A simple example of this happened recently when the spirit reminded a woman that she did not follow through on an auto manufacturer's recall notice. I was given only that information. If I had predicted a consequence or warned her, I think that would have been my psychic interpretation of the message.

It is in the medium's interpretation, I think, that errors arise. In my process I often know the information just as I am speaking it, rather than seeing a picture or knowing something and then putting it into words. I am always interested in hearing Charlie's messages because he is given detailed pictures, symbols and colors. He describes them with courage! For example, I remember the first message I ever heard him give as a student. He said that he saw a dresser in the woman's house that had a particular photograph in it. When the sitter smiled and said 'Yes," I probably would have taken the confirmation and stopped. (Student mediums sometimes "go where wise men fear to tread," ignoring ego's fear of being wrong). Charlie proceeded to describe the dresser's third drawer down; each item in its layers of contents, and then the photograph and frame! The woman seemed to make her own meaning with these facts and nodded.

Compare that example to an experience of using one's psychic sense and spirit teachers and guides as the basis for making various life choices and for reframing situations. From some source of psychic knowing, one medium had an image of the sitter jay-walking on a busy NYC street. The sitter replied that she was often in a rush and did indeed jay walk because it took too much time to walk all of the way to the corner. The medium's next mental picture was of a station wagon hitting the woman as she dashed out into traffic. (In my belief system it would be irresponsible to predict an accident or death.) After asking "spirit" how to word the message effectively, the medium said, "Just imagine how terrible it would be for a station wagon to hit you. Those parents and kids would have a lifetime of guilt to carry, just because you were rushing."

This point of view captured the woman's attention, and she replied that she had never thought about others, and she wouldn't want to create that kind of situation. That style of message is congruent with my natural gifts and with how I was encouraged in my use of intuition and spiritual counseling.

It has taken me a dozen years to move toward practicing the Spiritualist style of mediumship. Initially I thought that people don't get smart just because they "get dead" (as my father puts it), so why talk to them?

I was initially taught to "go up higher," to go to the one mind for information. I learned from my grandparents and metaphysical teachers to reach for the higher planes of consciousness. Go to the one mind, one consciousness, and one presence where all truth is known. I believed that it was preferable to commune with the Universal intelligence, Jesus or some other Master teacher in order to offer worthwhile spiritual service.

An event in more recent years reinforced my awareness of the One Mind. In the early 1990s I had some health challenges. In addition to seeing an MD who was an endocrinologist, I also went to the Ayurvedic center in Lancaster, MA. The MD ran the usual tests and exams, but also called me a "reishi", meaning knower or seer. A reishi is a person who is born with a highly sensitive nervous system, and in the Hindu tradition they often live a life of seclusion. From the silence they can offer insight, wisdom, health diagnosis and effective treatments to those people in the world who need healing.

As one of the doctors put different patients' charts in my hands, I would tell him about the person, and he would use pulse diagnosis to monitor my body system. I would take on the physical symptoms (e.g., blood pressure) of the person in the chart! It was then that I again realized that being a medium was a double-edged sword. The same qualities that make me able to give a message in private or in public, together or at a distance, can also allow me to have poor boundaries and unconsciously take on another person's symptoms. I want to "know", not "be", your stuff! One of the world's best mediums, Edgar Cayce, perhaps shortened his life by choosing to serve others when he needed to heal himself.

At this point in my life, I now take on different styles of mediumship or psychic message-work according to the needs, desires and expectations of the receivers. In the Lily Dale public services I set my intention to bring through relatives and friends. That appears to work well if the public knows the names of the deceased and had spent time visiting with them. When Spiritualism developed, people spent hours visiting, sitting around the table with all generations of family and friends. Now three or more generations, extended family and community friends are fortunate to spend time together at a once-a-year reunion, a wedding or a funeral.

I actually do know the names, personalities and professions of my relatives back three generations as well as many of my grandparents' and parents' friends who are in spirit. But like many of my friends and clients, I have no unrequited need or desire to talk with them. Once when my Dad visited Lily Dale and watched me work at the "Stump" he said, "You never take my advice now; why would you listen to me when I get dead?"

I try to take the best and leave the rest. I always ask spirit for content, but in the public demonstrations I also ask for identification of a spirit the receiver will recognize. I am often uncomfortable with the elitism that judges mediumship. This judging within Spiritualism claims that one school of thought is better than another, or that messages in the past were better than today. Elitism also happens outside of Spiritualism in metaphysical schools of thought such as Theosophy in which connecting with and channeling the higher consciousness of ascended masters is considered superior to messing around in the astral plane of discarnate spirits!

In our interviews I learned that many mediums consider private readings and spiritual counseling to be about content, and they do not specifically focus on discarnate spirits. I take my lead from how the information is given to me after I have set my intention for healing. Certainly I have observed healing when a loved one in spirit brings joy, encouragement and comfort to a client. I have also felt honored to be a part of healing grief when people did not have the opportunity to say good-bye.

I consider grief-healing to be one of the greatest gifts of Spiritualism. Modern Spiritualism was founded in the mid-nineteenth century and became strong after the Civil War and during the World Wars. At those times people's need was for completion and solace. From another perspective, I have an older cousin who lived with my grandparents and her mother during World War II. She says that she often worried that her Dad, a chaplain in Europe, might come through at my grandmother's circles, meaning that he had been killed!

While the Spiritualist understanding of mediumship stresses communication with those you knew or loved, to many other people mediumship simply is focused on the *content* obtained by utilizing the psychic senses of finest (clear) hearing, sight, sensing. They do not identify the *source*, because after all, everything is one.

So what about my perspective? Before I work I ask to be a channel of joy, love, truth, wisdom and understanding. It doesn't seem healing or a spiritual service to judge one belief system as more elite or right than another. It isn't love to become fearful of spirit realms. I set my intention, then "Let go and let God." I think of a childhood Unity prayer that my Mother insisted that I say whenever I left the house. It serves me well now: "The light of God surrounds me, the love of God enfolds me, the presence of God protects me. Wherever I am, God is." And then I give the message.

Daily I think of another saying that I do not know the origin of after so many years. It is, "God goes before me and guides my way through every moment of the day…." With this statement I want to differentiate between my concept of mediumship and my daily use of intuition. Many people call many experiences mediumship that I call intuition or using my psychic senses. I have discussed mediumistic experiences, and it doesn't yet reflect how I live.

I have an appreciation for intuitive knowing, for discovering myself and others, for the purpose of learning/teaching truths and for making everyday choices that is a foundation in life for any work I do as a medium. Some simple examples are that I believe I will always be at the right place at the right time to do what needs to be done by me. So one day I asked and knew it was the day for Charlie and me to travel to Gettysburg to find a house together. He had suggested we go earlier, but finally I knew the time was right. We arrived in town, and the house had just become available that day.

Another time I was taking an evening walk in Lily Dale and saw a pair of French doors put out for trash pickup. I immediately thought, "Oh, those are for my cottage." We had been happy renting in the summer, but I knew the doors were a sign to purchase a cottage. I asked my friend Connie to store them for me. Later that week I walked by a house that the owner was showing to a possible buyer. I toured it and later sat in the living room where I proceeded to have a mediumistic experience with past mediums who had lived there (none of whom I had known). By fall I purchased the cottage.

Every morning I ask Spirit (and my highest self), "What can I do to be truly helpful?" That way I know where to go, when, for how long and what to do next. I also use "tools" like a pendulum when I do not have adequate information to make a rational choice, but I believe that my highest self always knows. For example, Charlie decided to purchase a sound system and asked for my input. He went to the library, investigated systems through questioning and listening when we visited retailers. I dowsed with a pendulum and came up with the same answer several hours before his choice.

I also chose our publisher in similar fashion. Charlie rationally researched publishers. I saw the name of one that I "knew" was right. I checked myself by using the pendulum and received a strong yes. Charlie later chose the same one for rational reasons. This works for me because living with Charlie I have access to both the rational and intuitive, without taking the time for research! When head and heart meet, there is a sureness and rightness to decisions.

38

A Rainbow of Reasons

There is a wide range of goals and functions served by different types of spirit mediumship. I (Charlie) get annoyed when I hear people making narrow judgments about what qualifies for "proper" mediumship. I probably would not be so intolerant of other people's intolerance if I were not so involved in the subject, as a student medium. My attitude comes from being a member of a Spiritualist church and a sociologist/anthropologist at the same time. I can step back and understand the social reasons for members of different groups setting up boundaries and making rules, but I'm also close enough to the action to react emotionally.

The easiest way to get a broad view of the variety of purposes for mediumship is to look at some cross-cultural examples. Although the Chinese Communist Party makes it politically incorrect to say so, traditional Chinese usually take the existence of an afterlife for granted. Chinese don't use spirit mediumship to "prove the continuity of life"; they use it for the very practical purpose of finding out what their relatives on the other side want, and telling them how they want to be helped in return.

Spiritualists in Western societies, however, need to prove the continuity of the spirit after death because of the scientific skepticism that dominates the culture. By contrast, Louise Lone Dog provides another example of a non-Western medium who can take the existence of the spirit world for granted. She brings through prophetic visions for her people, channeling ancient Aztec and Inca ancestors from centuries back.[100]

Another example that would seem strange to American Spiritualists is the case of spirit mediumship in Zimbabwe in Africa. Through a long tradition, spirit mediums have been used there for political guidance and more recently to unite guerilla fighters in rebellion.[101]

Of course this book is primarily about mediumship in the United States and Britain. Even here there is a wide range of functions, and they are all controversial from the point of view of some group or other. First we will look at the purposes mediumship serves for the sitter (client), according to various mediums (and psychics etc.). Most of this information comes from our interviews with present-day mediums, since we could ask them such questions directly.

39

Entertainment: Parlour Tricks and "Comediums"

Especially to traditional Spiritualists, using mediumship for entertainment would seem to be the lowliest and least acceptable purpose. At the outdoor services in Lily Dale, for example, the chairperson of the session reminds people that this is a religious service. If newcomers start to applaud a medium, they are usually told that it is not appropriate.

Nineteenth-century British medium Bessie Williams said, "When these mediumistic gifts are used, it should be for some higher purpose than…an hour's entertainment."[102] Part of the reason that the prominent Spiritualist leader Emma Hardinge Britten left her work as a public "test medium" for a career in lecturing for the cause seems to be that her "spirit friends" told her not to turn mediumship into a show from the platform.[103]

Indeed some of the public demonstrations of mediumship created so much interest especially in the nineteenth century that they turned into what might be called traveling shows, as in the case of the "worldrenowned" Davenport Brothers.[104] Today the famous medium James Van Praagh says, "This is not a game. It is not my intention to teach you some *tricks* so that you can amuse others with your psychic abilities."

Behind this admonition some might see the shadow of fraudulent mediums that were so common at the turn of the century. Or one might think about Houdini and other trick magicians and "mentalists" who have entertained crowds with apparent feats of mediumship and psychic powers, often stating explicitly that they are not using psychic means. What they did and do use instead are hidden holes in blindfolds, message codes with assistants, and ways of gathering information about the crowd before they arrive.

Paranormal or not, such entertainments are usually considered inappropriate in the context of Spiritualist meetings. Nevertheless, there is a structural pressure put on a medium in a public demonstration to keep the crowd happy. It may not be easy to do this without at least a touch of humor. Not everybody is very interested in other people's messages, unless they are highly evidential and make the people who get them cry.

We saw a startled James Van Praagh come out on stage at a "whole life" expo in Baltimore to see 1200 people in the room. He had just been on the Oprah show to publicize his first book. Previously he had conducted small workshops and had never been before such a large live crowd. Although he was appropriate and respectful, he had to "play the audience" with some humor as well.

One of the weekly chairpersons at an outdoor service in Lily Dale kept telling people each day not to applaud, but it was clear that she was amused by one of the mediums who is well known as a "comedium" (comedian+medium). Does this seem inconsistent? Why else would one not applaud "in church" unless it is supposed to be serious and not an appropriate place for entertainment? Well, can the minister tell a joke in the sermon?

One British medium told us that some Spiritualist churches in England don't like it when people laugh during the message part of the service. They say, "This is a serious service."

I examined my (Charlie's) own attitude about this. Like many of the mediums in Lily Dale, I do appreciate a bit of fun in the service. And we often say that "spirit" has a sense of humor. The question becomes, under what circumstances do people (mediums here) feel that there is too much emphasis on entertainment? I perceive the norm to be this. The humor should not overshadow the mediumship, which would be like a minister telling jokes but giving no spiritual message. Also, it should not appear that the medium is engaging in self-aggrandizement, because the focus is supposed to be on the message and not the messenger.

Although several mediums at the public services in Lily Dale attempt to include a bit of "comediumship" in their messages, only two of them (which is about 5% of the regulars) frame virtually their entire "performance" that way. One of them reportedly does a standup psychic/mediumistic act elsewhere during the Lily Dale offseason (Lily Dale season runs from late June through early September).

One thing that makes such presentations look like an "act" is certain recurring motifs. I have attended hundreds of the services at the Stump and at the Forest Temple over the past six years, and I know these motifs by heart.

One is, "I'm not saying that you're going to win the lottery, but if you do, remember my name is…." Or when someone indicates that the medium is right about something, the medium says, "Yes, I know these things, dear. That's why you're there, and I'm up here."

As with any comedian, people's reactions vary as to whether their humor is appropriate. One comedium whom I do like and consider to be appropriate includes kidding people in the audience as part of his act. Not everybody agrees with me that it is always respectful enough of the sitter. For example, he'll say, "Would you recognize a relative named William?" The response was, "My grandfather was William." He replies, "Well, grandfather, that's a relative," as if to imply that the sitter didn't know that. To me it's obvious that he's pretending to make himself look foolish for thinking that. He will also look around at the chairperson, in Jack Benny style, as if looking for help when someone says something peculiar. This man is a good medium and very popular among audiences and mediums alike.

Sometimes he ends up as straight man for the audience. Once he told an old woman that a certain person was there in spirit for her. She looked amazed and said, "I didn't even know he was dead." Another time he told a woman that he saw her mother (in spirit) with some unidentified man. "What's she doing with somebody named Ralph?" he asked. "I don't know," she replied, "I'm not responsible for what my mother does."

Although having structured entertainment mixed in with message work may be controversial, there is no doubt that most Spiritualist gatherings have light elements. It is generally far from being a highly formalized and overly serious religion. A study by Gillen emphasizes the "pleasures of Spiritualism," including sociable gatherings and the fun of trying to decipher messages from spirit.[105] I have yet to see even an old traditional Spiritualist who did not appreciate a good anecdote about an amusing confirmation a medium got, for example.

There are also jokes, anecdotes and sayings that circulate among mediums, some of them not politically correct or for polite company (neither the mediums nor their jokes; now's your chance to skip to the next page if you don't want to be subjected to this). Some of this lore is critical of the style of other mediums. For example, a "shopping-bag medium" is always telling sitters who don't recognize their messages to "take it with them," as if the meaning will dawn on them later.

One medium was having trouble getting a woman in a message service to recognize the spirit. "I have a Dick here," he said. "I'll hold on to it," she replied.

One old-style way of asking permission of someone in the audience/congregation to give them a message is to say, "May I step into your vibration?" A friend of ours tried this in an organizational gathering (not a Lily Dale service, heaven forbid), "May I step into your shit?" It brought the house down.

A favorite source of amusement among some mediums is to caricature the style of other mediums (behind closed doors with friends). Sometimes this is even done at public fundraisers in Lily Dale. Each season there are events with names like "Twisted Message Service" or "Fun Night," in which the usual norms of mediumship are relaxed and parodies are allowed. People may take on the role of clown or do caricatures of fortune telling, channeling, and mediumship.

In spite of the lowly status of entertainment as a purpose of mediumship, it is clear that Spiritualists are not without a sense of humor. But asking people about the "purpose" of something is almost begging for an ideal, ideological statement. This results in what sociolologists call "social desirability response."

40

"Ed, Come and Help Me:"
Practical Magic

Another purpose of mediumship that is not supposed to be socially desirable is what we may call "practical magic." Many of these purposes are difficult to distinguish from one another and difficult to rank, but this one seems to be almost as low in rank, from the point of view of Spiritualists, as entertainment.

"Practical magic" refers to the use of any paranormal powers to accomplish mundane tasks, like finding lost objects; or to accomplish material goals, like making money. All societies use magical/religious means for practical purposes when their scientific means fail or do not apply. For example, bingo-players use magic, like cupping their hands while playing (to imitate receiving money), because they have no scientific way of controlling the outcome of the game to their own benefit.

In his book *Talking to Heaven*, James Van Praag asks readers what their motives are for contacting their spirit loved ones. He says that it is "frivolous" to ask for winning lottery numbers. Other purposes he disapproves of are finding lost wills, finding out who murdered one's child, and satisfying idle curiosity.[106] One of the traditional Spiritualists we interviewed said that the emphasis on material things, like getting lotto numbers or finding lost money was "prostituting mediumship." Sometimes there is a tendency to expect such fortune-telling in platform work (public services, as opposed to private readings), and that's why she dislikes doing such work.

This is a complex issue. One problem is that the term "fortune-telling" is found in many public statutes making various alleged uses of psychic powers illegal. It is also a stereotypic label that conjures up fraud, as in cases when a psychic tells the client that it will cost $3,000 to remove a curse. For Spiritualists especially, one question is whether messages of practical magic come from spirits or "merely" from the psychic abilities (clairvoyance etc.) of the medium or psychic.

Since most mediums began with very "psychic" childhoods before developing specifically as mediums, they often have used both psychic and mediumistic means of practical magic, at least in their past. As a child the famous medium D.D. Home told his neighbors where to find lost items.[107] Maud Lord, another nineteenth-century medium, told a neighbor where to find missing papers, helped her father escape Union troops in the Civil War, and later went to Iowa where she located coal and water by putting her head to the ground.[108]

Previously talked about Ray Torre using his psychic ability to know when there would be a pickup for him on his truck route. Hilda Wilkinson, a Lily Dale medium born in the first decade of the twentieth century, reports that as a child "My mother had pulled up some linoleum and a tack hit her eye....She was miserable....My sister went into trance (she was only a kid) and Great Bear, he says, 'Go get a yellow root (carrot) and then relieve the eye.' (My sister) mashed up (a carrot)...and put it on her eye. We got a lot of things like that from spirit."[109]

In recent years Hilda still gets practical advice from spirit. "I know my husband is in the house because (when) I'm struggling to put up a shelf or something and I say, 'Ed come and help me,'...I can go to the right tool and do it like magic. So I know his presence is with me."

This illustrates how traditional Spiritualists have used practical magic, often with the help of spirits. This happens even among those who emphasize that mediumship should not deal with such mundane matters. Partly this emphasis seems to be an ideological or "social desirability" response that does not match the full reality of their actual behavior. It is designed to separate Spiritualism from psychics and fortune-tellers. It is also worth noting that the practical message Hilda received from her husband, not only helped her with the shelf; it was also evidence of his loving presence, something of which Van Praag would no doubt approve.

Another type of practical magic involves the use of mediums (and psychics) in detective work. Even the great nineteenth-century spokesperson for Spiritualism, Emma Hardinge Britten, said that she was "frequently visited by detectives."[110] Although acting on precognitive warnings may be a difficult form of crime and accident prevention, it should be noted that twentieth-century American medium Caroline Randolph Chapman begged popular singer Russ Columbo to stay out of the room in which he was later fatally shot by accident.[111] Recall the case in Chapter 8 in which the medium was interrogated by police for her warning about the school child who was then murdered.

It may be difficult to mount a moral argument against mediumship as practical magic in cases that might save lives or solve crimes, but probably the most politically incorrect practical use of mediumship (or psychic ability) from a Spiritualist perspective involves gambling. This is apparently not because it would be an unfair advantage but more because financial gain is materialistic and not "spiritual". Potential contradictions abound here, because one aspect of New Age thinking involves prosperity consciousness. Some think that this prosperity should be achieved, but it often contains an element of windfall. Perhaps the biggest problem is that lottery numbers are associated with "fortune-telling" (more on this later).

Twentieth-century American medium Dorothy Moore tells about the following experience she had before her introduction to Spiritualism. In dire straits with her husband out of work and facing eviction, she got a number in her head. She played that "number" (in the days before the legal lottery) and won $90 (sometime before 1950, when this was a significant sum). This happened repeatedly with other numbers until she had won a total of $1,017. At that point she gave $5 to the Methodist Church and never played another number again.[112] The usual Spiritualist response would be that she did this "merely" psychically and that this has nothing to do with the proper use of mediumship.

In the 1990s at public message services in Lily Dale we have never seen a medium give anybody advice on gambling. However, practical magical messages are rather common. Some mediums concentrate on identifying spirit relatives but sprinkle in practical advice. A few actually focus on practical matters to the point of almost sounding like a horoscope, with advice on travel, jobs, relationships, cars and other material possessions.

There are two previous sociological studies of Lily Dale done in 1929 and 1974. In the former, George Lawton records actual public messages that give evidence of "practical magic" content, lest we think that such messages are only a recent phenomenon. To be sure there was also a lot of identification of spirit relatives. For example, "I get Aunt Minnie. I get Joe too...a tall and slender gentleman. You are going on a boat ride (and will) have a wonderful

and enjoyable trip." There are also references to physical health, material conditions, "lots of money", and a "transaction."[113]

Richard and Adato do not provide examples of messages but make it clear
that practical magic or "fortune telling" existed in 1974. They also note that
"fortune telling" is against New York State law, but not if it is "solely for the
purpose of entertainment or amusement."[114] Defining it as entertainment
satisfies the law but of course not the ideology of traditional Spiritualism.

41

Guidance and Teaching

It occurs to me that there are overlaps all along the continuum from the "lowly" entertainment function to the highest spiritual function of mediumship. We just saw that practical magic or fortune telling can be said to be for the purposes of entertainment. Next it would seem that fortune telling could also be taken as guidance, telling us for example to change jobs or "take that trip you've been thinking about." If a medium says, "I see suitcases around you," is that a prediction or advice? Mediums often say to the sitter that the future can be changed by free will, or that they don't have to take "spirit's advice."

Especially some traditional Spiritualist mediums said in interviews that people relied too much on the spirit world for advice. Betty Schultz, a long-time Lily Dale resident said, "We can give someone the proof that the one they love still exists, it gives them the ability to go on....That's our real purpose here. The rest is garbage people want because they don't have enough faith and trust in their own abilities."[115]

Anne Gehman, also of Lily Dale, said, "I'm not interested in pleasing people, telling them sweet platitudes...and talking about their romance, and all these other things they should be in charge of."[116] As noted in Chapter 7, Patience Worth disapproved of "looking to the spirits generally for guidance and help."[117]

And yet Anne Gehman said that "Every medium should be a teacher....I would say to spirit,...what is (this person's) greatest need? Then I would try to...help them to learn how to do that. What they need to do for themselves."[118] This suggests the idea of empowerment, mentioned by some other mediums as well. Lily Dale medium Pauline Kay's version of empowerment is to tell people to get their act together, sometimes rather bluntly. Her messages from spirit are generally, "Get in charge of your life," much moreso than "You'll be rich in three months."

42

Counseling and Healing

One of the most common responses on the open-ended interview question about the purpose of mediumship was to say a rather generic "to serve" or "to help people." Probably everyone would have agreed that mediumship is to "help people" if we had asked a simple agree/disagree question. "Helping" would seem to fit a wide area on the purpose continuum, certainly including "guidance and teaching" as well as "counseling and healing."

A couple of the mediums we interviewed discussed mediumship specifically as psychological counseling or therapy, and many of them do a type of spiritual or pastoral counseling as ordained ministers in various Spiritualist churches. Although most mediums do not want to be called psychics, many of their functions are similar. Anthropologist Geri-Ann Galanti interviewed psychics who had three major goals: making their clients feel better, bringing about attitude change, and providing insight. Galanti says that all three goals are "consistent with traditional psychotherapy."[119]

A response from our mediums about their purpose even more common than "helping" was "healing". This could be taken all the way from a basic physical meaning of healing to a mental and spiritual level, including an all-encompassing holistic sense of health. Spiritualists do "healing" in a variety of ways. One way is to bring through messages from spirit containing health advice and remedies. Another is a physical hands-on healing. Finally, any spirit message could be "healing" in a mental/emotional or spiritual sense.

Remember that the famous nineteenth-century Spiritualist Andrew Jackson Davis said that he saw the ancient Greek physician Galen in a vision. After that he did inspired physical examinations and prescribed unusual folk remedies like warm rat skins for a hearing problem.[120]

George Lawton reported on his 1929 observations of a Dr. C.A. Burgess (not an M.D.) who conducted spiritual healing classes at Lily Dale. Some of Burgess' training had come with Pawnee healers, and he had previously distributed his own medicines to leading drug stores. Burgess said, "Medicine is useless. You must help mentalities….Avoid operations; nine out of every ten are unnecessary. These M.D. doctors like to rob and bleed you."[121]

A Lily Dale camp program for 1902 had advertisements for 41 mediums, 7 of whom listed healing as one of their specialties. No one is permitted to set up as a private healer in Lily Dale today. And it is certainly taboo to criticize the medical establishment openly as Dr. Burgess did in 1929. Fear of legal problems seems to be the main reason for the current norms.

If mediums bring through anything related to health in the public message services, they usually give some type of disclaimer, such as, "We cannot diagnose or prescribe." Then they may say, "Make sure you see your doctor for a checkup." In private readings one medium gets a mental image of the Pillsbury Doughboy with indications of possible problem areas noted on his body. Then if she picks something up, she recommends that the sitter have the area checked medically.

Hands-on healing is supposed to be done only in the context of classes on the subject or in services at the Healing Temple. There are many dedicated volunteers who act as healers at these services, held 13 times per week during season. Many of the healers are mediums as well.

The overlapping roles of healer and medium reflect the core values of Spiritualism. Barbara Sanson, who conducts most of the services in the Healing Temple is also a medium and stresses a holistic view of physical and spiritual health. The same could be said of many others. Beverly Burdick-Carey says that her purpose in mediumship is to make people feel better and to share a sense of joy and happiness. "Healing is love in action," she says. Another medium, Marilyn Stafford, considers her mediumship an extension of her work as a nurse. One common sentiment among Spiritualists is that "it's all about healing" (both mediumship and healing in the narrow sense are healing of one sort or another).

Of course, on a world scale health has universally been connected with spiritual phenomena, and the emergence of a scientific medical model is what is new and unusual.[122] One common spiritual explanation for disease in many societies is possession by evil spirits. A 1969 study of Spiritualists in South Wales found that ill health was often explained by possession.[123]

However, there is great variety among Spiritualist groups, and possession is rarely discussed in Lily Dale. There are a few people in our area who talk about getting rid of "entities" or "elementals" that cling like ticks to the body's energy system and cause physical or emotional problems. Generally the Spiritualists we know emphasize spiritual cures much more than spiritual causes of disease.

In fact there is a general tendency to downplay evil and imperfection in Lily Dale, at least in public. Whoever chairs the healing service generally begins by finding something nice to say about the weather, rain or shine. One of the most delightful healing services happened by candlelight during a power outage in a lightning storm.

Many Spiritualists use the euphemism, "There is a lot of healing going on there," (instead of "I see a big problem there."), when bringing through a spirit message about a physical ailment someone may have. A few people have even begun to answer "How are you today" with "Only good things happen to me." Another "Accentuate the Positive" message is the bumper sticker, "Find the good—and praise it."

Consequently, if a medium says that the purpose of her work is "healing," this may mean any part or all of a broad spectrum of holistic well-being. And it will probably not be inconsistent with the next two purposes listed below (proving the continuity of life, and spiritual development).

43

Proving the Continuity of Life

If there is any dogma that traditional Spiritualists (ones not highly influenced by the New Age) take seriously, it is that the purpose of mediumship is to "prove the continuity of life." It is against this standard that merely psychic messages (ones from ESP and not from spirit) and "fortune telling" are condemned. Of course it also helps to establish the legitimacy of mediumship as part of the right to practice one's religion, protecting it from legal sanctions.

Apart from a strictly traditional and legalistic perspective, why would it be important to show that "so-called death" is not the end? We have already pointed out that many cultures, Chinese for example, take the existence of an afterlife for granted. In this skeptical, scientific culture, however, our concept of death leaves us with essentially two problems on a human level: grief and fear of death. This means grieving the loss of your loved ones, and fearing the loss of yourself.

One of the important reasons for the popularity of Spiritualism in the nineteenth century was a rebellion among women against the religious doctrine that sinless infants who died unbaptized were ineligible for Heaven.[124] And ever since then it has been very "healing" for mediums to bring through recognizable messages from the spirit world to the living. The mediums we have interviewed and observed get a great sense of satisfaction when they can do this.

Certainly it must have been very difficult for parents to cope with the death of so many of their children in days of high infant and child mortality rates. Although life expectancies are longer now, death of a relative at any age can be a cause of grief, and there are still significant numbers of parents who must cope with the death of their children, especially in unexpected accidents.

The best and most popular books about spirit mediums in recent years are significantly about grief management. This applies to books by Martin and

Romanowski about George Anderson,[125] and books by James Van Praagh,[126] Rosemary Altea,[127] and John Edward.[128] Other books discuss ADCs (after-death communications) apart from the use of mediums, in the form of apparitions, dreams, signs or synchronicities, showing how important they can be in providing comfort.[129]

Although the concept of the continuity of life after "so-called death" is supposed to make death more acceptable, it is generally considered inappropriate for mediums to bring through messages about impending death. They might be needlessly upsetting, whether they come to pass or not. If you see that somebody's grandmother is about to die, it would be alright to suggest more frequent visits and talks. Sometimes this is understood as a gentle hint.

One interesting violation of the death-forecast taboo, if there was one then, occurred when nineteenth-century American medium Maud E. Lord "helped a family in transition." She told the family of a mother of a newborn child that the woman would die. They all gathered at the bedside while she died, and Maud watched the spirit leave.[130]

A few mediums told us that one purpose of mediumship is to help people get a different attitude about their own death, fearing it less. Dr. Neal Rzepkowski said that knowledge of life after death, through mediumship, changes people's whole perspective on existence, reassuring them, and letting them find more joy in life. This type of change in perspective is especially powerful in people who contact the other side through an NDE (near-death experience). Several mediums told us about their own NDEs, which usually enhanced their mediumship.

44

Spiritual Development

Although few mediums told us explicitly that the purpose of their mediumship was to help people with spiritual development, it is unlikely that any would disagree if asked directly. Emphasizing spiritual development becomes more of an issue for mediums who are outside the Spiritualist tradition. This is especially true for people who are more involved in channeling higher spiritual beings. They may be influenced by the Theosophical notion (see more on Theosophy in Chapter 74) that it is not very important to bring through lower-level (astral plane) spirits like Uncle Harry.

One medium (channel) told us that information from spirit is to help heal the soul. He said that it's really not about giving a message; it's about getting us back into remembering that spirit is the primary cause of everything. We're spirit beings, but we think that we're separate from God. (This is a typical view in New Age philosophy in general.) He also said that it's OK for people who need proof to get messages, but we need more. We need greater spiritual development.

45

Mediumship for Mediums

Up to now we have discussed the purposes of mediumship under the assumption that it's to help the sitter. What do mediums get out of it? Is it supposed to be just a selfless endeavor, a labor of love? Is it OK to charge for the service, and how much?

Several mediums made a special point in the interview of saying that they got a lot out of it themselves. Some state this in terms of the Spiritualist notion of natural law, "What you give you get back," some would say three-fold or even ten-fold. If you give out good things, you get good things back. The same with bad things.

Sometimes the benefit is perceived as immediate. Both in hands-on healing and in mediumship, healers and mediums often feel as if the energy is coming right through them and benefiting them first.

It is clear that many mediums are very sincere in wanting to pass on their own feeling of healing or redemption to others. One said that "the healed heal healers." This applies especially to three people who acknowledged having received a lot of help and who therefore feel that they can and want to help others. For some mediums/healers it seems to be their whole life, somewhat like college professors who have difficulty distinguishing their work from their leisure.

Passing one's own benefits on to others seems like the natural law principle mentioned above, except that the medium receives before giving in this case. Another New Age saying applies here, "You don't have to give in the same place you receive." Mrs. J.H. Conant, a nineteenth-century American medium, went to see a medium when she had a serious illness at the age of 21 (in 1852). He told her that she had strong mediumistic powers. He said that he would cure her, and his fee would be that she should "give your powers to the world (hereafter)."[131]

Is it acceptable for mediums to be paid? This question could be answered legalistically, looking at various state laws that prohibit fortune telling or "telling the future for money." When there are such laws, mediums have a variety of safeguards, including stating that they are providing entertainment only, or doing spiritual counseling as a minister, taking "donations" for their time (the information is free) etc.

In Britain there is the "Fraudulent Mediums Act of 1951" which prohibits deception in the exercise of mediumship, unless it is done for entertainment purposes only. This act is a great improvement over the Witchcraft Act of 1735 under which mediums were actually prosecuted into the twentieth century (to the outrage of Winston Churchill).

Of greater interest here is whether mediums consider it moral or ethical to charge for private readings. We never interviewed or observed a medium who said that it was not. Among the 80 biographies found through library research, only three mediums made a point of objecting to charging for mediumship, and none of these three were active members of a Spiritualist organization.

One of the mediums who objected was Louise Lone Dog, who said that she would lose her power to channel her Native American ancestors if she gave spirit messages for material gain.[132] It makes sense that mediums coming from a communal shamanistic tradition might object to charging for sacred activities. In modern, industrial society, however, few people outside of monastic and military settings can afford to work without pay. It should be noted that few mediums make more than a working-class or middle-class yearly income.

More controversial are the very few who charge very high fees, such as one famous medium who reportedly received $1,200 for forty-five minutes sometime in the late 1990s. By contrast, John Edward, certainly a famous medium, stated recently on television that he charges $300 for a reading, however long it lasts. He could get much more, but he says, "I can't abuse my abilities by charging an obscene fee for a private reading just because that's what the market will bear."[133] He also feels that although there is nothing wrong with financial success, the emphasis must be upon the work itself and the good it does.

46

Serving Spirit

There is a custom among some Spiritualists for the medium to finish a platform or public-service appearance by turning to the chairperson and saying, "Thank you for letting me serve spirit." Probably to most mediums "serving spirit" means helping the spirit world to help the living to receive help through one-way messages from the spirit world.

However, one of our forty mediums specifically mentioned in the interview that "It helps those in the spirit world too." Rosemary Altea, in her book *The Eagle and the Rose*, states that her spirit guide told her that people in spirit "want to communicate, and they need you."[134] James Van Praagh asks, "How can the living help the dead?" and then discusses how spirit communication can help the souls of those who have committed suicide find peace.[135]

Sometimes mediums (and psychics) are invited to haunted houses by "ghost hunters" (amateur apparition researchers), and they try to release unhappy spirits by telling them to "go to the light." This is reminiscent of the practice of exorcism. There are also spirit-rescue groups, some of them concentrated on the fate of the souls of victims of mass murder, as in the "ethnic cleansing" in the Balkans.

At least one medium says that spirits don't need that kind of help, because they get help from spirits on the other side. Recalling our Chinese example, those who practice ancestor worship are clearly in the business of helping their spirit relatives by burning effigies of paper money and of other things needed in the underworld. Of course they expect help in return from their ancestors.

47

Serving Society

Five of our interviewees said that mediumship serves society. Tom Rugani said that it can make for a better, safer, and more loving world. Another talked about it raising people's consciousness. Three spoke on a global level, saying that mediumship could "heal the spirit of the planet" or bring about a "holistic healing of the planet."

Another function seldom mentioned by our mediums has to do with informing society. One talked about channeling scientific information from the spirit world. Another wanted to provide proof of mediumship for science, so that the rest of society would accept it. And a third used the term "paradigm shift," in the sense that the culture would move toward spiritual awareness.

It seems likely that a sample of mediums from a century ago would have talked much more about convincing society of the truth of spirit communication. Emma Hardinge Britten, for example, was a "test medium" before she concentrated on lecturing.[136] Mrs. Leonora E. Piper of Boston was the first mental medium to provide impressive evidence to parapsychologists in the 1880s.[137] About that time Spiritualism roused strong passions, on both positive and negative sides, leading to the necessity of mediumship to defend itself through convincing demonstrations. Such conditions also convinced some mediums, like the British Spiritualist William Eglinton, "to abstain from mediumship as a means of living."[138]

In one fascinating case, a woman referred to as E. d'Esperance agonized in her 1897 autobiography over the problem of validating mediumship to the world. When she was tested outside the context of her supportive group, her abilities faltered. "I wanted to convert the world, but the world did not want to be converted." Eventually she came to mistrust both herself and her assistant, horrified by the possibility that she was cooperating with fraud while in a trance state.[139]

48

What the Sitters Want

This has all been a jolly discussion of the purposes of mediumship mainly as seen by spirit mediums. But what do the "sitters" want, the people who come to the public message services and church services, and who pay for private readings? Frankly there is not much information about the sitters, not nearly as much as on the mediums. This study is no exception. However, we can say a little, some of which is based on the observations of the sitters by the people who know them best: the mediums.

In their 1974 study of Lily Dale, Richard and Adato surveyed 57 visitors, with a methodology that probably oversampled more serious or committed ones (for example, 14 were Spiritualists). "Only two respondents mentioned the death of a relative or close friend as a reason for coming to the Dale, although 42 percent said they had recently lost a friend or relative." The most commonly selected category of purpose for coming was "guidance and knowledge" (47%). Although visitors also came for the lectures and healing services, 84% did consult a medium privately, and 77% attended public message services.[140]

Of course these results leave much to be desired in terms of our more detailed analysis of the purposes of mediumship given above. From our observations and interactions with both sitters and mediums, it seems that the "guidance and knowledge" most people seek falls mainly into what we called "guidance and teaching" above. People especially want to know what to expect and what to do in the core areas of their lives: relationships and family, jobs and money. "Counseling and healing" are probably close behind and intertwined with the previous matters. With especially some mediums/counselors, like Penelope, counseling is the main service for which they are sought out.

Connecting with departed loved ones may be next. Many people are less aware of the benefits of doing this, and they probably benefit unexpectedly when relatives and friends come through, even if they did not seek out the medium for this reason. At certain times in history, demonstrating "the continuity of life" has been of greater importance to the sitter than at others. For example, there was a jump in interest in Spiritualism during and shortly after World War One as grieving parents tried to contact the spirits of their sons. This probably influences changes in the number of churches affiliated with the National Spiritualist Association of Churches: 454 in 1906, 343 in 1916, rebounding to 543 by 1926.[141]

Ranking below the above reasons seems to be "practical magic". It is certainly not insignificant, but most people do not think to consult a medium for this reason, and they may not even be aware of a particular problem before it comes through in the reading. They are often amused when such a message comes through, however, which overlaps the "entertainment" function. Sometimes they are very grateful.

A friend of ours was given a message in her Spiritualist church that she should not sign a contract with a neighbor. This meant nothing at the time, but later on her husband presented her with a contract to sign involving their neighbor and an energy company. She refused to sign before looking into it, although pressured to do so by others. Her delay uncovered other information which saved them thousands of dollars.

I (Charlie) had an experience that illustrates people's interest in practical magic from a medium. Once I gave a little demonstration of mediumship at a paranormal interest club. In the question period a woman said to me, "Ask your mother (who was acting as my spirit guide) to help me find some important papers." I felt a little foolish, but I gave it a try. I had a mental picture of boxes of magazines and such at the bottom of a closet, although the papers were supposed to be somewhere in a desk. This impressed the woman because previously a psychic had told her virtually the same thing, but she had not wanted to bother looking through all of the boxes. Whether my location was correct or not was still unknown, but it led to two other people asking me to find things for them.

Although psychics do not emphasize contacting the spirit world to the extent that spirit mediums do, it is interesting to compare the two, especially since the general public probably tends to lump the two together. In anthropologist Geri-Ann Galanti's article "Why do people go to psychics?" she found that "most first visits to a psychic are for fun or curiosity."[142] This is based on interviews with only 20 Los Angeles area residents. However, it shows the importance of the "entertainment" function, which is probably associated more strongly with psychics than with mediums.

However, Galanti found that people who make return visits to psychics "usually do so in times of stress." In other words, once people go beyond the curiosity level, they look for "direction or help in decision-making" (which seems to fit our "guidance and teaching" category) and for answers to "spiritual (and) metaphysical questions" (which fits our higher-level purpose categories, like "spiritual development", if not so much "proof of the continuity of life").

49

Control Issues

There is one more important sociological/anthropological thing to say about the "So What?" of spirit mediumship. This chapter is supposed to explain the purposes of mediumship, mainly from the perspectives of the mediums themselves. This is mostly a "micro" view, but there is also a "macro" view, that recognizes the importance of the wider social/cultural context. This will be discussed more in Part Seven, but we need to say something about it now.

Whatever mediumship is as a natural ability in human beings, it tends to be shaped and molded by social organization. Spiritualism has been a very loosely structured religious social movement over the past 150 years, but it has also had its tendencies toward order and organization. Bret E. Carroll's controversial book *Spiritualism in Antebellum America* stresses the structure more than some other historians would like.[143]

At any rate, both Spiritualists and others put a lot of energy at times into defining, controlling, and labeling mediumship and related psychic/spiritual phenomena. My (Charlie's) bias is to say that the social rules and theories about such phenomena greatly exceed our actual knowledge about them. However, there are social reasons why such rules and definitions exist.

The main reason, as I see it, is that the various groups involved have their vested interests. Mainstream scientists condemn psychic/spiritual claims because they threaten to undermine the dominance of the scientific establishment and its rational methodology. Parapsychologists are willing to study psychic phenomena, but they are cautious about any kind of spiritual explanation for fear of being rejected completely by "normal" science.

Practitioners of the "paranormal" have their own boundary issues. Although different groups argue about their place in the continuum, there tends to be a hierarchy of respectability with fortune tellers at the bottom, psychics just above them, Spiritualists a rung higher, and Theosophists and other miscellaneous New Age spiritual groups above that.

This gets messy because "New Age" covers so many things, including astrology, for example, which some people would stereotype as being of lower status (down with fortune telling and psychic reading) but which others would place in higher spiritual realms. Michael Brown's book *The Channeling Zone: American Spirituality in an Anxious Age* discusses how "channeling", the currently more popular term than "mediumship", involves elements of spirit communication ranging all throughout our list of purposes (for mediumship) but with emphasis on personal identity and the development of new spiritual and global consciousness.[144]

Back to the hierarchy. Some New Age channels, especially ones with Theosophical roots, say that they bring in only more highly developed spirits than Spiritualists do. Why would you want to contact the lowly energy of Uncle Henry the alcoholic?

Within Spiritualism there are debates about the right way to do mediumship and how to keep it above the level of "merely psychic" reading, and of course above "fortune telling," in spite of the fact that some mediums do these things, as we pointed out earlier. Internal conflicts in Spiritualist churches and communities are common, partly because of the structural problem of it being so difficult to control a group in which so many people are constant sources of revelation (the mediums). The Roman Catholic Church, for example, has far fewer problems like this because of its control over doctrine.

Skultans, in her study of Spiritualism in South Wales, found considerable competition and conflict over styles of mediumship and accusations against other mediums of self-interest instead of the desire to serve spirit.[145] In Lily Dale there is a certain amount of control over what mediums do, especially in public message services, where mediums are sometimes reminded to identify spirit instead of giving just a "psychic" message.

Sometimes a medium will tack on a spirit identification to what is primarily a message of advice or practical magic. No doubt mediums experience some pressure to alter their messages, partly due to the expectations of the Lily Dale Assembly board and partly due to the expectations of the public. This means that there are bound to be some tensions due to a conflict between the goals of the Spiritualists on the board and the personal goals of visitors to Lily Dale.

If Spiritualist mediums may have negative stereotypes about psychics (and fortune tellers), psychics in turn may stereotype fortune tellers (the lowest of the low). Mary E. Leonesio who has "put on many of the popular psychic fairs" writes that "throwbacks from the 'bad ol' days' still exist. They are the ones I call 'fortunetellers.'" She never gives a precise definition of either, but she uses words like "fakes" to describe fortunetellers, saying that they are not "true psychics". "Fortunetellers tell you what they think you want to hear" and may claim that they are always right, or try to "bilk you out of a lot of money" by saying that you need to have a curse removed.[146] It appears that the term "fortuneteller" is used more as a label for readers who fail to obey a set of norms for psychics, rather than for any particular cultural group.

Spiritualists are not referred to directly in her article, but she makes certain comments that seem to suggest that psychics do not necessarily accept the higher status of mediums. For one thing she says that "religion and belief systems should not enter into a reading. (Doing so) frequently indicates that they want to show you how 'spiritual' they are." When she says that "it's considered unethical for readers to ridicule forms of divination other than the ones they use," this could also apply to Spiritualists, who sometimes say that messages should come from spirit rather than from tarot cards etc.[147]

In case you were wondering if there are rules and social control among fortune tellers, who seem to occupy the bottom rung on the psychospiritual ladder, there is a sociological study on "Fortune Telling Practice among American Gypsies."[148] According to Marlene Sway, gypsy fortune telling is an important ethnic business, controlled by the ethnic community in terms of territories of operation to maximize profits and to see that all practitioners can earn a living in the trade.

50

So, "So What?"

As you can see, there are lots of answers to the question, "So what?" Take your pick. I (Charlie) would not be so bold as to claim that certain purposes are clearly more noble than others. As I said before, as a sociologist, I see the apparent social reasons for the rules that human groups devise about proper purposes and methods of mediumship. As a scientist, however, I doubt that we know enough about claims of the paranormal to make definitive and dogmatic statements about how mediumship does or should work.

But I am also a "student medium," and my involvement in the activity of mediumship gives me certain biases and preferences. What is more important for this study is that my involvement helps me to understand "the mind of the medium." Next we need to look at how people become spirit mediums, followed by how they do what they do.

PART V
ON BECOMING A SPIRIT MEDIUM

51

Shamans and Mediums

In a sense this entire book is about becoming a spirit medium. However, the focus of this part is on how people in this "rational" society manage to take on the role of spirit medium. How they "do" mediumship is more a subject for Part Six ("How Mediums Get the Message").

Data for this chapter come mainly from interviews we conducted with 40 mediums and from written accounts of 82 other mediums going back as far as the early nineteenth century. If it were possible, we would have interviewed all 122 of them. Since we couldn't, we do not have information on all aspects of each one's experience. Nevertheless, it is still possible to make interesting comparisons this way, and to get an idea of what it has been like to become a spirit medium over the past century and a half, mostly in the United States and England. Also keep in mind that these 122 mediums are not a random sample, and therefore we cannot claim to generalize about all mediums.

A more general study of the subject of mediumship would begin with the topic of shamanism in anthropology,[149] although the word "shaman" is sometimes reserved for a practitioner who controls spirits in order to heal the body, leaving the term "spirit medium" for people who contact the spirit world for information. Most shamans (or mediums) throughout the world begin with spontaneous experiences in altered states of consciousness. However, sometimes the role is hereditary, and usually there is some type of training, followed by an initiation ceremony to recognize the shaman's special role, even if other members of the society have occasional spiritual encounters too.[150]

What is most strikingly different about spirit mediumship in modern Western societies is that the dominant culture is often hostile or ridiculing in its attitude toward mediums. By contrast, shamans in training in a Native American society would be highly respected. Although people would consider the possibility that a particular shaman might be a fake, they would not doubt the validity of shamanism itself.

So, we are interested in finding out how people manage to become spirit mediums in our society in spite of the fact that it seems to be a deviant activity in the minds of many. Who would want to do mediumship if they are going to be considered superstitious, bizarre or fraudulent?

52

Childhood Experiences

The logical place to begin is with the early paranormal experiences of people who eventually become mediums. We hasten to add that we do not claim to be able to know whether spirit mediums have generally had more paranormal experiences in childhood than other people have. Even if we had random statistical samples of both groups, it would be difficult to measure paranormal experiences in any objective way.

We suspect that virtually everyone in this society has childhood experiences that could be interpreted as paranormal, until they are socialized to ignore them or to explain them in a rational way. Nonwestern societies in general encourage more spiritual and mystical approaches to reality. Based on our data, we are inclined to think that "natural" mediums do have lots of unusual spontaneous experiences as children, more than most people. However, a few of the greatest adult mediums seem to have had rather ordinary childhoods. Also, mediums may be more likely to recall their early unusual experiences more and to label them as paranormal. Certainly some of their accounts are very interesting and deserve further study.

Out of the 105 mediums for whom we have the information, 93% had paranormal experiences as children; and of the ones who had them, 72% had a high level, that is, more than just one or two significant ones. Mediums we studied from library sources were more likely than our interviewees to have had a high level (85% compared to 51%, counting only people with experiences), probably because the ones who appeared in print were generally more prominent mediums.

However, a higher percentage of the mediums in library sources (9%) had no childhood experiences, compared to our interviewees (3%). Four of these six in the former group were quite famous mediums: William Eglinton, Arthur Ford, Pearl Curran, and Mina Crandon ("Margery"). Evidently it is possible to become a medium without exhibiting any talent for it in child-hood.

Among the 98 mediums who reported paranormal experiences in child-hood, the most common type of experience was apparitions or visions (73% had one or more). This means that 69% of all mediums for which we have the information claim to have had some kind of "ghost" sighting or unusual sensory experience involving visions, voices etc. Various surveys of the general population in Europe, England, and the U.S. have indicated between 4 and 12 percent of adults claiming to have had an apparition experience sometime in their lives.[151] So in this case at least we *can* make the claim that spirit medi-ums do have an unusually high level of one type of paranormal experience, not even counting ones they have as adults. Apparitions or visions are an especially important type for a medium to have, considering that such experi-ences are sometimes referred to as "seeing spirit."

The next most common childhood experience for our mediums is ESP, in which we include telepathy, precognition and clairvoyant knowing (but not including apparitions, which may also be included under ESP by parapsy-chologists). Among the childhood experiencers, 42% had ESP experiences (39% of all the mediums). If anything, this seems low after the apparition fig-ure. It may be that biographies of mediums tend to emphasize the more dra-matic apparitions or visions, leaving out some of the more ordinary ESP accounts.

However, the same pattern is found even with our interviewees, when we were in control and could ask explicitly about both apparitions and ESP. Only 45% of our interviewees reported ESP as children compared to 63% reporting apparitions. This is a very interesting finding and makes one won-der whether an especially heightened awareness of spirit is involved in medi-ums, even as children, and not just a developed psychic sense (which manifests as ESP). Certainly among the general population, the percentage claiming to have ESP (19% and higher) tends to be far higher than the per-centage claiming to have had apparition experiences (4% and higher).[152]

The third most common experience (after apparitions and ESP) is acting as a medium in childhood. This goes beyond mere apparitions to getting information from the spirit world and passing it on to others. Surprisingly 27% of the childhood experiencers were already doing this before becoming adults (25% of all). Even more interesting is the fact that 47% of the mediums who began their mediumship by the end of the nineteenth century were childhood mediums, but only 8% of the twentieth-century mediums were.

The reason for this is likely to be that Spiritualism in the nineteenth century was largely an informal social movement based on home circles and seances. Mediums commonly arose spontaneously from these circles, or even without a participating in a circle. Highly intuitive children who had not yet learned to be "rational" might make very good spontaneous mediums. By the end of the nineteenth century Spiritualism was becoming more institutionalized into churches with formal mediumship classes for adults (and children), who sometimes developed for years before performing as mediums.

Another important difference between our mediums by century is that 25% of the nineteenth-century mediums experienced physical phenomena (table-tipping or some type of psychokinesis) compared to only 3% in the twentieth century. These data confirm the commonly stated claim that there has been a decline in physical mediumship over the years.

People suggest various reasons for this decline. One is that the professionalization of science by the end of the nineteenth century left Spiritualism without any legitimate authority for providing "scientific" evidence of the spirit world through physical phenomena. Another is that physical mediumship fell out of favor by being associated with fraudulent mediumship displays, such as drawing "spirits" through a darkened room on pulleyed ropes. Some claim that physical mediumship requires a consistent weekly commitment over years by a group that sits to raise the energy for one medium, but now mediumship is more individual and such group commitment is rare.

Other paranormal phenomena reported by our experiencers include out-of-body experiences (OBEs) (9%), automatic writing (4%), near-death experiences (3%), and past-life memories (3%). Many of their accounts are quite fascinating, but we must be selective. The most significant for our purposes are in these categories: "imaginary playmates" (or spirit friends), visions of spirit guides, and childhood mediumship.

53

Spirit Friends

Altogether 13% of mediums, for whom we have information on whether they had childhood experiences, reported having spirit friends or "imaginary playmates." They began to have them in preschool years, at a median age of 4 (range 3 to 5 for those six who mentioned an age), although they just may not remember earlier incidents. Generally they fade in later years of childhood, although one mentioned them lasting until age 17. We are not including here the majority of mediums' experiences of occasional apparitions, but only cases in which the same spirit people are seen many times and interact with them.

They uniformly describe them as "real" to them, although not necessarily entirely realistic. As pointed out in Chapter 2, Eileen Garrett said that the children in her "imaginary" world consisted entirely of the light that made up other people's "surrounds" (or auras). Ellen Cook (also in Chapter 2) said that she only heard children's voices at first, soon after accompanied by visual images.

English medium Ena Twigg said that she visited and played with her "misty people," who were her "best friends." In spite of their evidently unusual appearance, she stated that "They didn't seem imaginary—they seemed quite real."[153]

Famous nineteenth-century medium Madame Elizabeth d'Esperance wrote about her "shadow friends" who used to pass through the unused rooms of her family's decaying mansion in the east end of London. She said that they were sometimes so real-looking that she mistook them for living people. However, she notes that some of these "people" took no notice of her attempt to show them things, which makes them sound more like the apparitions in a haunting, sometimes called "dumb ghosts" by parapsychologists in reference to their lack of interaction with the living. Nevertheless, her "shadow friends" were real to Elizabeth and helped her not to be afraid when she had been badly frightened by ghost stories read to her by a nurse. She never considered the shadow friends supernatural.[154]

Louise Lone Dog, whose ancestry is Mohawk and Delaware, said, "What some people call imaginary playmates in childhood are indeed very real spirit playmates." She had one for several years, and "then one day he went away and never came back again." When she spoke to her sister about his long absence, her sister replied, "No one has ever seen your playmate you call 'Johnny'...except you. Now we can tell you that he was a spirit...." She was startled to hear this because the experience "had been so vivid and real to me, as if he were exactly like any other living pal of mine." [155]

Although "imaginary playmates" are the core of this phenomenon, these spirit people are not always children, as for example in the case of Madame d'Esperance. One of the mediums we interviewed said that she used to hide in the attic at age 3 or 4, when her alcoholic father went into a rage. There she encountered a fantasy world in which a lady came every day and said, "Come to my house." She could see the house and hear the lady sing "In the Garden." We are not passing judgment on the reality status of such experiences and understand that they may at least in some cases represent only a psychological escape and not necessarily any contact with the spirit world.

At any rate, this fantasy world continued until she was age 14. It felt as if she were making it up in her head, but it was very realistic, as in a lucid dream. One thing the woman did was to bring in her ancestors. Then at age 14 our interviewee's uncle died. Three days later he appeared in the fantasy world. At this point the girl told her mother about the lady in the fantasy world. Her physical description matched that of the girl's mother's mother, whose favorite song was "In the Garden." The mother cried...then took her daughter to a psychiatrist.

As pointed out in Chapter 2, Estelle Roberts' brother Lionel, who died before she was born, allegedly appeared to her and talked to her over the years. She "watched him grow" over time.[156] This is another case of a relative acting as a perpetual "spirit friend" rather than showing up only occasionally as an apparition.

Clifford Bias, a twentieth-century American medium, had imaginary friends as a child. One of them, "Pepper," grew up with him and became one of his spirit guides.[157] This shares the "growing-up" feature of the previous case but is somewhat unusual in terms of lasting until adulthood and becoming a permanent part of mediumship. Indeed this provides a bridge to the next category of experiences: visions of spirit guides.

54

Visions of Spirit Guides

Ten percent of mediums met a spirit guide in visionary form in their child-hood. This does not include cases of a guide coming through in a seance or in some temporary trance connected with mediumship. Visions or apparitions with no special significance for the future medium's spiritual career are also not included. Only two of these cases involve individuals who also had imag-inary playmates or spirit friends, just about the amount of overlap to be expected if these two phenomena are *not* related statistically. Altogether 21% of our mediums experienced at least one of the two (spirit friends or visions of a spirit guide).

As usual there are some cases we have included that are somewhat border-line but interesting nonetheless. One of the mediums we interviewed said that at age 3 or less she saw and heard spirit guides and teachers talking to her in her crib before she went to sleep. She didn't know who they were, but they looked as real as anyone.

Another woman received a guiding message first at age ten. Lying in the grass on a nice day, looking up at the sky, she heard and saw a vision of a Native American who said to her, "Don't think that this is all there is; there's much more." About that time she also began to have out-of-body experiences and mystical experiences with golden and white light.

Children (and adults) often associate bright lights and certain colors with spiritual visions. In Chapter 2 we described Estelle Roberts' "White Knight" who first appeared outside her window, pointing his sword in salute. Pene-lope (in Chapter 10) discussed her "Turquoise Master" with whom she con-versed on a daily basis from age 4 to 9, and later in life during a serious illness.

Twentieth-century American medium Geraldine Pelton often saw and heard spirit people as a young girl, but her first vision of her spirit guide, who claimed that he had been with her from her birth and would be with her always, came at age 16. A bright light appeared during her evening prayer. It was the "materialized figure of a wondrous man," tall, dark-skinned, wearing a white robe and a purple cape lined with gold. He said, "I am Pondoroza, your Guardian Angel."[158]

A skeptic might wonder at the generally exotic and multicultural character of spirit guides, the culture of which might be picked up even by young children. It's true that one seldom runs across White Protestant accountants as spirit guides, for example. Then again, if spirits are not limited by time and space, why should they always be from here and now?

Native American and Asian guides have been common since the early days of American Spiritualism. Nineteenth-century medium Maud Lord was sent home from school one day for receiving spirit raps on her school bench. After a beating at home she woke up blind the next day. Her "Oriental Master" appeared to her and told her to go down to a tree by the creek where she learned from invisible teachers.[159]

Famous contemporary medium George Anderson's most important spirit visitor in his childhood was his "Lilac Lady." Notice the main colors we have so far: white, turquoise, and lilac; all spiritual, high-chakra colors. George's Lilac Lady, "a woman in lilac robes and bathed in purple light, would appear to George in his room, especially when he was despondent," and once at a psychiatric center when he was afraid he was about to be admitted.[160]

Popular TV psychic and medium Sylvia Browne first encountered her spirit guide, a South American Indian named Iena, at age 8. Standing in the middle of Sylvia's bedroom she said, "Don't be afraid, Sylvia, I come from God." Sylvia was frightened until reassured by her psychic grandmother. However, she decided to change Iena's name to Francine. Francine is still her guide in adulthood.[161]

John Brown, "the medium of the Rockies," was born in 1817, lost his parents early in life, and joined a company of trappers. At age 7 he heard voices talking to him when he was alone in a field. They said, "'John we have come to help you, we love you, we love to be with you....'" Then one day he met his guide "Mopoloquist" who opened the door and walked inside. He had John hold a two-foot rod, a symbol of truth and honesty, then took it back and left; but he was John's "guiding angel" from then on.[162] This account is reminiscent of Andrew Jackson Davis's claim that a spirit guide gave him a "magic staff" and took it back again (Chapter 3).

55

Childhood Mediumship

Certainly the first case of childhood mediumship to discuss is that of the Fox sisters (Margaret aged 14 and Kate 11) that began in 1848 in Hydesville, near Rochester, New York. This story is the spark that set wildfire to the "burned-over district" of western New York State (and to much of the U.S. and Britain), and is known as the beginning of modern Spiritualism.

For about two weeks the Fox family cottage was the scene of rapping sounds and noises like moving furniture. Kate asked the power behind the knocks to respond to the snapping of her fingers, which it did, a knock for each snap. Mrs. Fox and a neighbor asked it questions which were then answered correctly in number of raps (e.g., "How many children do I have?").

This case goes on much further, and the noises persisted even without the Foxes present, which is one of many reasons why Margaret's later claim to have hoaxed the phenomenon by cracking her toes and knees seems insufficient even if partly correct. At any rate, this spontaneous event was the beginning of the mediumistic careers of Kate (apparently the better medium) and Margaret Fox.[163]

In the fervor of the craze that followed the "Rochester rappings," Ira Davenport Sr. of Buffalo, a bit of a skeptic, saw a 5-year old boy levitate. As a new convert, he tried table-tipping at home and got results. After his house had attracted followers, his teenage son Ira began to do automatic writing. Next the boy allegedly levitated nine feet from the floor, as did his younger brother William and sister Elizabeth.[164] According to Doyle, "Hundreds of respectable citizens of Buffalo are reported to have seen these occurrences."[165] The Davenport Brothers went on to become famous mental and physical mediums, touring Europe and entertaining royalty.

Perhaps the most interesting cases of childhood mediums are ones who were only babies when they were considered to be mediums. Such an example is James "Farmer" Riley, born 1843 in Philadelphia. While sitting in a highchair at the neighbor's house, Jim put his hands on a table set before him. "The table would begin to move and twirl about, and no man in the room, though he tried, was strong enough to hold the table down and keep it still." This apparently happened before the Fox sisters became known. Then at ages 7 and 8, when table-tipping was all the rage, the neighbors watched him table-tip. "Often three men would sit on the table and try to hold it down, but they could not do so."[166]

An anonymous author wrote in 1921 about her own baby mediumship that also occurred in the early 1850s. "Francis", born in 1851, sat in a home circle that was getting table tremors and raps. It was a custom at that time to have individuals leave the table one at a time to see who was the medium. When she, the baby, was the only one left, sitting on the table, she got a "joy ride." The table ended up putting a dent in the plaster on the wall.[167]

At some later point in her childhood, Francis would go into trance and begin to lecture on anatomy, botany, or history, from 10 to 40 minutes, "correct in every particular." A doctor observed her and was stunned.

For a similar case of a child who lectured in trance, see the story of Cora Richmond in Chapter 5. Cora began platform speaking at age 10 and did automatic-writing mediumship at age 11.

Madame d'Esperance (born 1849), the English medium we discussed earlier, also seems to have done automatic writing in her sleep as a child, as did Cora Richmond. Once she prayed for help with her homework. She awoke to find a fine essay written mysteriously in her own hand. She was also a sleep-walker, which is another type of physical movement during sleep.[168]

One other childhood medium deserves special mention: Eusapia Palladino, born in 1854 in Naples, Italy, probably the greatest of all physical mediums (in spite of a few cases of childish fraud in trance apparently). At age 14 her mediumship first surfaced when she sat at a table with a group of spiritualists. "At the end of ten minutes the table was levitated, the chairs began to dance, the curtains in the room to swell, and glasses and bottles to move about. Each sitter was tested in turn to discover who was responsible for the movements...." It was determined that Eusapia was the medium, but she took no interest "and only consented to have further sittings to please her hosts and prevent herself from being sent to a convent."[169]

Before she died in 1918 Eusapia Palladino went on to be tested at great length for physical mediumship (levitating tables and herself, writing at a distance etc.) by prominent parapsychologists, generally with very convincing results. What is especially fascinating in terms of childhood mediumship is that she seems to fit the classic pattern for being a poltergeist focus, as studied by modern parapsychologists.

The classic type of individual to become a poltergeist focus (a living center of psychokinetic activity) is a 14-year-old girl who is unhappy with her social surroundings but too inhibited to complain, and lashes out unconsciously with physical psychic energy. Eusapia was 14 when her physical mediumship began. She was a foster child in the home of friends, her mother having died at her birth and her father having died when she was 12. The fact that she was in danger of being sent to a convent against her will is another clue that she might have fit the frustrated adolescent model.

Whatever structural reasons there may be for physical mediumship declining by the twentieth century, such as a lack of development classes focusing on it, there may well be an age-related reason as well. In the nineteenth century, especially from 1848 to 1860, there was such a craze of interest in Spiritualism that many natural mediums could surface in home circles. Perhaps children are the best spontaneous mediums. So, if more mediums were being born than made at that time, perhaps the physical mediumship connected to the psychokinetic or poltergeist-focus activity of children like Eusapia Palladino was more likely to emerge. By the time a person tries to develop mediumship as an adult (as was more common in the twentieth century), it may be too late especially to begin to cultivate the physical aspect.

56

Religious Background

Aside from paranormal experiences in childhood, another factor we might expect to influence potential spirit mediums is religion. Of course not all mediums are Spiritualists, and especially in the nineteenth century, many people who practiced spiritualism informally in their home circles might easily have belonged to some other type of church.

Out of the 86 mediums for whom we have information about their family's religious preference when they were growing up, only 2 had no religion. Among the other 84, 55% were Protestant, 21% Roman Catholic, 17% Spiritualist, and 7% other (including 2 Jews, 2 Native Americans, one Christian Scientist and one "eclectic"). We assigned the 21% who had more than one religious influence in the family to the one affiliation that seemed strongest.

Of course we would expect the Spiritualist percentage to be higher among mediums than in the national average. Estimates of membership in such a diffuse social movement are very difficult, because it often has not involved official church membership. Some inflated estimates in the nineteenth century reached nearly 50% of the population.[170] Formal Spiritualist church membership then and especially today is only a fraction of one percent.

Our percentages of Protestants (55%) and Catholics (21%) among mediums are not far from national estimates of the overall population (there are no official figures from the U.S. Census, which is prohibited from collecting data on religion). The most common denominations among our 46 Protestant mediums were Episcopalian or Church of England (10), Presbyterian (9), Methodist (7), Baptist (6), and Lutheran (4).

It is interesting to divide the group by century. Among the 18 nineteenth-century mediums in the sample there are 56% Protestant, 11% Catholic, and 33% Spiritualist. Among the 66 twentieth-century mediums there are 55% Protestant, 24% Catholic, 12% Spiritualist, and 10% other. The increase in percentage of Catholics probably reflects the greater immigration of Catholics beginning by the end of the nineteenth century, and of course the decline in Spiritualists reflects the decline in the popular Spiritualist movement.

These figures are exciting to have because the only other data on the religious affiliation of spirit mediums we know of come from Richard and Adato's study of Lily Dale, New York, in 1974 in which they encountered 7 Protestants and 1 Jew.[171] Of course this is a very small sample. If anything there should have been more Catholics, especially because Catholics are over-represented in the northeastern and midwestern regions of the country.

Looking deeper into our data it becomes clear that the importance of family religion is much more complicated than just listing a main preference. Sometimes the nominal religious affiliation of parents has virtually no importance. For example, Justin Hulberd was a Jesuit priest in Scotland who had a son named Little Justin Hulberd (i.e. Justin Hulberd, Jr.), born 1828. Since the boy's foster parents had no religion, we coded him "none" rather than Roman Catholic of course.[172]

One of our contemporary mediums told us that her mother was a Spiritualist, but she had no conscious influence from Spiritualism while she was growing up. In fact she and her sister used to sit in the car coloring while their mother was in church. At times she would go into church, but she'd rather stay in the car. Any influence she did receive was probably diluted by the fact that she ended up attending Sunday schools and church picnics in a number of denominations.

We list Pearl Curran (who channeled Patience Worth, see Section Three) as an Episcopalian by background. Her family was not religious, but she went to religious schools and was confirmed Episcopalian. One might suspect that her Spiritualist uncle might have influenced her into mediumship, but in fact she never knew about his Spiritualism until she was 13. At age 18 she visited him in Chicago and played the piano in his church for about a month and a half. "I didn't like the crowd that came," she said, "and the whole thing was repulsive to me."[173] She wanted to make it clear after she became famous that she was an Episcopalian, not a Spiritualist. Ironically she was buried by a Spiritualist minister.

The sociological lesson is that social life is too complex to be captured in an objective survey, and that we need qualitative studies to complement quantitative ones. Just the fact that 21% of our mediums had a mixed religious background says something. Some of the combinations were rather involved and often contained some element of "free-thinking" mixed in with the formal religious base.

One of our interviewees had an Irish Catholic father and a Methodist mother. Her mother's mother was a Buddhist. At age 15 she herself attended a Spiritualist camp and started doing platform mediumship.

George Wehner, born 1891, was brought up as a baptized Episcopalian. However, his father studied to be a Baptist minister, then labeled himself a Free Thinker, "worshipped nature," and liked Greek mythology.[174]

Sylvia Browne's father was Jewish, her mother an Episcopalian. However, they converted to Catholicism so that they could put Sylvia into a convent.[175]

Sometimes the less religiously dominant parent sneaks in some influence, or some other member of the extended family, especially a grandmother. One medium told us that her father was a fundamentalist Protestant, but her mother taught her a bit of spiritualist philosophy and told her not to tell her father or people in church.

Another woman had a Southern Baptist father but a Cherokee grandmother with very different spiritual ideas. Penelope was raised Presbyterian, but her grandmother taught her a great deal from her New Thought and Spiritualist perspectives. Twentieth-century American medium Caroline Chapman had Presbyterian and Southern Baptist parents, but she learned about reincarnation from her grandmother.[176]

Finally there is the pattern in which the child converts the parent. We know of several cases of this happening with adult mediums and their parents. But in at least one case the medium was only 11 years old. Cora Richmond was born in 1840. In 1851 her father, an "independent free thinker," said he had found his religion (Spiritualism) after witnessing Cora's mediumship.[177]

57

Family Reactions

Next let's see what kind of support (or lack of it) our mediums got from their families if they had paranormal tendencies in their childhood. In order to code or classify the information we have on this subject for 70 mediums, we had to make some judgments. We put their accounts into degrees of reaction from "very negative" to "very positive", with "mixed" in the very middle if there was a close balance between positive and negative. This has to be very rough and is only the beginning of the story of course.

We came up with 49% getting mostly positive reactions, 16% mixed, and 36% negative. Positive reactions could be anything from verbal approval of a child's ghost experiences to holding a seance. Some negative reactions were mild censure, but others were very severe. Out of the 70 mediums, 7% were told that their experiences were the work of the devil, 6% were warned that they might be going crazy, 6% were considered physically ill, and 6% were spanked or beaten.

Next let's compare by religious backgrounds. Of course the ones in Spiritualist families got the most positive reaction (11 of 12, or 92%; and only one negative, 8%). Fundamentalist families (6, including Southern Baptist, fundamental Methodists, and strict Mennonites) were most negative (83%, with 17% mixed). Nonfundamentalist Protestants (20 of them) were 65% positive, 10% mixed, 25% negative. Roman Catholics (11 of them) were 27% positive, 27% mixed, 45% negative.

It appears that the reasons for different levels of support in different religious groups are complex. The high percentage of negative response among Protestant fundamentalists (83%) is to be expected, where the paranormal is taken seriously as the work of the Devil. Other Protestants may have less focus on interpretations of evil. Roman Catholicism celebrates miracles more than Protestantism does but is ambivalent about spirit mediumship.

In Chapter 29 one Catholic woman thought that going to a spirit medium was a mortal sin. Other Catholics feel that the church tends to discourage paranormal practices outside of the church context, but they may not take that as a serious prohibition of mediumship. John Edward's Catholic extended family was generally interested in and supportive of psychic reading, even though he himself ridiculed it at first.[178] Later when Edward worked as a psychic medium, he felt alienated from the church, but he has remained a strong believer in Catholicism. Eventually he received support from a nun and a priest who praised his work as a gift from God, even if the church would prefer people to see Jesus Christ as the only medium.[179]

If we compare the nineteenth-century mediums to the twentieth-century ones, we see a great decline in family support for paranormal abilities after the hey-day of the Spiritualist movement. In the 1800s (21 cases) we find 62% positive, 14% mixed, and 24% negative. In the 1900s (40 cases) we find 30% positive, 20% mixed, and 50% negative.

Now, you're going to say, "Of course, because there was a higher percentage of Spiritualist families in the nineteenth century." However, if we take out the Spiritualist families, 6 in each century (all positive except for one oddity in the 19th c.), we still see a big decline. Here we have 53% positive, 20% mixed, 27% negative in the nineteenth century (15 cases); 18% positive, 24% mixed, 59% negative in the twentieth century (34 cases).

Whether they were actually Spiritualist or not, there were probably a higher percentage of families in the nineteenth century who were willing to be open to the paranormal experiences associated with Spiritualism. We must remember that our mediums are an unusual group of people, not necessarily representative of the general population in either century. If their families generally tended to be more liberal about the paranormal, this does not necessarily mean that the wider community was that much more accepting of Spiritualism in the nineteenth century, even though there was a Spiritualist craze going on. We will return to this point later.

By the way, we also checked to see if there were differences in support for our mediums by gender (we have 75 women and 47 men), and there were not. Percentages for both family and community support were very close for women and men. This argues that although there have been more women mediums (consistently about 60% at least, even among the ones appearing in books), there is no significant difference in the acceptability of being in the role of medium by gender.

Usually the best examples of support come from Spiritualist families or family members. One of our interviewees said that if she told her mother that she saw a man in the corner (an apparition), her mother would say, "What's his name?" Sometimes adults will cultivate psychic/spiritual abilities by asking children to play games. Penelope's grandmother, for example, asked her to find a key she had hidden. Penelope was supposed to imagine that she was the key, and then to describe what she could see from that perspective (see Chapter 10).

Twentieth-century American medium Millie Gordon made a prediction to her brothers that they would not have to fight in World War One because it would end on her birthday, November 11, which it did. Her father, a rabbi, who might not have been expected to approve of such precognitive goings-on, chose to frame it positively. He said that she had a gift of prophecy, like Elijah.[180]

An English medium born in the late nineteenth century, Mrs. A.E. Perriman, saw an apparition of her mother in the same room where her mother lay dead. In an alleged example of post-mortem family support, the apparition said, "When I was a little girl I saw pictures just as you do. Don't be afraid of these pictures....You have been blessed with a great gift. Use it for the good of others."[181]

Although we were able to categorize 84% of our cases as predominantly positive or negative in terms of family support for childhood experiences of the paranormal, it was common for people to have experienced a combination of positive and negative reactions. For example, Ena Twigg, English medium born just before World War One, considered herself very fortunate for never having been considered "eccentric or peculiar" at home, but she managed this by never discussing her "misty people" with the family. "Our whole family was psychic, but nobody wanted it, nobody could bear it, nobody talked about it."[182]

By tacit example Ena's family supported her belief in the paranormal, but their fear of it led her to suppress it. Her mother was clairvoyant but didn't seem to know it. Her father used to rub a glass paperweight and feel things through it as if it were a crystal ball. When her brother Harry appeared to her as an apparition, her father protested, "It's got to stop."

Sometimes one family member's influence is counterbalanced by another's. One medium's Southern Baptist father beat her for displaying psychic ability. However, her Cherokee grandmother, who worked with her on her spirituality and mediumship, intervened to protect her.

Madame d'Esperance found confidants in her grandmother (grandmothers are nearly all supportive in this study) and in an old servant when she wanted to talk about her "shadow friends" in the house. Her mother, however, would scold her for telling stories about them. Her father, a sea captain, told her fanciful stories which she connected with her own experiences. On board his ship once she saw a "ghost ship" on an apparent collision course disappear right before the crash, then reappear behind them. Her father didn't believe her and told her not to say such things again.[183]

Parents concerned about their children's psychic tendencies sometimes attributed them to physical illness. A.B. Whiting, born in Massachusetts in 1835, used to see "the people," spirit beings around him, especially in his room at night. His parents told him it was just "vapors", or maybe something wrong with his eyes or brain. His mother patiently suggested that he would get over such sights when he got older; she had seen such things when she was a child too.[184]

The mother of Dorothy Moore, twentieth-century American medium, was seriously worried about her daughter's apparitions and took her to an optometrist. Told there was nothing wrong with her eyes, her mother said, "I want her to have glasses anyway." When the glasses didn't solve the problem, a doctor was called in, who removed Dorothy's tonsils right there on the kitchen table. Dorothy never saw or talked with her "imaginary friend" Susie again.[185]

George Wehner, born in Detroit about 1891, told his father about his apparitions and other psychic experiences. Doctors were consulted who said that there was nothing wrong with him. However, they said that he was far-sighted, making near objects blurry, and he imagined that he saw spirits.[186] But wait, here comes the grandmother factor: once the spirit of his great-great-grandmother Anne gave him her name, and his grandmother rewarded him with ginger cookies.

In many cases the explanations for these childhood "fantasies" combined physical and mental illness, and mental illness with Satanic influence. The case of Daniel Home (see Chapter 2), born 1833 in Scotland but moved to Connecticut, provides a good illustration. After his apparition of his friend Edwin he was told, "Nonsense, child—you are ill, and this is the effect of a fevered brain." Later he was accused by his aunt (with whom he lived) of bringing the devil to the house.[187]

As we noted in Chapter 3, Emma Hardinge Britten's mother was also worried about the devil. She was afraid that her daughter's mediumship might even end in "permanent lunacy or death."

One of our interviewees was taken to the psychiatrist for having a persistent evidential apparition that answered the description of her mother's mother. The psychiatrist didn't know what to do with her and recommended taking her to the pastor of their church. The pastor decided that she was evil because she talked to dead people and kicked her out of the Southern Baptist church. The responses of the psychiatrist and the pastor fall under our category of "community reaction," but the actions of the mother fall under "family reaction."

English medium Rosemary Altea's mother's mother, whom she never met, used to hear voices that no one else could hear. They frightened her so much that she checked herself into a psychiatric hospital, "The Towers." Both she and her daughter thought that she was mentally ill. Then when Rosemary started seeing and hearing things, her mother screamed, "'You'll end up like your grandma...in The Towers.'" Rosemary grew to fear for her own sanity, and these words "were to haunt me for a very long time."[188]

At least part of the time such warnings seem to have had a dampening effect on the child's experiences. As we pointed out in Chapter 2, Estelle Roberts was spanked with a belt and told that hearing voices was evil. She was afraid she might be crazy. Gladys Osborne Leonard, born in England in 1882, regularly saw visions of a place she called "Happy Valley." When the family realized that her detailed descriptions went beyond ordinary imagination she was forbidden to look at it any more. "With an effort she was able to suppress her visions, and they gradually stopped coming."[189]

Little Justin Hulberd, born 1828 in Scotland but raised in New York by foster parents, was a tougher case. His grandmother whipped him for lying about "the old lady" who helped him pick gooseberries he couldn't reach, because the woman he described had been dead for over 200 years. The grandmother's mediumistic daughter-in-law visited from England and verified Justin's claim, leading to some inconsistent child-rearing.

Dismayed by his imaginary playmates and apparitions of dead relatives, "His foster parents believed him possessed of the devil and attempted to beat it out of him." His grandmother often told him that he was fit only for the

Gypsies and the show people. So, he ran away with the circus, was retrieved by his family, went with the Gypsies, and was brought back again. Justin finally received family vindication of a sort when his foster father had a vision at age 83 and converted to Spiritualism just before he died.[190]

58

Community Reactions

If some of the family reactions to the childhood paranormal experiences of the future mediums in their household seemed grim, community reactions tended to be grimmer. We have only 43 mediums with information about community response, in contrast to 70 for family response, no doubt because there was a tendency to keep such things within the family. However, for those who commented on community response, only 33% were generally positive, 12% mixed, and 56% negative. Family responses were 49% positive, 16% mixed, and 36% negative.

Positive responses were essentially from people who were involved in Spiritualism or who crowded around to witness phenomena or to get information from the spirit world. Negative responses were more heavily in the "evil" category and less in the illness category compared to the negative family responses.

Among the 43 mediums who got community reactions as children, 19% were told it was the devil or a demon, 9% were called witches, 5% were told that they were damned (e.g., "The devil has a mortgage on your soul."), and 5% were excommunicated from the church. Two were subject to violence (5%), two were called crazy, and two were told they must be ill. One was referred by the doctor to a medium for an exorcism.

Let's compare mediums who were from different religious backgrounds and see how they fared. This should not be as meaningful as the connection between religious background and family reactions. However, at least in some cases the surrounding community might be rather similar to the medium's family in their religion and attitudes.

It turns out that Roman Catholics received the highest percentage of negative community responses, 71% (5 of 7, with one mixed and one positive). This is probably because the formal church and religious school reactions would be more authoritarian (in spite of the theoretical possibility of miracles being more recognized by Catholicism). Spiritualists (7 of them) got the best reactions (43% positive, 29% mixed, 29% negative), but this is way below the 92% positive family response.

Among the Protestants there was not much difference this time. Of the 6 fundamentalist Protestants, 17% positive, 17% mixed, 67% negative. Of the 9 nonfundamentalist Protestants, it was 33% positive, 11% mixed, 56% negative. Of course this is a very small sample, but the same expected difference is seen. It's just that we expect the community not necessarily to have homogeneously the same perspective as the family.

Probably the most interesting comparison is between nineteenth and twentieth-century mediums in the level of community support. Recall that there was a much lower level of family support in the twentieth century (30% positive) than in the nineteenth (62%). And taking out the Spiritualist families, the decline was about the same or even greater (18% down from 53%).

In the case of community reaction the two centuries show almost identical percentages. In the 19th (with 21 cases): 33% positive, 10% mixed, 57% negative. In the 20th (with 22 cases): 32% positive, 14% mixed, 55% negative. Granted this is a rather small sample, it still suggests a possible interpretation. One wonders just how much different the two centuries were in terms of popular support for Spiritualism.

Being more specific, we thought that the mediums in the middle of the 1800s might have gotten more support, when the Spiritualist movement was taking off. However, checking the birth dates of all the nineteenth-century mediums shows no change in community reactions throughout the century. And of course our twentieth-century mediums were nearly all adults by the time the New Age or New Spirituality movement picked up in the 1970s and 1980s; and even the youngest ones had to deal with adults raised before that. One would think that the (early and mid) twentieth-century reactions would be more negative than the nineteenth-century ones because of the decline in the Spiritualist movement.

The fact that they are not suggests an interesting hypothesis. Maybe there never was that much support for Spiritualism, even at the height of the movement from 1848 through the Civil War. Certain families were deeply into it, and their sympathies show up in our nineteenth-century family data, whether they were ready to call themselves Spiritualists or not (and they would probably still belong to some other church anyway, because the movement had very few actual churches).

But for most people, even ones who experimented with table-tipping, it may have been merely a curiosity. Beyond the core of families who took serious spiritual lessons from it, all the other millions may have been merely curious. It may have been first a craze at the height of the phenomenon, then a mere parlor game, as the ouija Board is for many people today. Some of our case material suggests this. For example, Pearl Curran, who was vehemently opposed to Spiritualism, tried a ouija Board just for amusement. She got more than she bargained for obviously (see Chapter 7 on how she channeled Patience Worth).

What does this mean for our data? It may mean that the climate for Spiritualism was largely negative even throughout the nineteenth century. Childhood mediums who let people outside the family know about their paranormal experiences sometimes generated positive reactions, in the form of curiosity seekers and sometimes from people who really wanted information about their dead relatives. However, there was also a backlash against Spiritualism. Sometimes social control was exercised by mobs and by organized religious protest. It was clearly a mixed bag.

Looking at specific cases, we coded the Fox Sisters' community reaction as mostly positive. As described above, their 1848 raps in their Hydesville, New York cottage started the great public attention to the phenomenon of spiritualism. Within a month hundreds of people had visited the Fox home, and the neighbors, who were sympathetic and respectful, had formed a committee of investigation to record and test the communications, including digging in the basement for remains of the peddler whose spirit was allegedly coming through. In 1904 a skeleton and peddler's tin box were finally found in the cellar walls, according to the *Boston Journal*, a nonspiritualist newspaper.[191]

However, once the Fox sisters began to become famous and do public demonstrations, there were outraged reactions especially from some clergy and at least some minor violence in nearby Rochester. In their defense a Quaker, Mr. Willetts, declared at a public meeting, "'The mob of ruffians who designed to lynch the girls should do so, if they attempt it, over (my) dead body.' There was a disgraceful riot, (and) the young women were smuggled out by a back door."[192]

Over in Buffalo, beginning in about 1855 the Davenport brothers, also discussed previously, attracted many people to their home to see their levitations and table-tapping messages from dead relatives. Of course this is several years after the Fox sisters had begun the craze. We coded their experience "mixed" because it apparently included even more negative reaction. Not only was there some violent opposition and hooliganism, but the family was threatened by arrest, imprisonment, and law suits.[193]

One of the groups more supportive of spiritualism in the early days was the Quakers. In fact many spiritualists were fallen-away Quakers, some of whom were influential in the founding days of Lily Dale in the 1870s. When Little Justin Hulberd's childhood mediumistic powers became known, about 1835 (before the Fox sisters), he was "a great favorite" among Quakers, who "asked him to go into 'the state'...and see what he could for them...which he always did."[194]James "Farmer" Riley was about 7 or 8 (about the same age as Hulberd was in 1835) when his table tipping caused great excitement among the neighbors in about 1851.[195]

In the twentieth century, which is of course beyond the days of the popular spiritualist craze, a child's psychic or mediumistic feats are not likely to cause a community uproar. Some mediums did however get some notable reactions. Millie Gordon, for example, at about age 16 (in the 1920s perhaps) told a boy in front of 22 witnesses that he should not drive to a fishing trip because there would be an accident. He went anyway and was killed in a car crash. People were astounded and sought her out to have their fortunes told.[196]

It is interesting that having such a reputation could be a double-edged sword, causing both positive and negative reactions, sometimes in the same people. As pointed out in Chapter 2, Mrs. Cecil Cook, American medium born in the late 19th century, complained about being shunned in public by people who were eager to get spirit messages from her in private. American medium Maud Lord, born 1852, stated that some people who came to her for information on the coming Civil War also advised that she be punished for having the information.[197]

What these cases illustrate of course is the tendency for people to conform publicly and deviate privately. Especially people in prominent community roles are expected to voice the prevailing morality. This leads us to examples of reactions by the clergy.

D.D. Home, born 1833 (see Chapter 2), experienced apparitions and physical effects between 1846 and 1850 in the house in Greeneville, Connecticut, where he lived with his aunt and uncle. Aunt Mary accused him of bringing the devil to her house and called in three ministers to check him out. The Congregationalist refused to come. The Methodist attributed it to the devil. The Baptist prayed for it to stop.[198] It didn't help. Daniel started telling neighbors where to find lost items and giving them proofs of "spirit identity." He was kicked out of the house in one week.

Mrs. J.H. Conant, born in New Hampshire in 1831, had experienced haunting phenomena in their house prior to her mother's death when she was 11. Her mother, a member of the Baptist Church, had experienced them too and was thought by the neighbors to be possessed by a "wild delusion" and to be involved in "dealings with the devil." Consequently the Baptist minister refused to officiate at her funeral. Fannie (the daughter) said, "A strong disgust took possession of me, together with a desire to *kick* the reverend bigot."[199]

Fannie's spirit guide appeared to her and told her to ask the Methodist minister, who she said would come. Fannie went into trance and found herself at the minister's residence. A sociologist might not be impressed by the trance claim, but the first minister is certainly a good example of a negative "reference individual," someone who influences you to be unlike him.

Mary Garrett Shaw, born into a Catholic family in New Orleans in 1848, went to her bishop at age 13 to share a clairvoyant insight. She said that he should send Father Coppinger away because his ruin was being sought by "a beautiful devil in the garb of a handsome young woman." Although the priest confirmed the issue, the irate bishop said it was the devil's work and sent Mary away. "I'll have none of this foolishness in my parish," he declared. Wondering if the bishop was right, Mary asked St. Michael to keep the devil from her and said "Hail Mary" for protection. The young priest, who was being seduced by a Society woman, was sent away to a monastery.[200]

Mrs. A.E. Perriman, English medium born in the late nineteenth century, saw a vision at age 8 in the school garden pool of her mother falling off a horse and getting injured. She reported it to a nun who said, "It's wicked, wicked,...you must never talk about such things. Those pictures you have seen are things of the devil." The next day the news came in confirming the accident, but the Mother Superior agreed with the other nun that she shouldn't talk about it.[201]

Nearly a century later, George Anderson's Catholic school experiences were not much different. At about age 11 he told another student about a vision he had had. "Someone reported it to George's teacher, a nun, who ridiculed him in front of his classmates." Another time he saw such a vivid vision in class of a spirit in clerical garb that he announced it to the whole class. A nun hit him over the head with a thick book, saying that she intended to "'beat him sane'" by the end of the year.[202]

George had other unpleasant experiences in school as well, with other nuns and with classmates who called him a "weirdo". Of course he learned to keep things more to himself, but he did find one sympathetic teacher, Sister Bartholomew. She even seemed comforted when he gave her a spirit message from her recently deceased father.

It is interesting to compare George Anderson to another famous contemporary medium, James Van Praagh. He told his first-grade teacher in Catholic school, Mrs. Weinlick, that he knew (clairvoyantly) that her son had just been hit by a car, and that he had broken his leg but would be alright. When the news came in she was shocked, but later she had a calm talk with him. She told him that he had a special gift that might help people some day, but that he should also be careful with whom he shared it. Now he says, "If I had had a nun for my homeroom teacher instead of a layperson, my life might have turned out a lot differently."[203]

It is clear that Van Praagh would expect a more negative response from individuals in a formal church authority position. But there are also the Sister Bartholomews, especially when they get messages in private instead of in front of the entire class.

Not all church authorities respond in the stereotypical way. Not only are there differences based on whether there is some public expectation for social control, but sometimes there are also interesting alternative ways of framing things.

One of our interviewees said that her parents were a little "freaked out" by her precognitive statements. They took her to the fundamentalist preacher who labeled it as coming from "religious figures." He saw it as positive, like the prophecy in the Bible. What a surprise, considering our earlier examples of especially fundamentalist Protestants who labeled paranormal phenomena as the work of the devil.

In a similar case, one of our interviewees stood up in her Southern Baptist church at age 8 to report on what happened in summer Bible school. She proceeded to channel information that included an admonition to apply their lessons to their own lives instead of just studying old Bible stories. The congregation was speechless. Then the preacher said, "Spirit is moving today."

What one preacher might have labeled the devil's work if it were thought of as Spiritualist mediumship, another might label the influence of the Holy

Spirit (as in "speaking in tongues"). Miraculous healing is also found in both fundamentalist Protestant and Spiritualist churches in somewhat different forms.

One last example of unexpected clerical reactions comes from twentieth-century American medium James M. Laughton. At age 9 he had a vision of a little girl in a casket. Later he recognized the same girl in church (denomination unspecified); she was the daughter of the minister. At some point he told the minister about it, and six months after his vision the girl died of scarlet fever. Instead of being angry or upset, the minister was fascinated and paid James a quarter each time he came to visit his study and talk about visions. The quarter was hush money.[204]

59

Adult Experiences

We have made the point that it has generally been considered deviant to be a spirit medium in the United States (or England, since several of our mediums are English). How then do some people manage to become one anyway? So far we have looked at the childhood paranormal experiences of mediums and at the reactions to them from family and community. Although about half of our mediums had more positive than negative reactions from their families, that means that about half did not. And community response was even worse, only one-third mainly positive.

Of course our sample is of mediums, most of them performing in some kind of public setting. Most people who were discouraged enough from being mediums would have given it up and not been interviewed or had books written about them. The question is what happened to the mediums who stuck it out.

To a sociologist, the answer would likely be found in "differential association," which generally explains why some of us are socialized one way and others of us another way. People who manage to associate with enough influences heading them in the direction of mediumship will become mediums, even if most people think it is deviant.

Clearly there are too many discouraging associations for most of the mediums in our sample to explain why they became mediums, if we look only at childhood experiences. Therefore we must look to other types of influence as well, namely aspects of their adult experiences. Of course, some mediums may have been curious enough about their experiences to persist in spite of negative social reactions. Most of them, however, manage to find like-minded people, either in Spiritualist churches or elsewhere.

We coded eight different types of adult experiences that helped move people into the role of medium, and 91 people (75%) had at least one of these factors. Most of the other 31 people can be accounted for probably by the fact that we could not get sufficient information from their biographies.

Among the 96 who had not done mediumship as children, 83% reported at least one of these influencing factors. Among the 26 who *had* been childhood mediums, only 11 (43%) reported one or more adult influences. This shows that the childhood mediums at least sometimes needed further direction. Some even had to revive their spiritual path because it had been squelched at some point in their childhood.

Our eight factors are as follows in order of how frequently they were mentioned: significant others (69%), group influences (59%), adult paranormal experiences (57%), medium calling (mediums telling them they should do mediumship) (20%), crisis illness (20%), crisis social experience (12%), reading about Spiritualism etc. (12%), and spirit calling (being told by a spirit to do mediumship) (8%). Of course the percentages total more than 100 because many mediums reported several factors; they represent what percentage of those reporting adult influences had experienced each type of factor.

Beginning with significant-other influence, the most frequently mentioned type, this shows the great importance of social factors of course. It is surprising perhaps that most of these influencing individuals were only acquaintances or strangers (mediums, church acquaintances, professors, speakers etc.), 42 mentioning these, compared to 19 relatives and 12 friends.

Of course it may be that the relatives and friends, though fewer, had more continuous contact and influence. The most frequently mentioned relatives were wife (5) and husband (5), followed by father (2), sister (2), and four others mentioned only once (including only one grandmother this time).

Our focus here is on factors that influenced people in the direction of doing mediumship, but some people mentioned contrary adult influences that had to be overcome. One woman's husband was opposed to her being a psychic, and one man's father argued that mediumship was trickery, but in both cases the individuals said that they were guided by spirits toward doing mediumship anyway.

Another woman said that she left the Episcopal Church as an adult and went searching elsewhere because she knew that the bishop was "restricting himself," holding himself back from telling the whole truth about spirit.[205] Although the previous two examples don't count as significant-other influences toward mediumship, this one does because the bishop was a "negative reference individual" as mentioned before.

Sometimes the potential medium treats the significant other in this negative way but then becomes converted. William Eglinton, English medium born in 1857, as a young adult ridiculed his father's home circle. "'I refused to join them, on the plea that "it was all humbug," thus setting myself up as an authority on a subject of which I knew nothing.'" After 7 or 8 nights of no results, Willie put ridiculing signs up on the door of the seance room, "'There are lunatics confined here; they will shortly be let loose; highly dangerous' etc."[206]

Willie's father was offended and asked him either to join the circle or stay out of the house. He decided to join the circle and had the following conversion experience. "'A strange and mysterious feeling came over me, which I could not shake off....The table began to show signs of life and vigour; it suddenly rose off the ground, and steadily raised itself in the air, until we had to stand to reach it. This was in full gaslight.'"

Some young adults have had experiences before (Willie Eglinton had not) but spend their childhood baffled by them and being labeled as weird by family and community members. One of our interviewees was like that until she met a Spiritualist friend and her mother (the pastor of the church) who helped put psychic phenomena into a Spiritualist framework. She felt that she had "found someone like me." Another woman asked her spirit guides to lead her to people like her, and she met a man in a store who introduced her to a Spiritualist church.

Another example of reframing as an adult the experiences one has had as a child can be seen in Emma Hardinge Britten (see Chapter 3). A couple told her about spirits of the dead, which made her think about the ghosts she had seen and the voices she had heard, none of which she had associated with spirits. At that point she was skeptical about a Spiritualist interpretation, but this new perspective got her to investigate.

Some conversions occur when the person is not really searching. One of our interviewees was a college professor who did a service to an hysterical college student by taking her to Lily Dale to find some explanation for her spontaneous experiences with channeling. This led to the professor getting an evidential message from a medium and to both of them attending development class.

Another woman describes what she considers a series of synchronicitous events involving the actions of a number of people who steered her along, even though she had no notion where she was going. A friend of hers wanted to get a reading in Lily Dale and asked her to make an appointment for him. She didn't even know what he was talking about. But soon she happened to see a newspaper article on Lily Dale; then a fellow airplane pilot turned out to be a Spiritualist and explained a bit about it to her.

She made the appointment in Lily Dale, but as it turned out her friend didn't show up. She got the reading herself, which turned out to be excellent, from a medium who ended up being her mentor in mediumship later on. After many other twists in the story, working with healing, rather than mediumship, she became a professional medium five years later.

Another example of significant-other influence involves a complex set of relationships. This potential medium's grandmother was a medium in Lily Dale. When our interviewee moved to Lily Dale with her husband, it was her husband who was influenced by her grandmother to become a medium. Then she was influenced by her husband. After she was divorced from him, she influenced her second husband to become a medium.

In many cases the individuals we are calling "significant others" influenced people not only by what they said but also by introducing our mediums to organizations, or our mediums found these people in the organizations. Therefore, these previous cases are often linked to our next category, "groups or social events."

Among the 54 mediums who were influenced by groups or events, 33% mentioned Spiritualist camps (especially Lily Dale), 31% churches (mostly Spiritualist of course), 30% classes (including a couple of college classes, but mostly spiritual/psychic classes), 30% circles or seances, 9% psychical research organizations, and 7% psychic fairs. Although only 30% (16 mediums) specifically had classes as an important influence getting them into mediumship, many more of our mediums had formal training in mediumship than that. It's just that many were already socialized into taking on the role of mediumship before that.

As we pointed out earlier, formal training in mediumship was seldom available in the nineteenth century but became much more common in the twentieth century. Therefore, let's look at one century at a time. None of the 27 nineteenth-century mediums for which we have the information had a high level of formal training (an extended program or ordination as a Spiritualist minister), 4% (one person) had a low level of formal training, 56% had informal training in circles only, and 41% had no training at all. The Fox sisters and the Davenport brothers are examples of spontaneous mediums with no training. They just did it.

Now for the twentieth century. Among the 73 mediums for which we have the information, 23% had a high level of formal training, 38% a low level of formal training, 21% circles only, and 18% no training.

Let's look at a few of the interesting reports about group influence. One of our interviewees moved to Canada in middle age. Although she had had psychic experiences throughout her life and had even had some association with a Spiritualist church in England, she was not especially looking for one in Canada. She didn't know anybody and went to five different churches before people spoke to her…in a Spiritualist church. Within three months she was giving spirit messages and lectures in that church.

Twentieth-century English medium Leslie Flint had had apparition experiences as a child, and became interested in survival and started reading about Theosophy as a young adult. He was told at a Theosophical Society meeting that Spiritualists only contacted "unevolved entities." This was supposed to discourage him from getting involved with Spiritualism, but it had the opposite effect. He ended up at a Spiritualist church getting an accurate reading from a medium who encouraged him to become one too.

Finally, one American medium born in 1851, was a child medium and did both trance work and healing. However, she stayed away from Spiritualist meetings and circles as an adult. She healed the sick and helped other mediums develop but was not willing to go into public work or start a Spiritualist church.

"Spiritualism, as I understand it," she said, "did not come to the knowledge of man to establish a new religion…but to prove (survival of the spirit)." Here is a medium who withdrew from group influence. It may be in part because she was "too timid…(ever to) be a public platform medium," as her father said. "Francis" published her autobiography in 1921 with the anonymous byline, "Written by Herself."[207]

Our next category of adult influences is "medium calling," that is, being told by another medium that you are or should be a medium yourself. In the early days the labeling of mediums was often done as part of the process of discovering "who's the medium," or who was responsible for the phenomena occurring in a table seance, the tipping or rapping especially. As mental mediumship became more common, the medium responsible for the circle or seance might identify a potential medium in the group.

In this sample of mediums, 20% (18 people) had a medium calling. People were told such things as, "You can do this too," or "You're very psychic," or "Someday you'll be a (great or famous) medium." Three were told this by a medium in a Spiritualist church setting. In our participant observation of church services and platform demonstrations we have seen this many times. Whether it is calculated or not, it serves as a recruiting device. Keep in mind that in most Spiritualist churches probably at least 20 or 30 percent of the members take mediumship classes and do at least "student" mediumship in services.

Of course not all of our mediums are or always were Spiritualists. One of our interviewees stopped in a crystal store to shop for a geode. The woman in the store told her that she was there for a reading, not for a geode, and proceeded to tell her that she would be giving readings as her life's work in six months.

A couple of weeks later our interviewee started doing spontaneous automatic writing that set out her life purpose and path. Six months later, the day after she took her first money for doing a reading, she was laid off from her regular job, and indeed her primary source of income became giving readings.

Mrs. J.H. Conant, an American born in 1831, had a severe case of "consumption of the blood" with no hope of survival at age 21. A healing medium told her that she had strong mediumistic powers and said that he would cure her. However, his fee was that she should "'give your powers to the world thereafter.'" His medicines cured her in three weeks.[208]

Only 8% of our sample (7 people) had a "spirit calling," some kind of vision or other communication from a spirit directing the person to become a medium. We referred to two good examples earlier in Chapters 3 and 8: Andrew Jackson Davis' vision of Swedenborg, Galen and his spirit guide; and Ray Torrey's vision of himself being "initiated" in a Native American ceremony in his driveway.

One woman had such a calling *prior* to her call to become a medium, so it doesn't count, but it's an interesting parallel. At age 26 she heard a voice coming from the corner of the room one night saying, "Go be a nun." Although she left the convent after five years, she thinks that it makes her more credible as a medium to some people that she was once a nun.

Louise Lone Dog communicated with spirits and spirit guides since childhood, and she received informal training in Native American spirituality from her Mohawk and Delaware family. However, she also received a special calling and preparation for trance mediumship when she heard "the Voice say, 'trance, trance.'"[209]

Ena Twigg, English medium born just before World War One, reports an experience that apparently occurred in her young adulthood (date unspecified). One night some time after her heart had been damaged in an operation, three transparent, apparitional people came into her room, took a medical history, and injected something into her neck which left a visible mark there the next day. Every Tuesday night they came to see her. She recovered in six months, and then they told her that their job was done. However, she needed to repay the favor by "giving to others that which you have received."[210]

They gave her an address on a piece of paper, which her husband also saw later. The house at that address turned out to be the location of a mediumship circle. People there told her that she was a natural medium, and that she would replace the medium they had just lost. In the circle a spirit message came through that she would demonstrate clairvoyance on a Spiritualist platform. Soon she was called by a Christian Spiritualist church to fill in for an ill medium.

There is no way to check the reality status of this experience at this point, but it is interesting how similar her account is to ones of alien abductions that have been first published decades later. Consider the medical exam, the physical mark on the body afterwards, and the "sense of mission" in the abductee or "experiencer". One thing that does not sound typical for an abduction account is the apparitional quality of the people, but notice that the piece of paper was no apparition.

We have two additional cases in which a spirit of some sort guided the person to a particular address. Back to Mrs. Conant again, referred to above in the case of the healer whose fee was that she should help others with her mediumship. Later she channeled the spirit of a doctor who told her to go to a boarding house to get a room for seances. When she got there she found that there was a room available that conveniently had been "already magnetized" by another medium who had just left.[211]

Another woman met a spirit guide in a near-death experience (NDE, which we will discuss later), who told her, "If you will follow me, I will show you a new way of life." She felt guided to the residence of a man who answered the door and said to her, "I don't know who you are, or where you came from, but they told me you were coming." She ended up going to this man's house most afternoons for many years to learn about the principles of Spiritualism.

60

Conversions and Crises

So far we have considered social and spiritual influences in adult life that have been important to our mediums in establishing their role as medium or in reinforcing their childhood inclinations to be mediums. Some of them were already rather comfortable with the role due to a supportive environment in family and/or community. However, since the role of medium is often labeled as deviant, many people need a significant shift or break with "normal" reality before they can be receptive to suggestions that they take on such an atypical lifestyle.

Sociologists who study "conversion" to fringe religious groups, or to other nonmainstream subcultures, tend to emphasize that people who find themselves in some kind of crisis or major life change are more likely to be receptive to conversion.[212] We hesitate to embrace this idea fully for two reasons.

First, we are uncomfortable with labeling spirit mediums as deviant, and then implying that something must "snap" physically or emotionally or socially before anybody would be willing to do something so crazy. Participation in any group or role involves some amount of socialization or resocialization, and it is never completely "rational". It is not clear that there is anything so special about becoming a spirit medium compared to anything else, except in how society looks at it.

Second, calling the adult socialization to mediumship a "conversion" is a bit strong for many of our cases. Many people are redirecting or reaffirming tendencies they had established in their childhood.

Having said all of that, it does appear that some kind of crisis or major life change was significant for many of our mediums. Altogether 29% (26 individuals) had either a crisis social experience or a crisis illness or both (3 people had both) that moved them toward mediumship. Once they were in that condition they were also more open to the social and spiritual influences we have already discussed.

Among the 12% (11 people) who had a crisis social experience, the most common type was divorce (4 people), followed by death of a close relative (3), loss of a job (2), and one each with "dissatisfied life" and depression (the last one overlapping with crisis illness). Alfred Askin Wright, American medium born in 1869, was living in New York when he got divorced. He moved to Los Angeles, "But (I) still found myself depressed and in need of a mental lift. I was attracted one day to a Spiritualist meeting." Soon he was attending regularly and developing his mediumship.[213]

More common than a crisis social experience was a crisis illness, experienced by 20% (18 people). By far the most prevalent type was a near-death experience; 10 people, including 2 who had two each. In addition to the NDEs, there were 4 with various illnesses, 3 with surgery, 3 accidents or physical traumas, and 2 mental illness.

Certainly the NDEs are interesting, especially the fact there are so many. Thinking back to the childhood experiences, there were only three then. Also there are no significant differences by century or gender.

Two of the NDEs took place in the nineteenth century, long before Dr. Raymond Moody called attention to this phenomenon in the late twentieth century. The accounts sound very much like the ones described today.

Mrs. J.H. Conant had one in 1851 at age 20. When ill she was prescribed a large overdose of morphine and went unconscious. The doctor thought she was going to die. She went into trance and channeled a simple medication, and recovered. While in trance she went to "some beautiful place; she thought she was in heaven." There she met her mother, begged to be allowed to stay there, and was told she must return to earth life because "she had yet a mission to perform."[214]

John Brown, the "medium of the Rockies", born 1817, seemed to have one (sometime around 1850 perhaps), although without a vision of "the other side." They had not thought him to be "unusually ill," but then he had an out-of-body experience, looking down on his own body. He heard the doctor say, "He's dead." However, he revived.

One of our interviewees had an NDE at age 24 when she was in a car accident. While she was "out", she felt as if she were experiencing "oneness" (how we are all one). She heard a voice say, "You can stay or return and teach. We'll help you." She came back, started a home circle, and went through formal mediumship training.

Both the previous and the following individual had two NDEs, of which the first was more significant in both cases. The second individual "died" of a bee sting and other complications. She heard the doctor say, "Oh that's too bad, she's got lots of kids." Then she came back and said, "Oh my God, I'm dead." The doctor lifted the sheet and said, "I don't think so." After that her mediumship got really intense.

Serious operations without any mention of NDEs are also recorded as preceding the development of mediumship. Mrs. Piper, American medium born 1857, had two operations shortly before falling into trance unexpectedly when in consultation with a healing medium.[215]

One of our interviewees had a severe hemorrhage when her stitches broke while recovering at home after cancer surgery. She was in a horse barn when it happened, and put her hands on the wound and prayed. Then she saw a spirit form in the corner; she thought it was a spirit coming to take her away. It became the face of her grandfather, who had died when she was 6. He said, "Don't worry." After that life-changing experience she changed her life purpose and career, taking classes to become a healer and medium.

In Chapter 6 we related the story of Molly Fancher who fell off a horse and later was very seriously injured when she caught her dress and was dragged by a streetcar. These traumas led indirectly to other complications and to periods of unconsciousness. Just before going into a nine-year "trance" (or coma), her "second sight" began to develop.

There are also cases in which illness seems to hinder mediumship, although it may not be exactly the same as these "crisis" examples. Doyle states that D.D. Home's mediumship "went with the tubercular diathesis."[216] Arthur Ford is reputed to have experienced a decline in his mediumship due to the effects of alcoholism.

We notice by comparison that there are only 3 cases of illness that seemed to affect mediumship or other paranormal experiences in childhood, compared to 18 in adulthood. The most significant case of childhood illness was that of George Anderson, whom we discussed earlier as developing visions after a severe case of chicken pox that attacked his central nervous system.

One wonders if paranormal experiences in childhood are an easier way for mediums to be turned toward mediumship in the first place, before they are socialized against it in this society. Then, as adults, influences are more likely to come from crisis events, physical or social, accompanied by social influences from sympathetic spiritually-minded people.

Nonetheless, 57% of our mediums who had significant adult influences report adult paranormal experiences as significant (third in importance behind "significant others", 69%; and "group influences", 59%). Remember that 93% reported childhood paranormal experiences, and that 100% had adult paranormal experiences in the sense that they are all mediums.

Within the group of 52 mediums with influential paranormal experiences as adults, apparitions or visions were most common (31%), followed by mediumship (25%), NDEs (19%), PK or physical mediumship (13%), ESP (13%), synchronicities (6%), automatic writing (6%), and a few minor others. People with more than one type of experience make the percentages go over 100.

Two important examples are found in Part One (Chapters 4 and 7). Arthur Ford first experienced precognition as an adult while serving as an officer in World War One, dreaming of a list of his men who would die the next day of influenza. This could fit the pattern of a crisis event or trauma triggering psychic or mediumistic tendencies. The other previous example of an adult experience is Pearl Curran's unexpected channeling of Patience Worth at the ouija board.

Patricia Hayes, well-known teacher and medium, was a student of and later the personal liaison for Arthur Ford. Three years after he died he appeared to her as an apparition in 1974 in a car she was riding in. He very quickly showed her in pictures a system for mediumship he wanted to pass on to people. She went home and wrote down these charts for doing a kind of healing mediumship.

James "Farmer" Riley provides a good example of a childhood medium who did nothing for many years as an adult. Thirty-five years after his father had discouraged him from doing table-tipping, he sat with his wife at a table. For six months they got nothing, but one night the table began to move, and they used a code of raps and movements to bring in a message from her brother. Farmer Riley was back in business.[217]

There is one other allegedly paranormal example we find especially amusing. One of our interviewees was working on a thesis in comparative religion for his training to be a Methodist minister. A book literally fell off the library shelf and landed on his foot. It was about Spiritualism, and it resonated with him. The seed was planted. This is an example of a synchronicity, and we have heard many very similar examples, even specifically about important books oddly falling off shelves.

This example also overlaps with our final category of adult experiences, namely reading about Spiritualism or other subjects relevant to mediumship. Only 12% mentioned this as an influencing factor, although we suspect that a far greater percentage did significant reading as adults that helped convince them to be mediums. We did not ask specifically about this in our interviews, and it probably was not included as often as it should have been in the written biographies. The most common type of reading was about Spiritualism (45%), then parapsychology or psychic phenomena (27%), followed by individual mentions of other things like mesmerism (hypnosis) and Theosophy.

This concludes our discussion of how people get to be spirit mediums. The next question is, "How do they do it?"

PART VI

HOW MEDIUMS GET THE MESSAGE

61

Variations on the Theme

At first we thought that this part of the book was going to be mostly a technical account of the procedures used by spirit mediums to bring through what they considered to be messages from "spirit." We'd count up how many mediums were clairvoyant, clairaudient etc. And discover whether they had to look up to see pictures, look down to feel things kinesthetically etc. It would almost be like a manual of how to fly an airplane.

Well, some mediums do have a system they can describe almost like a manual. However, others are much less aware of how they do what they do. Also, there is a great deal of variation among mediums. The more we looked at the data, the more we realized how complicated it is to explain how mediums operate. At this point we stood back and began to ask some basic organizing questions.

First of all, what sort of communication is this spirit mediumship? Who's contacting whom, and who's in charge? Some mediums really don't have much of a conception of what is going on. Also, even some mediums who do think they know, are nevertheless very passive in their role and have no system for controlling it.

In the broadest sense, there is a range of apparent communication with passive trance at one end and an active blending with others at the other end. In full trance the medium loses consciousness and is apparently occupied by a spirit who speaks through her/him. In semi-trance or "light trance" the medium is somewhat aware of what is happening and can remember channeling the spirit when it's all over.

Especially mediums today, who want to be more in control, are less likely to go into trance. In the middle of our continuum from passive to active we next have the typical communication with spirit in which the medium gets impressions sent from the spirit and relays them to the sitter or audience. Let's call this the "relay" system.

So far we have trance (full and semi-) and relay mediumship. There is one more we'll call "blending." This is the most active. In blending the medium moves into, or "becomes one with" the sitter or a spirit in order to understand what that other soul knows or feels. Only 4 of the 40 mediums we interviewed are blenders at least part of the time.

In trance the other spirit comes into or possesses the passive medium in order to express information. In relay the medium exchanges information with the spirit and then passes it along to other people. In blending the active medium moves into the soul or field of the other in order to retrieve information. Although any such typology is bound to be an oversimplification, we think that it is a useful beginning in the adventure of trying to make sense out of how mediums get the message.

62

Trance

Altogether 59% of the 98 mediums for whom we have such information did some trance mediumship. If we leave out the 8% who did it very little, this leaves 51%. Among the ones who specified whether it was full or semi-trance, 15 did the former and 13 the latter type.

It is very important to divide our mediums into three groups here in order to show how much trance mediumship has declined over the years. Among nineteenth-century mediums 87% did trance, 8 individuals specifying full trance and only 2 semi-trance.

Among the twentieth-century mediums in library sources (many of whom were earlier in the century), 51% did trance, and only 40% if we leave out those who did it very little. Among our interviewees, all contemporary mediums, only 33% have done trance, and only 18% if we leave out those who have done it very little. Moreover, only 2 of our interviewees specify full trance, 6 semi-trance.

It is not surprising that trance was much more popular in the nineteenth century. Beginning in the 1850s, Spiritualist women were able to speak in public in a trance state at a time when women in general, even feminists, were not. Since the spirit was in charge, women trance speakers could not so easily be accused of stepping out of their legitimate passive domestic roles. This practice resulted in both the spread of Spiritualism through enthusiastic audiences and some loosening of the restrictive role of women.[218]

The down side was that the trance state fell under the medical definition of psychological abnormality. This was one of many ways in which Spiritualism was labeled as deviant, part of the social control process mobilized against the spread of Spiritualism as a religious social movement in the nineteenth century.[219] Even in the twentieth century, until recently anybody who spoke as if channeling another spirit entity was a good candidate for the diagnosis of multiple personality.

Of course trance mediumship has not existed merely for the purpose of allowing women to speak in public. Trance has been common in mediumship in many cultures. For example, Chinese mediums may go into trance, imitating the gestures, dialect and the sound of the voice of the deceased.[220] If a "medium" is a go-between, connecting the spirit world with the land of the living, it might be expected that the most direct way of being a medium would be to be possessed by the spirit, going into unconsciousness to get one's own mind out of the way.

In looking at specific examples of mediums who were said to be in trance, it is clear that the word "trance" has been applied to a variety of conditions. For example, one of Molly Fancher's "trances" (see Chapter 6) lasted for nine years. Today we would say that she was in a "coma." When Eileen Garrett said that she could go into trance by "sleeping away from" her aunt's voice (see Chapter 2), we now suspect that she was experiencing some type of dissociation or having on out-of-body experience (OBE).

People were also said to be in trance when they were "mesmerized" or "psychologized," in other words, "hypnotized." Today many psychologists think that hypnotic trance is really just suggestion in a normal state and not even an altered state of consciousness.

Generally speaking, when spirit mediums are "in trance," this means some type of altered state of consciousness, presumably with another entity at least partly in charge. Whether this other entity is really a spirit or just another personality of the medium is difficult to know.

Buhrman studied 18 Lily Dale mediums in trance and found that 11 were in full trance, 7 in semi-trance (and had some memory of events and of how their body felt). Of the 11 in full trance, 7 were completely unconscious, but 4 surprisingly continued to have and to remember an inner awareness after waking up. These latter 4 were said to be in "conscious full trance," which seems to be a contradiction in terms. Interestingly Buhrman also studied 18 meditating yogas, 6 of whom had amnesia during meditation (like the typical full-trance medium).[221]

Since this study is mainly an attempt to understand mediumship from the medium's point of view, let us leave the puzzling psychological and physiological questions of what trance is now, and look at some accounts of the subjective experience of trance from mediums themselves. Sometimes mediums go into trance unawares, as in the case of Mrs. Leonard who awoke from a little nap in a seance to find that she had been in trance, channeling her guide or "control" Feda.[222]

Other people watching a medium go into trance can observe behaviors such as the following. In the case of Mrs. Leonard (when she was actual *trying* to go into trance), after "a brief period of silence,…she begins to breathe slowly and regularly as if sleeping. In a few moments sighs are heard, and then whispers come from the medium's mouth."[223] And then the spirit speaks.

In the case of Mrs. Piper, "The onset of the trance (in the early days of her work) was often accompanied by unpleasant spasmodic movements, grinding of the teeth, etc."[224] This is the sort of thing that was taken by nineteenth-century physicians as evidence of pathology.[225] One wonders about the people who tested her to see if she was really in trance, but she "could be cut, blistered, pricked and even have a bottle of strong ammonia held under her nose without being disturbed."[226]

When I observed a spirit medium in Hong Kong in 1980, they said that she went into trance in the morning and stayed in it all day long when giving individual readings. She would greet me and speak as if she were Sam Gu ("Third Aunt," her control or spirit guide). Sam Gu would go find the spirit I wanted to contact, and give an appropriate descriptive identification, to which I agreed. Sometimes the description would be all wrong, and she would have to try again.

When it was decided that the correct spirit had been identified, the medium lay her head on a pillow that sat on a table containing a red bulb, a framed sacred writing in red, a statue of Sau ("Long Life"), and offerings of oranges and grapes. In about half a minute her whole body shook, her head especially rocking back and forth. She made a gurgling noise, sat up, and began to speak as if she were the spirit.[227]

As I think about this today, I would say that she probably went into light trance in the morning by meditating. Her guide Sam Gu spoke through her in semi-trance. But when she wanted the spirit to speak directly, she went into full trance while her head lay on the pillow.

Now for the subjective accounts by the mediums themselves. The similarities among them are evident. Arthur Ford would "breathe slowly and rhythmically until I feel an in-drawing of energy at the solar plexus." Then he would feel Fletcher's (his guide's) face pressing into his, and he would lose consciousness.[228]

Mrs. Cecil Cook began to be "controlled" at about age 7. She felt a tingling in her arms and felt cooler. As the feeling spread, her vision faded, and everything went blank. Other kids said that she stiffened, groaned, and seemed to fall asleep. "When I was controlled, it was feeling some stronger influence coming INTO me. It came much as though some one had walked right into my body....Then I must have gone someplace else."[229]

This sounds like full trance. Then it could take several seconds to adjust when coming back into her body. She was upset that she couldn't hear the things that the controls (guides) told people.

Going into trance as an adult, Dorothy Moore had the feeling of "being elevated, of spinning, of losing awareness of my surroundings." She went unconscious and had no awareness of what happened while she was out.[230]

James "Farmer" Riley had a similar experience in terms of the notion of elevation. He reported the "sensation of floating away; his head feels light and swollen to twice its size; as though it is expanding—going up, and carrying him with it, and then he knows no more until he comes out from under the influence."[231]

George Wehner described his trance process like this. "I relax utterly....I wait for the touch of my guide...(then) I let myself 'go' completely." He would get a numb sensation in the back of the head, and his hands and feet would usually be very cold; there would be icy waves up his spine. Then his body would be flooded with warm currents (concentrated around the solar plexus). Usually there would be gas in his stomach. Usually he would have a sensation either of sinking fast or rising rapidly. He would lose consciousness, but just before that he might see auras around sitters and spirits.[232]

In spite of all his awareness of the process, he said that he could not go into trance at will. Apparently this means that he could not force it, only relax and wait for it to happen *to* him. On rare occasions he would become conscious after a while, still in trance. Then he would feel the personality of the controlling spirit. He could watch the thoughts of the spirits inhabiting his physical brain. Sometimes when awakened by someone while he was in trance he would go out of body (have an OBE).

We have been looking at examples of full trance, and in Wehner's case he could rarely observe what was happening in his controlled brain, which might be called semi-trance, or be like one of the cases Buhrman described as full trance with some consciousness. Pearl Curran, who channeled Patience Worth (see Chapter 7), seemed to be always in semi-trance. From the alleged spirit's point of view, Pearl sometimes got in the way. Patience complained that Pearl's conscious mind would make substitutions, changing the word "portions" to "bits", and "rocks" to "stones."[233]

It is interesting to note that some mediums could do two things at once in trance. Mrs. Piper sometimes brought through two different spirits at once, one through automatic writing and one by speaking.[234] Mrs. J.H. Conant could do automatic writing with both hands at once, writing down a medical prescription with one hand and bringing in another spirit with the other.[235] Once Katie Fox "was talking and laughing while her left hand was doing backward some very serious mirror-writing...." Sometimes she would write with two hands at once, on separate sheets.[236]

Of course these claims are consistent with the explanation that trance mediumship represents multiple personality. Two or three different aspects of the medium's personality could be doing different things at once. We are not interested in debating the issue at this point, but you may well be thinking about it when we present the next point: what the spirits think about the process.

Spirits trying to communicate through Mrs. Leonard talked about two kinds of difficulties. One was their failure to remember things due to being constrained by the use of a brain foreign to them. The other was their incomplete control over the medium's brain, making it difficult for them to get her to say things. One spirit said that it was easier to communicate when locating not in the brain but just above the eyes in front (which sounds like the pineal gland or "third eye").[237]

Arthur Ford said that his control/guide Fletcher was needed to act as a "master of ceremonies" to give order and precedence to "the crowds of discarnates who pressed about me."[238] And of course this is the apparent purpose of having at least one dominant spirit who will "control" not only the medium in the sense of taking over his/her body in trance, but also the many spirits that might come through a medium who is in trance. Remember that this is not just a custom in one culture. Chinese mediums do the same, as in the case of my Hong Kong medium who used Sam Gu as her control or "master of ceremonies" as Ford put it.

However, one of the spirits who spoke through Arthur Ford said a curious thing. "Ford is his own master of ceremonies. He is here with us, on what you call our plane. He feeds his impressions to Fletcher who reports them. However, it is to his own memories that Fletcher has access....From Ford he gets only such impressions as Ford communicates and they appear to him as his own."

We're not sure that that makes a lot of sense. Also, Ford was surprised to hear about the communication later, because he had thought that his own mind was "knocked out" during trance and would be unable to participate as the spirit claimed. If the spirit's explanation were true, it would mean either unconscious participation on Ford's part or conscious participation followed by amnesia.[239]

As we saw in Chapter 2, the famous medium Eileen Garrett was not at all certain that the spirit guides Uvani and Abdul Latif who came through her in trance were real. She thought that they might be part of her own consciousness, a case of multiple personality. Even when the messages they brought in were highly evidential, this did not prove that her own mind or "higher self" was not responsible for bringing in the information. Next we should find out more about how mediums experience their spirit guides.

63

Spirit Guides

Recall that we found trance to have declined greatly over the years. Only 18% of our interviewees have done much trance compared to 87% of the nineteenth-century mediums. However, spirit guides are alive and well.

Since spirit guides tend to be very important in "controlling" a medium in trance, especially in full trance, you might think that they would have outlived their usefulness as the popularity of trance declined. However, only our four mediums who tend to blend actively with the soul they are trying to get information about, seem to have no use for a guide when doing their own blending. Relay mediums still find a spirit guide handy for organizing the communication with the other world.

Among the nineteenth-century mediums 75% of those for whom we have the appropriate information had spirit guides; still 72% of the library-source twentieth-century mediums had guides, as do 74% of our interviewees. If anything there may be an increase in the percentage of mediums with guides who have more than one guide: 52% in the nineteenth century, 54% in the twentieth-century ones from library sources, and 61% of our interviewees. By the end of the nineteenth century Spiritualism was becoming more institutionalized, and there was more of a culture about how many guides you might have in your "spirit band."

However, it is interesting that the percentage of mediums who claim to have any personal knowledge of the identity of any of their guides has declined. Nearly all, 95% (20 of 21), of the nineteenth-century mediums claimed to be able to identify the name or characteristics of one or more of their guides; but 86% (24 of 28) of the twentieth-century library sample could, and only 69% (20 of 29) of our interviewees with guides could. This does not include mediums who were merely told who their guides were by some other source, such as another medium.

We suspect that the decline may reveal that spirit guides may have lost some of their importance after all, in spite of the strong notion in the mediumistic culture that one ought to have spirit guides. Some mediums have a vague feeling that they are there or "must be there," but cannot identify them.

Next we thought that it would be interesting to see if people who can identify their guides tend to be women, on the hypothesis that women might be believed less and need to legitimate their work by claiming to have a spirit guide. As it turns out, this seems not to be the case. Overall 61% of our mediums are women, and 63% of those who can identify at least one of their guides are women, a small and insignificant difference.

However, we did find an important gender difference when we made a list of all of the identified spirit guides, grouping them by the gender of the guide and by the gender of the medium. Altogether there were 112 guides, of which we could determine the gender (or probable gender) of 93; of these 93, 76% were male and only 24% female. Nor is there any tendency for female guides to show up more frequently in more recent times.

Among the nineteenth-century spirit guides, 73% were male; among twentieth-century spirit guides (excluding contemporary cases) 74% were male; and among our interviewees and other contemporary mediums taken from library literature, 79% are male. In our total sample of mediums (rather than guides) from these periods there are 41% male in the nineteenth century, 50% male in nonrecent (noncontemporary) twentieth century, and 26% male in the contemporary group.

What does this pattern of predominantly male guides and predominantly female mediums mean? In the nineteenth century, especially in the 1850s, women were not expected to speak in public, but women mediums were more likely to get away with it, especially if they were channeling a male spirit. Ironically, however, we see the percentage of spirit guides who are male increasing somewhat, not decreasing, as we move through the supposedly more liberal and liberated twentieth century.

Could part of the problem be that we have a biased sample of mediums? It is highly likely that there have always been more female than male mediums in the U.S. and in the U.K. ever since Spiritualism took off in 1848. Our nineteenth-century sample of mediums consists of every single usable biography in all of the books in both libraries in Lily Dale (we looked at every one); this should be as good a sample as one could get, and it shows 41% males.

Probably this is an overemphasis on male mediums, however, since males probably were more likely either to be famous or to get into print or both, due to a general sexism in the culture.

In the twentieth-century noncontemporary sample there are 50% male, also no doubt an exaggeration of male participation in mediumship as a whole, maybe even more pronounced as Spiritualism became more institutionalized. In our interviewed and contemporary library sample we have 26% male, which might be a slight undercount of males due to our accidental sampling technique. Nevertheless, both in Spiritualist churches and in the overall New Age community of channels and mediums, women clearly dominate (except among TV and print celebrity mediums).

As it turns out, however, it doesn't seem to matter much whether we have an overrepresentation of one gender of medium or not, because there is not much difference in the tendency of male or female mediums to have male or female spirit guides. Both genders are more likely to have male spirit guides.

This is true in all three of our time periods (19th century, earlier 20th, and contemporary). Sample sizes are small, but ironically mediums were more likely to have a spirit guide of their own gender in the nineteenth century than later. In one way this makes sense, because there was more gender differentiation in more traditional times. But what makes it ironic is that women became more likely to have male guides in the twentieth century (as if they were being more dominated by the male part of the spirit world rather than less).

Getting specific, in our nineteenth-century group, the guides of male mediums were 91% male (10 of 11), and those of female mediums were 63% male (12 of 19). In the earlier twentieth-century group, guides of male mediums were 57% male (4 of 7), and those of female mediums were 81% male (13 of 16). In our contemporary group, guides of male mediums are 60% male (3 of 5), and those of female mediums are 83% male (29 of 35).

In spite of the small sample sizes, the overall pattern is fairly clear: moving from nineteenth to twentieth century the male mediums (if anything) are moving in the direction of having a smaller majority of male guides, and the female mediums (if anything) are moving in the direction of having a greater majority of male guides. There is no indication that the women are becoming "liberated" by picking up a higher percentage of female guides.

What might this mean? Perhaps it represents a combination of tendencies. It might be different for male and female mediums. For one thing, among mediums who could identify their guides, the female mediums identified more guides than the male mediums did. The 39 women identified 82 guides (2.1 per medium), but the 23 men identified only 29 (1.3 per medium). This suggests that the women relied more on guides to help or control them.

There is some other evidence that female mediums have used guides as authority figures more than male mediums have. Neither male nor female mediums had a single female guide who was mentioned as being in a role of authority (such as "Doctor" or "Master"). Among the male guides, however, there were 12 doctors (or "physicians"), which might be expected due to the importance of healing in mediumship; three "masters"; and one Native American "chief". By the way, there were no lawyers. There was also a "council of men," whom we counted as one guide, as in all cases when a group was mentioned with no specific names.

Interestingly these authority figures were highly concentrated among the male guides of female mediums. They were 26% (14 of 54) of all the male guides of female mediums, but only 18% (3 of 17) of all the male guides of male mediums. They were the most concentrated in the contemporary female mediums' male guides, 38% (11 of 29), which is another counter-indication against a liberationist theory of modern female mediumship.

However, there are some problems with this sociological perspective that seems to indicate male dominance in spirit mediumship continuing into if not growing in the twentieth century. We seem to be implying that female mediums choose their guides (whether they exist "objectively" or not), and that they predominantly choose male ones, often males in authoritative roles. Most mediums, however, especially Spiritualist ones, have given more emphasis to the voluntary participation of the guides. Usually they choose the medium, although there must be mutual acceptance.

If this is the case, ironically it might be that these spiritual authority figures are showing preference to women as spirit mediums. Why most of the guides should be male, however, is another difficulty, especially in a world view that professes the need for balancing female and male energy, and that historically protested the dominance of males in mainstream churches. Of course, in spite of the prominence of women in nineteenth-century Spiritualism, there was a tendency for women to lose out to male authority when groups of Spiritualists tried to organize the movement formally in the 1850s and 1860s especially.[240]

In contemporary Spiritualist churches, as well as in New Age groups and gatherings, there seems to be a very prominent presence of women both in membership and in active authority roles, certainly in comparison to mainstream churches. Although both female and male mediums seem to have predominantly male spirit guides, there does not seem to be any significant preference for or differential treatment of male or female mediums in these organizations.

The fact that there are more female than male mediums would seem to be a reflection of the greater percentage of women among the general membership. If male mediums are overrepresented in mainstream media, this is probably not particularly a function of the Spiritualist or New Age subculture.

Looking back at the spirit guides, there are some other interesting patterns aside from gender. Altogether 27% of the guides are clearly Native American, and there are others that sound as if they might be. There is no gender difference on this (28% for male mediums, 27% for female mediums). This pattern is also remarkably stable over time: 26% of nineteenth-century guides are Native American, 26% in the earlier twentieth-century group, and 28% among the contemporaries. Obviously this is not just a recent New Age phenomenon.

Overall 71% of the Native American guides whose gender was specified were male (compared to 77% of non-Native Americans). Although the numbers are very small, all four of the Native American guides of male mediums were male, and 11 of 17 (65%) for female mediums were male.

As a group the Native American names are often rather similar. For example, ten of the thirty involve a color: Black Bear, Grey Eagle, Blue Mountain, Blue Feather, Gold Feather, White Feather, White Cloud, White Wing, Red Cloud, Turquoise.

There are also 14 other nonEuropean-sounding names or identifications: a Chinese, an Oriental, an Oriental Master, a Hindu, Abdul, Abdul Latif, Dr. Rohun, Moses, Master Morah, Zabdiel, Uvani, the "Old Man" from Egypt, Star-and-Crescent, the "Little Prophet" from India. Some others that may well belong to the Native American total are Crystal, Running Fox, Thistle, Winona, Snowdrop, Bright Face, Pink Rose, and Feetheart. If we added all 8 of these to the Native American group we would get 38 (34%). And the non-European total would be 52 (46%). We might see this as a culture of the exotic. Or, from a spiritual perspective, it might indicate that spirit guides are culturally nonrestricted, and that Native Americans are especially tuned in to spirit.

Relatives of the medium are rarely spirit guides. None of the 35 guides in the nineteenth century fall into this category. In the earlier twentieth-century and contemporary groups two men have their mothers, and one has his daughter as a guide. Two women have their brothers, one a grandfather, and one a daughter as a guide. Note the predominantly cross-gender connections here. One contemporary woman has an "archetypal grandmother" as her guide.

One other interesting pattern is that there are five guides named Harry, all in the contemporary group. There may be no connection, but it reminds us of the common saying among mediums that Spiritualists typically contact "your uncle Harry" as opposed to higher beings.

A few other miscellaneous names that might be notable are Mopoloquist, Chlorine (a Native American woman), and the guardian angel Pondoroza. Sylvia Browne had a guide named Iena, an Aztec/Incan woman from the sixteenth century, who first visited Sylvia when she was eight-years old. Sylvia decided to change her name to Francine, which she liked better than Iena.[241]

We have decided not to include the alternate personalities of Molly Fancher (see Section Three) among the spirit guides: Sunbeam, Idol, Rosebud, Pearl, and Ruby. They are all female and would change the percentage of guides who are male somewhat. However, they were rather obviously a case of multiple personality. Some of the spirit guides that we did include might also be alternate personalities. However, Molly Fancher did not consider them to be or use them as spirit guides. In fact in spite of her apparent psychic and mediumistic abilities, she did not even categorize herself as a medium.

Next, let us take a few examples of how mediums talk about their guides and use them for different functions. One contemporary medium, a Spiritualist, who is an expert on spirit guides, states that all mediums should have a minimum of five spirit guides from birth. The three main ones are the gatekeeper (hers is an Iroquois woman named Turquoise), the teacher (hers is Master Carnelian), and the healer (Dr. Carlyle in her case). In addition her protective guide is Long Arrow, a Native American, and her master teacher is Master Shannon.

Turquoise appeared to her when she was a child. Before Master Carnelian her teacher was Dr. Carmichael, her primary philosophy teacher who also works with other mediums now. Dr. Carlyle the healer was not always there when she was a child. All five were there at least sometimes during her childhood.

Long Arrow first materialized when she was meditating shortly after taking formal mediumship classes. She wanted spirit to come in, then heard a voice that said, "Open your eyes." Seeing the magnificent vision of him, she reached out to touch him, but then he dematerialized (something that typically occurs when people try to touch an apparition according to parapsychologists). All of these guides work closely together, she says, not just for her progress but for their own as well.

Another one of our interviewees had a guide named Water Lily, a Native American woman, who was gentle and slow. They say that your guides are usually like you, but she was the opposite, too slow with the information. For a few months she had another guide named Henry Williams. However, for over twenty years now her guide has been Harry from Ireland, a real character. When she is giving a message or reading she ordinarily hears everything from Harry, but there is also another guide Michael in the background, and she can hear him sometimes.

This medium talks about a division of labor among guides that is similar to the previous medium's system. She says that every band has five members plus five others that come and go. Harry is her protector, but he also serves in the role of chemist (healer). Michael does the leg work and sets up appointments in the spirit world (the functions of runner and message bearer). There are also the roles of teacher, master teacher, and gatekeeper (or control).

Another woman has an Iroquois guide named "Black Bear," which she says may not be his real name. She has seen him move through the room, and has seen him during meditation and in an astral state (when out-of-body). He is her protector and teacher, the one with whom she has the best rapport. She has three other guides, however: Crystal (a woman who is around a lot, but she's uncertain that that's her real name), Running Bear (a runner), And Dr. Blackmore (chemist or healer).

One British medium talks about her spirit band as a "rostrum team" during a platform mediumship appearance. There may be more than this, but the ones she knows the most are Abdul (who provides humor), Harry (who brings forth evidence), Maria the nun (an overseer), and Running Fox (who helps her with her public presentation style).

We found two people who say they prefer not to reveal everything about their guides to others. One woman says that she knows the name of her guide but keeps it "sacred". She has seen him only three times, but he is always there, and she can hear his voice. He is Oriental, has a distinct laugh, and speaks fairly good English but with an Oriental accent. He will say, "And you tell them this…," then give a direct quote from the spirit world.

She also has a group of spirit guides, "They," who never identify themselves but help her find the spiritual vibrations. She knows when they are there because they appear as a blue-white light. She also sees a dot of blue light flash to confirm that something is true.

Another medium has had one guide since she was seven. "Names are not important," she says, but her guide shows her a symbol to identify him/herself; she does not tell other people what it is. For the last 25 years she has had another guide, a doctor, who tells her what's wrong with people.

For people who are unaccustomed to the idea of spirit guides, these examples may appear fanciful. It is important to stress that our interviewees seem to be very sincere and truthful in talking about their guides. Sometimes, however, it is not clear whether the medium is certain about the reality status of the guide.

As mentioned earlier, one medium says that in her "imaginal experience" she conceives of a Jungian archetypal grandmother who collects the relatives and brings them in to the reading for the sitter. She does not necessarily mean that the grandmother is "just her imagination" when she says "imaginal." "What is imagination, anyway," she asks? She is at peace with not understanding what mediumship is all about, as long as it is healing and helpful.

Through meditation she has also envisioned a spirit band, not necessarily exactly 5 or 10 guides as in a traditional Spiritualist conception. What she saw was a roomful of unusual beings, not unlike the characters in the bar scene from "Star Wars." She finds this amusing but not necessarily ridiculous.

Penelope has been trained in a number of traditions, not just Spiritualist. When learning to do mediumship in the Spiritualist style, however, she decided to ask Moses to be her guide, i.e. to go round up the (spirit) relatives before a public message service. It occurred to her that if Moses had spent 40 years wandering in the desert, he probably had developed expertise in finding things (or people). Since she had channeled the Civil War hero Joshua Chamberlain before, she thought that she would ask him to give the rounded-up relatives order and inspiration at the Stump service, just as he had done with the mutinous soldiers from Maine at Little Round Top at the Battle of Gettysburg.

When I quizzed her about the reality status of her conception of this, she said that she was not sure that it was really the same Moses of the Bible who was helping her; he might not be available. Nor has she actually sensed Moses and Joshua (Chamberlain) during the services. She also seems to find her vision amusing but not necessarily ridiculous.

Finally we talked to one medium who thinks that her guides are a council. She has no particularly Spiritualist conception of who they are. On one occasion she recalls standing before them, all men sitting at a table. They were talking, but she could not hear anything. In her thoughts she felt that they were programming her, improving her "usability." She has had many different kinds of spiritual and paranormal experiences, some of which seem to fit the pattern of the UFO phenomenon, including this scene with the "council."

64

Mental Modalities

Next let us examine the kinds of input that spirit mediums experience in the process of "getting the message" that they bring forth from the spirit world. If a medium goes into trance, especially full trance, she may have little or no concept of how the information comes through. If she goes unconscious, another spirit (or personality of the medium) takes over.

Also, in the beginning stages of learning mediumship these days, students try to identify and practice different quasi-sensory modalities (clairvoyance, clairaudience etc.), but after they have had more experience mediums tend to just "get into the flow" without much awareness of what they are doing. Consequently, for many of our interviewees, it involved some difficult introspection for them to try to describe how they actually do get their impressions. Their process may also change significantly over the years.

We have much more information on the modalities from our interviews than from the library sources. Out of 122 mediums, 24 gave no information at all on any of the following: clairvoyance, clairaudience, clairsentience (or kinesthetics), or trance (which might obviate the need for the first three). All but 2 of these 24 were in the library sources. In other words, 95% (38 of 40) of the interviewees gave some information, but only 73% (60 of 82) of the library sources did, and many of the latter were very sketchy.

Among the 98 mediums for whom we have information on these things, 72% were clairvoyant (literally, "clear-seeing"), meaning that they got information from the spirit world visually, either as an external image or vision (rather unusual), or internally ("subjectively") as if it were a dream image, or both. If we leave out the 2% who were seldom or rarely clairvoyant, this leaves 70%.

Next most common was clairaudient ("clear-hearing"), meaning that they got information by hearing things, either externally (very unusual, sometimes called "objective", or if others can hear it, "direct voice"), or internally ("subjectively") as if they were imagining someone's voice, or both. Altogether 66% had some clairaudience, but only 61% if we eliminate those who had it seldom or rarely.

The next category, clairsentient ("clear-feeling") is the most problematic. It can be a catch-all for any other sense: smelling, taste, or touch. However, especially when people use the near synonym "kinesthetic," it tends to include any kind of "feeling" either on the body or emotionally.

Sometimes clairsentience or kinesthetics also includes "just knowing" or "thought forms" that people have no clue where they came from. Some people joke that they just "g-know" (pron. "guh-know") things intuitively. This word "g-know" is apparently based on the word "gnostic," which refers to the Gnostic heresy in the early Christian church that advocated individual intuitive understanding of the divine.

Altogether 42% said that they were clairsentient or kinesthetic. Subtracting the 2% who said that they had this sense little or rarely, this leaves 40%. Out of the entire 98 in the group with information about modalities, 24% said that they had body feelings or emotional sensations (it's difficult to distinguish between the two); and 7% (7 of the 24 in this feeling category) specifically commented that they had to learn how not to feel sick or had asked not to get these feelings. Also 13% said that they "just knew" or "g-knew" things, including sensing but not really seeing auras. There were 8% who could smell things, jokingly called "clairsniffance" sometimes. And just 1% (1 person) who could taste things (paranormally of course). The latter percentages total more than 42% because some mediums had multiple kinds of clairsentience, and some did not specify what type of clairsentience they had.

Not very many mediums stated which modalities were dominant, if they had any dominant ones. However, 10% were dominantly clairvoyant, 3% dominantly clairaudient, and 2% dominantly clairsentient. This ranking matches the frequency of the three modalities (70% clairvoyant, 61% clairaudient, and 40% clairsentient).

Remembering back to trance, which we discussed earlier, 51% did trance more than just a little, which could also involve these sensory modalities if they're not unconscious. Only 6% said that trance was their dominant technique, but we think that this is very much undermeasured because there are so many trance mediums in the library cases that give little information about techniques.

Now let's consider some subjective descriptions of clairvoyance from our mediums. We could ask various questions about their experience, such as, where the image is, what it looks like, whether it moves or not, and how realistic it is.

One of our interviewees apparently has eidetic imagery, a "normal" but unusual psychological ability. This means that she can visualize things completely realistically, as if they were really in front of her. In mediumship she sees what appears like a TV screen about one foot in front of her face. The image is in color and realistic. She can also see another (real) image in the same direction at the same time, such as a person sitting in front of her. There is not much limit to her ability to visualize. She can make herself see an elephant *behind* her head, a pink one with purple ears.

Of course hers is an exceptional case. Among our 40 interviewees, 13 can at least occasionally see things external to themselves, not counting people who have had only a rare vision or two. Typically this external seeing is much less spectacular than in the eidetic imagery case. One woman gets an occasional very brief flash of a picture.

The great majority of the clairvoyance is internal. One medium said that it is as if a black curtain opens in her mind, and she sees colors and faces. Another medium said that he sees snapshots (stills) in his mind.

I (Charlie) am dominantly clairvoyant in mediumship, and I see internally, but I feel mostly as if I am "there", as if in a dream, not as if it is a photograph or movie screen. On rare occasions I have seen something that seems to be "out there," like a green light, or a box in front of the sitter, but it is hard to tell if I am really seeing it externally or just having another image in my mind appear intermingled with my external vision. Of course, my rational mind tells me that it must be the latter.

Another medium says that he can see things both with his eyes open and closed. However, if he closes his eyes it improves the image, like turning the lights down in a theater. When I saw my green light, twice in a couple of minutes during one outside message service, I closed my eyes to check if I were seeing some kind of after-image, and I could not see it with my eyes closed, but opened them again and it was still there.

One of the students in a class we were teaching was startled to see a clear photo-like image in front of her while she was doing a mediumship exercise. She had never seen such a thing before, and it made her think that maybe she really could do mediumship. It was an image of a class member in a city environment, and it verified the message that she was getting about her, which the student also confirmed.

Another medium sees images in front of her that look like a strip of film, some of them not very clear, wavy as if they were under water. During the interview she practiced the phenomenon and gave me an uncannily accurate description of my house back in Gettysburg, which she was seeing on her film strip.

One medium told us that earlier in her life she often saw what looked like movies in front of her. They disturbed her so much that she meditated in order to make them go away. This is an interesting contrast to people who use meditation in order to *stimulate* mediumship.

Penelope can see movies with her eyes closed just before going to sleep. It seems similar to lucid dreaming, because she can generally manipulate things in the "dream" to suit herself, such as walking into a different area of the scene.

Andrew Jackson Davis claimed to be able to see the internal organs of sitters (as if he had x-ray vision) and flames of light coming from the organs.[242] One wonders if he saw this as some kind of internal mental image rather than out in front of him Superman style. Once I got a mental image of a person's left knee that looked somewhat like an x-ray view. I told him that I was picking up a problem with too much lateral movement and that he should be careful. To my surprise he confirmed that he had just been diagnosed with a left-knee problem similar to what I had described.

One of the most interesting examples of mental visual images is in the case of Pearl Curran's channeling of Patience Worth (see Chapter 7). "The scenes become panoramic…not confined to the point narrated (by Patience Worth), but (taking) in everything else within the circle of vision at the time….e.g., I see not only (two people walking on the street), but…the buildings, stones, dogs, people and all, just as they would be in the real scene." At the same time she would be picking up clairaudiently the voice of Patience Worth interpreting what was going on over the sounds of people in the street scene talking a foreign language.[243]

Apparently it was like a small screen view inside her head, as we see from the following. "One very odd and interesting phase of the phenomenon is the fact that (while watching) the tiny panorama unfold before me, I have often seen myself, small as one of the characters, standing as an onlooker, or walking among the people in the play."[244]

This sounds like what we might call an "in-the-body experience" (an IBE rather than an OBE) in the sense that her sense of self gets inserted within her vision rather than going outside of herself and looking back down. If she wants to investigate part of the scene, "This tiny figure of myself would boldly take part in the play…walking to the bin-side of a market man and taking up the fruit and tasting it….It was as real to me as any personal experience…recorded by my sight, taste and smell as other experiences…."

Pearl Curran's experience also combines clairvoyance with clairaudience (and other senses). By contrast we noticed in other mediums who are not regularly clairaudient that the clairvoyance sometimes has to compensate. Two mediums told us that they see writing. One of these said that she sees names that look like airplane writing in the sky; she is never clairaudient. Another, the woman with eidetic imagery, sees words in her pictures. Although she is sometimes clairaudient, usually she is heavily focused on the clairvoyant image.

The most interesting thing we noticed in the data from clairaudient mediums is that 5 of the 60 especially noticed that clairaudience is associated with their spirit guides. One man said that he was clairaudient usually when getting information from his guides. One woman said that she always hears the voice of her spirit guide first; this is her first input, and it verifies for her the accuracy of the information to follow. Another woman said that information from her spirit guides is typically clairaudient; the information from other spirits is clairvoyant. Nobody said that *clairvoyance* was especially connected to her/his spirit guides, although one woman did say that the presence of a blue-white light was a clue that they were around.

I (Charlie) am especially fascinated by this finding because for years I wondered why my first spontaneous mediumship consisted of the voice of my mother in my left ear (but internally, inside my head). As I learned to give messages to other people in the Spiritualist church, however, most things were clairvoyant. This pattern could explain the difference. In essence my mother is my spirit guide.

Only 8 of our 40 interviewees experience clairaudience outside their head, sometimes called "direct voice" (especially if others can hear it too); and even for those who do, it tends not to happen very often. It may be just a short calling of a name, an impression that might be a normal psychological phenomenon, especially when waking from sleep.

Skeptics studying Spiritualism have often been suspicious of direct voice in seances, as in the case of Mina Crandon (known as Margery), who would bring through her brother Walter's voice (another spirit guide and clairaudience example). However, sometimes Walter's direct voice could be heard even when Margery could be heard simultaneously snoring in the cabinet (a closet-like device used to focus the medium's energy, and sometimes a place to hide fraudulent maneuvers).[245]

Seances with Eusapia Paladino, the Neapolitan physical medium, also produced direct voice. It is difficult to attribute the voices to the medium herself because one voice spoke in the Genoese dialect, and another in Arabic, with which she was not familiar.[246]

One other medium provided another interesting association with clairaudience. She said that most information she brings through for business and career comes through clairaudiently (inside her head), even though she does not get very much that way in general. One wonders if the auditory channel with voice represents a rational approach, as in business, as opposed to the intuitive which might be more visual. In like manner, a spirit guide is an organizer of the mediumship process, and may represent another rational element to be communicated more through speech rather than clairvoyantly.

We have already discussed the main components of the "catch-all" category of clairsentience or kinesthetics: body feelings or emotions, "just knowing," and the miscellaneous senses of smell, taste, and touch (all three of which are uncommon or rare). We tend to stick anything in this category that is difficult to explain or pin down. It was common in the earlier stages of Spiritualism merely to say that a medium was a "sensitive" or that she got "information from the vibrations."

Part of the problem is that it is often difficult for a medium to know exactly where the information is coming from. One of our interviewees said, for example, that she seems to hear things internally with no sound quality to it, as if it wasn't really a sense, just something spiritual. This may be like saying that the "perception" seems more like a thought form.

I (Charlie) can relate to this from my own experience. I used to hear my mother's voice internally, but the sense of what her voice sounded like faded over the months and years to the point where I now seem to be picking up thoughts directly, sentences with no sound attached. I can still remember what her voice sounded like if I just think of that, as if I were trying to run a

Sinatra song through my head. However, when I seem to be tuning in to her as a medium, I don't hear her voice (except rarely).

Some of the spirit communication in the clairsentient category could be labelled "ineffable," that is, very difficult to explain to someone else who has not had the experience. As a sociologist, I claim that doing mediumship myself has made the ineffable more accessible to me.

For example, one medium says that she "senses" but does not actually see colors. I remember one time giving someone a spirit message in which I said that something "feels green." Before that I found it very peculiar when people said that they could sense the colors in a person's aura without actually seeing them. "Ineffable."

Another example of ineffable is the experience of a medium who says that she can tell whether a person is in spirit or alive by the "feel or texture of the name." Or how about the medium who feels things "in her soul," what she calls her "ninth sense." Another word for such ineffable or indescribable ways of knowing is "g-knowing", as we said earlier.

65

Physical Mediumship

Our discussion of mental modalities has of course been concentrated on ways of getting information for mental spirit mediumship. Very little of this book concentrates on physical mediumship, although we have given a few examples of it earlier.

The main reason for dealing with it so little is that very little physical mediumship is done today. We argued previously that one reason for this may be that there is relatively little opportunity for childhood mediums to develop spontaneously in home circles at an age when they could learn to control their natural psychokinetic tendencies.

Whatever the reasons for the decline, we are able to document what Spiritualists all say, that there has been a big decline in physical mediumship since the nineteenth century. In our nineteenth-century sample, among those for which we have any information about their type of mediumship, 63% did some physical mediumship.

This includes things like table-tipping, using the trumpet (a metal megaphone-like device that would allegedly move or through which spirits would speak), levitating tables or people (including themselves), slate writing (without touching the little slate or blackboard), and bringing in apports (gifts from spirit, like flowers that materialized on the seance table).

By contrast only 44% of the twentieth-century library sample did physical mediumship. And among our interviewees only 11%. We have heard some rumblings about how it is about to make a comeback, but there isn't much evidence of this. We don't think that there is the right climate for physical mediumship. Very few people sit in circles regularly enough and long enough to build up the energy for what is a very slowly developing phenomenon in most cases. Physical mediumship, like trance mediumship, was thought of as being "developed" in the medium by the spirit world. Today, people want to be more in control and to make mediumship happen more quickly.

66

Regimen

One way to make things happen in the modern world is to condition one's body and mind, whether the activity is athletics, romance, or mediumship. This is not to say that mystics have not engaged in a regimen for millennia, but most of the people who became swept up by Spiritualism in the nineteenth century did it more spontaneously rather than training for it. In fact we have no information at all on regimen from the nineteenth century, and very little in the library sources for the earlier twentieth century. What little there is in library sources is similar to our interview data.

By far the most commonly mentioned aspect of the conditioning regimen for our mediums was meditation: 75% (21 of the 28 who gave information on their regimen). Next in popularity was prayer (61%), followed by diet (including water and alcohol intake) (50%). Only one person mentioned exercise, and only one said "not smoking." This last sentence is not a surprise in light of the mediums we have known.

Our sole exerciser is Henry L. Stern, born in Austria-Hungary in 1899, who moved to the U.S. In 1912. He said that the following were required for mediumship: controlled eating, little or no liquor, exercise, relaxation, a rested mind, concentration, imagination, prayer, faith, and expectation.[247]

One of our interviewees said that she meditates twice a day, prays, studies, and goes by the following diet. She takes no dairy, eats little red meat, eats light, eats after doing mediumship, and takes only moderate alcohol, none at all from 24–48 hours before working.

Another said that she meditates daily; she considers this the most important, because it sets the energies. She also does inspirational reading and discussion. Her diet emphasizes fruits and juices; also pasta if she is doing a lot of reading.

By contrast another medium said that she has no meditation regime, because that puts you too inward. She walks in the woods (which we might argue has a meditative function), prays every morning, and avoids alcohol before doing mediumship (because it stops her from going out of body). Otherwise she has no dietary restrictions.

The medium who had the most to say about regimen confessed that you can slack off after you get the skills. However, he does a little meditation, prayer, fasting, walking in the woods, and sweat lodges (which he organizes). On diet, he says that if you have a heavy meal, it's harder to get things to come through. He's been moving in the direction of vegetarianism, especially on days he does mediumship, although some people may need some meat to ground themselves.

His rule is to follow your inner guidance on all this. He drinks less (for his health in general). Following Edgar Cayce, he recommends "mummy food": figs, dates, and corn meal. Smoking makes it harder to be accurate on details, although it may ground some people.

Another medium has a daily meditation routine and practices her ESP, which you can use to train yourself not only for telepathy but also for communicating with spirits. When she sits she follows some dietary restrictions, but she admits that she is not good with it on other days. This and some other cases above point to the tendency for a medium's regime to become situational, used on days they do mediumship, but not always as a matter of regular conditioning. Then there are practices that are used just prior to a reading, which we will consider in the next section on "preliminaries."

There are also some interesting points in the responses of mediums who say they have no regimen. One says that she "just lives." And yet she is as tuned in as anybody we know. Another medium acknowledges that it is a problem for her mediumship that she smokes and drinks.

67

Preliminaries

We move now from the issue of whether and how mediums condition them-selves with a regular training regimen, to the question of what they do just before making contact with the spirit world. When we talked about trance earlier, we noticed that mediums would relax into it, letting it happen to them. This was vaguely referred to as "going into the state." Sometimes this altered state of consciousness was encouraged by hypnosis (mesmerism).

Even without going into trance, some mediums still describe their prelim-inaries as a rather passive process. Whether going into trance or not, some mediums talk about "getting out of the way" or "getting smaller," visualizing themselves as removing their ego from the process and just letting the infor-mation come through. It used to help me (Charlie) in mediumship classes at first to imagine stepping outside of my body, which is a pale imitation of hav-ing an out-of-body experience or becoming possessed by a spirit. Penelope talks about becoming a straw through which the information flows.

Many mediums do not have very much in the way of an active system of preliminaries to make mediumship happen. For example, one medium doesn't have to do anything because she is in "constant bonding" with the spirit world, she says. Spirit is with her every second; her mind is theirs. Even at night she wakes up, and they're there instantly.

Some mediums have very little awareness of the process. We observed one medium go into her reading mode and commented on what we saw. She said that she hadn't noticed what she did and felt that mediums "should be involved minimally." This is similar to the idea of getting out of the way per-haps. Another woman said that she just gets her "boys" (spirit guides), and they get her "geared in." Without specifying how it should happen, one medium just desires information and lets spirit give it in whatever form.

Mediums often say that when students begin to learn mediumship they need a system. It's like learning scales on the piano. However, once they have it down, they just let it come without analyzing what they are doing. They get into the flow, finding it easy to plug in or to trigger the appropriate responses.

One system for students to remember when starting out is the 5 Cs. Clear your mind, center yourself, climb (open up to the higher realms), call on your guides, and connect. There are variations on this formula, usually with fewer steps, such as "clear, center, and call." One woman put it this way: she clears her mind (imagines zeros on an adding machine), raises her vibrations, looks for her higher self, and calls on her guides.

For some mediums, there is no problem triggering this process. In fact, they may have to put a lid on it. One woman says that spirits often talk to her before she comes up front at a message service, and she asks them to wait.

Another medium says a prayer, and before she can finish, pictures start flooding in. She used to try to get one or two whole messages before going up to the platform as a security thing, but she felt guilty about it. Since then she has asked for that not to happen, and it seldom does.

I (Charlie) found her statement rather comforting, because I used to get all of my messages before going up front, also as a security thing. In fact, I was so afraid of looking like a fool that I got mine in the bathtub before going to church. I would often get a mental picture of what the person looked like who was supposed to get the message, and where they would be sitting. When I arrived and saw the person sitting there, it gave me more courage to give the message.

I think it is interesting that we both felt guilty about predelivered messages. Nobody actually said that it was a crime, although we were taught in classes to go through a certain process, getting up there first. Other mediums have talked about picking up things as they sit in the audience, but typically they just wait until they have actually called on the person before bringing through the message.

Library sources contain very little information about preliminaries, especially for the nineteenth-century mediums, except for things about getting relaxed for the onset of trance. Now however, there is more system and more of a conscious attempt to make mediumship happen, at least in classes for students.

For the 25 interviewees who gave specific information on their preliminaries, we coded several different activities. It was apparent that they all boiled down into two categories: getting into an altered state of consciousness, and asking for help. Altogether 40% of the mediums did altered-state preliminaries, and 72% asked for help. Of course any ritual can end up serving as a trigger for the mediumistic state, once the medium has practiced the routine enough.

Nevertheless we included the following things under the category of getting into an altered state, understanding that they often overlap: centering, "raising vibrations," clearing the mind, meditating shortly beforehand, singing, and "stepping aside" or looking into space. Under asking for help we included: prayer (60% did this, the single most common activity of all), calling on guides (28% did this), asking for a white light of protection, and setting an intention or desire. By the way, the medium who is in "constant bonding" does none of these things specially as a preliminary.

68

Access System

If it is difficult to get mediums to explain the preliminaries that trigger their mediumship, it is even more difficult to get them to explain their system of accessing the information once they begin. By access here we mean more than just the modalities of clairvoyance, clairaudience, and clairsentience we discussed before. Now we are looking for a system of knowing where to look for the information and how to sort it, according to direction etc.

Only 20 of our 40 interviewees could give us usable information on this (compared to 28 on regimen and 25 on preliminaries). We were hoping for a complex analysis based on such perspectives as NLP (neuro-linguistic programming, noticing how mediums look up for visuals, to the side for the auditory, and down for kinesthetics). A few people could sort things out this way, or we could observe them doing it with a sample message. One medium said that she used to have a system like that, but under the advice of a recent teacher she "broke her habits of sorting."

Although there is much more instruction for mediums today than in the nineteenth century, much of mediumship is still very "intuitive" (not surprisingly). Even if mediums have preliminaries to trigger the mediumistic state, they may not be very aware of what happens after that. This is most obvious with full trance.

One medium who used to do semi-trance earlier in his career now stays fully awake. However, after he sings on the way up to the platform, he has no particular way of dragging out or analyzing the information. "They just give it to me, simple as that," he says.

Another medium says that the information "just flows." She is passively unaware of the process. One woman says, "I open my mouth, and the words come out." This is way too scary for me (Charlie). It reminds me of the 1850s when some mediums in trance came out with obscenities. I want my conscious mind to do a little censoring, just in case.

255

When I asked other people about this, including Penelope, some said that when they get information clairaudiently they often "just talk" without reprocessing it. That is, they hear it and say it simultaneously. This does not mean that they have no system at all for other aspects of the process.

However, one of our mediums who "just talks" in fact has no system at all. She asks to get everything simply in words that come out of her mouth. No symbols, no pictures, etc. And she has no understanding or even interest in the process. There is a long-standing element in Spiritualism that resonates with this attitude, that is the idea that the simpler and less involved the medium the better. There is also a counter attitude, more prominent recently than ever, that spirit needs to use the medium's talents and intelligence in creative ways.

Aside from mediums who go into trance, and mediums who get information passively and relay it automatically, there is another type who would need very little if any system of sorting information. That is the "blender" who becomes one with the person or spirit in order to pick up information actively (rather than being controlled by the spirit). One blender talked about just feeling what the other soul is feeling, as if it were one's own experience, not something that has to be relayed and analyzed.

One medium, however, seemed to be informed about the NLP perspective on mediumship. He said that he looked up for visuals (things on the left representing the living, on the right for spirits), looked horizontally (usually to the right) for hearing, and down (usually) for kinesthetics.

Another medium had some sense of the direction or location of information, saying that she felt the presence of her guides behind and above her head, and sometimes as warmth coming across her right shoulder and down her arm. With the "blender" mentioned above, we watched for whether he looked one way or another for different types of modalities, and he said that he just closed his eyes and the information came in a split second. He knew about NLP but did not notice it working in himself.

Aside from an NLP perspective, recall that we already discussed some things about where images appeared for people who were clairvoyant, such as internally, in a filmstrip in front of them, or even behind the head for the eidetic imager. Another such example is the external screen with a fuzzy image that one medium sees and then tries to draw on paper for the sitter.

Two mediums have a special way of locating information when working on the telephone. They work off the name or voice of the person and imagine tuning in with a radio dial.

Twentieth-century American medium Caroline Chapman had an interesting way of sorting clairaudient information from regular hearing. She knew that it was spirits speaking in her right ear, because she had been deaf in her right ear from birth.[248]

If sorting input is difficult, imagine also the problem of knowing which sitter is supposed to get the message. We did not focus on this a great deal. However, most mediums just seem to know where it goes (or they may choose people because they like what they're wearing, and then ask for a message for them).

Some people envision a light over the head of the right sitter, or imagine an arrow in that direction. In my case, as I said, I sometimes came to the service with a picture and location of the sitter already in my head.

Twentieth-century English medium Ena Twigg "felt as if her hair were electric wires attached to a switchboard near the ceiling. Her scalp pulled, and there was a click when she found the right person."[249]

69

Symbols

Some of the information carried in the access system we have just been talking about can also be conveyed through symbols. For example, if some mediums bring through information about mother's side of the family on the left, and father's side of the family on the right, this means that direction (left or right) carries symbolic meaning.

However, we find that there is considerable variation in this symbolism among mediums. Some of it may be rather standard, such as the color pink standing for love, indicating the influence either of the general culture or of some specific aspect of Spiritualist or New Age culture. Nevertheless, to a great extent mediums have separate "psychic dictionaries."

One medium says that in his psychic dictionary a horse means ground transport. This may be due to his fondness for horses. When he sees (clairvoyantly) an oak in the wind, this means "unyielding." Usually these are symbols from his own psychic dictionary, but then the spirits may try their own or ones that the sitter will recognize. When spirit speaks, he says, spirit speaks very fast (a Native American saying). And spirit likes to conserve energy. For example, he once saw and described a face on a strawberry, which the sitter readily recognized as a grandfather associated with strawberries.

For another medium, visuals off to the left represent the past, center is the present, and the right is future. Messages from a higher spiritual plane come from higher up. I (Charlie) sometimes get visuals that appear to be far away, at a great distance, which seems to represent the distant past. At other times spirits at a distance seem to be having trouble connecting with the sitter, or do not tune in to their earthly affairs. I cannot explain how I know how to distinguish these two meanings of distance.

Another medium who told us about her psychic dictionary said that her symbols just came to her, and she didn't have to ask what they meant; she just knew. For example, a red car means speed, a wall represents protection, and the Statue of Liberty strength. At one point she asked spirit to change the symbols for variety. She didn't want people to hear her talking about the same symbols over and over again in public services. They might think that she was giving different people the same messages.

The famous medium Eileen Garrett said the following about symbols in 1943. "The symbols appear, they have to be interpreted, and the interpretation occurs through a 'flash' or 'click' in understanding, by means of which the perceiver knows."[250] This seems to reflect both the speed mentioned above ("Spirit speaks very fast.") and the idea that it may be difficult to explain how symbolization works.

Spirit mediums often say that you should just bring through the message without interpreting. A good example of this is Gretchen Lazarony's message (in Chapter 8) about a dog with a lit cigar in its mouth, which was apparently absurd until the sitter explained how her deceased dog used to pick up a cigar thrown away by the milkman and run around with it.

However, some symbols are difficult even to pass along without some kind of interpretation on the medium's part. For example, I did a church reading once in which I saw, or rather did not see, something that rapidly shrank to nothing and disappeared right into the heart area of the sitter. Somehow I just "g-knew" what that meant, although I have never seen the same symbol before or since. I said, "You have a secret, don't you?" My next image was a ring hovering above the end of a finger. That one I could not interpret, but the sitter knew immediately what it meant. She told me that her boyfriend had asked her to marry him over Christmas vacation. She had said no, and had not told even her mother; that was her secret.

We say more elsewhere about the theories of how mediumship should be done and what it means. However, we want to pass along one interesting thought about all this right now. One medium, John White, asks, "Can you dream wrong?" In other words, much of the content of spirit mediumship is apparently symbolic. What it means is often a mystery. Just because the medium and/or sitter may be baffled by it or may misinterpret it, this does not necessarily mean that it is "wrong".

70

Confirmations

Because of the problematic nature of mediumship, both in terms of its social acceptability and in terms of the elusiveness of its interpretation, mediums are often interested in getting confirmations that what they have said is accurate or useful. This subject harks back to Part Five as well, because one of the ways in which developing spirit mediums survive the doubts cast upon them by a disapproving society is to get confirmations.

Out of the 41 contemporary mediums for which we have the information, 29% found confirmations to be very important, 51% important, 12% not very important, and 7% not at all important. Although the numbers are small, of the 11 male mediums, 36% found them very important, 55% important, and 9% not at all important. Among the 30 female mediums, 27% found them very important, 50% important, 17% not very important, and 7% not at all important.

This means that 91% of males considered confirmations important or very important, compared to only 77% of females. We have no good explanation for this gender difference, which is not very great. We considered the possibility that our sample might contain more females with more experience who might feel less dependent upon confirmations, but that does not seem to fit the data very well in all cases.

It is clear from the responses that mediums are more reliant upon confirmations earlier in their career. However, this does not mean that all or even most mediums stop wanting confirmations after they have gained experience and confidence. Some pointed out that confirmations help clarify things for the sitter and help the communication during the reading or message. Someone said that it's good to know when you're "tuned in." In platform work confirmations also demonstrate accuracy for bystanders, as one medium pointed out.

Some mediums said that confirmations are still fun, even after they have gotten confident in their work. One said that it gives him a sense of awe; "How did I do that?" Another said that she is always in a growth pattern, even when she doesn't doubt herself, and confirmations help.

When asked whether she looked for confirmations, one medium said, "Of course; everybody does." She needs it for confidence. Another woman said that she "constantly (needs) a boost." Some said that this is just human, or our ego needs it.

However, it should be emphasized that mediumship is more problematic than other performance endeavors. One reason of course is that it rests on a way of knowing that is generally considered deviant in this society. One interviewee said that it is absolutely important for her to know that her mediumship is not just her imagination, because she is a very rational person.

Another reason is that even if a medium has seen strong evidence that she has done good mediumship in the past, there is no guarantee that it will happen again. Each message or reading is a new leap of faith, and no one is 100% accurate. As one medium said, "Anybody who is more than 80% accurate must have a trick."

Perhaps the comments of the minority 19% of our mediums who say that confirmations are *not* important are more interesting than those of the mediums who think they are. Mostly they say that information from your spirit guides should be trusted. This is an interesting way to escape or ignore the criticisms of rational skeptics who doubt that mediumship is even possible.

Remember the medium who asked, "Can you dream wrong?" He is saying that his intuitive system must mean something, even if we fail to interpret it correctly. He shows no tendency to integrate ("contaminate"?) intuition with rationality. When he gives a public message, he even closes his eyes to keep from seeing body language clues from the sitters.

Another medium who thinks that confirmations are not at all important says that you need to *know* that what you are saying is correct. If sitters say, "Yes but" to her, she doesn't want to hear it. She insists to people who say she's wrong that she's always right. "You don't want to *trust*, you want to *know*. Ask your spirit guides for certainty." This is an unusual statement, because other mediums who say they trust their spirit guides do not claim to be so certain.

Now for a few examples of confirmations from those who value them. Some of the best ones appear in Chapter 8, including Gretchen Lazarony's cigar-smoking dog case. Also recall Penelope's Raggedy Ann and Andy doll message in Chapter 22.

The medium who said that confirmations were essential to her because of her logical mind told us this one. In a development class taught by a medium with a reputation for excellence, she gave part of a message she had for another student. However, she could not bring herself to mention a silly thing she was picking up about a giraffe. "I'm not going to tell him about the giraffe," she was thinking.

Her teacher, who was standing beside her then said to her, "Are you going to tell him about the giraffe?" Admittedly this is not proof of survival (it might be telepathy), but it was enough to shake our medium out of her resistance to considering the possibility of the paranormal.

Some confirmations demonstrate the possibility that even messages that are rejected by the sitter may eventually be verified. When one medium told a woman that she would go to Las Vegas in October, the woman was "adamant and defiant," saying that she had no money and hated airplanes. However, within a week the sitter called back and reported that a family member with a ticket to Las Vegas ended up not being able to go and that she was going instead.

In another case a woman was told that she would move to New York City, marry a Latin man and have a little boy. Although the woman indicated her aversion to all three notions, two years later she came back to visit the medium and verified the prophecy.

Another medium had a vision of a man in a work uniform leading a race-horse right between her and the sitter, a young man who upon being told what the medium was seeing replied, "That's my dad." A month later the medium saw the same apparition when giving a reading to an older woman, who identified the man (whom she could not see) as her husband. The sitter then revealed that the young man who had been for a reading the previous month was her son.

One favorite confirmation occurred when the medium was being interviewed by a reporter who wanted to test her, giving her only her first name. Without any feedback whatsoever, the medium told the reporter what she was picking up from the spirit of her fiancé who had died before they could get married. She gave the reporter's birthdate, the fiancé's birthdate, the location of the engagement ring, and the date they were supposed to have been married.

For three months before the reporter's article came out, the medium was told nothing. Then she discovered that she had gotten all of the details mentioned above correct, even to the dates being exactly right. There were only a couple of things in the reading that she could not recognize.

It is common to read about really good cases of confirmations. All of the library sources we collected on mediums have them, even though they rarely talk about the importance of confirmations to the mediums personally. The books themselves are largely extended confirmations, although they often contain sections about how they were skeptical at certain stages of their lives.

But certainly not every message turns out to be a confirmed "zinger." Therefore, it may be useful to have a *bad* example of a confirmation to illustrate some of the process a medium may go through when there are doubts. I (Charlie) gave a reading in my church in which I got a very strong but strange message about a rotund man in overalls who wore glasses but didn't like them and often took them off. He had a barn only the corner of which I could see. It was smooth white and did not fit my stereotype of a red barn. I told the woman I was reading for that he seemed to be an uncle or something on her mother's side. To my annoyance he kept on moving to the left out of the field of my vision. There was also a tractor and some animals.

She couldn't place this man at first, saying that there were farmers on her father's side only. I couldn't let go of it and insisted that it must be on her mother's side. She said that there might be somebody really far back, but she didn't know. Then I picked up that the man claimed that he did see her when she was little. Also he was very a nice man but could not express his emotions. He kept walking away. I also got the name Orville.

Right about that point she had an "aha" moment and was sure that it was her mother's cousin, whose last name was Ogilvy. He was a large man, nice but not expressive, and had a farm with a barn. She did not know or remember whether he had glasses or whether the barn had a white base. She had really enjoyed visiting there, probably several decades ago.

I found this intriguing. I was glad that I had not given up on it, and glad that I had not just said, "OK, sure, must be your father's side then." But I also wondered, was the fact that he kept disappearing to my left some kind of clue? And if so, did it represent his shyness about communicating, or that I needed to go farther off to the side to get to mother's cousin rather than mother's brother? Also, was "Orville" a garbled version of "Ogilvy," with which it has four of its five sounds in common? Or is this too much of a stretch? The sitter was convinced and happy. Is that enough?

One medium told us not to mention her name with this quote, but I am sure that many mediums would say the same thing. "If you can make someone cry, you've got a hit." This especially applies to platform work, when you often do not get very much confirmation from the person sitting in the audience (although they will sometimes come up to you later to explain the "hit").

I gave one more reading in church that day, after the farmer "Orville" message. I told a woman (who gave no particular clue to me as to her national origin) that she had one part of her family who were Italians from New York (the church is in Erie, Pennsylvania). When she confirmed that, I gave a sigh of relief. Then I said that I saw the color red. She said, "That's my uncle. We called him Red." With a few more statements I had her crying (happily). She told me that I should not worry so much about being wrong.

I don't think that the rational side of me will ever stop worrying about being wrong. Ironically the first reading I gave that same day began with my telling a young woman that I saw a picture of her carving up a steak on a plate. She proceeded to tell me that she was a vegetarian. I replied, "Me too." For some odd reason I considered that apparently wrong image to be correct, and went on to talk to her about people criticizing her for being a vegetarian, including somebody she was going to meet who had an interest in a beef farm or something.

Shortly thereafter I told her other things that made her cry, but that just made me feel bad, because I was picking up her feelings of hopelessness and helplessness, and I couldn't figure out how to fix it for her. Things are complicated.

Finally there is one other type of confirmation that mediums often get that has nothing to do with the sitter: "goosebumps," also known as "goosepimples," and "tinglies." Although we did not ask specifically about them, 6 of our 40 interviewees told us that they got them as an indication (usually thought to be from their spirit guides) that they were getting the right information. A seventh person said that the right side of her body gets cold when she was receiving a clear message; that sounds similar. I also saw another one of these 40 interviewees giving messages in a public service when her arm became covered with goosepimples. I was sitting close enough to see it develop. When I asked her about it later, she confirmed the phenomenon.

We have not done a study to establish that what these mediums experience as a goosebump confirmation corresponds to what the sitters consider confirmable. However, Penelope goes so far as to say that she has never been wrong when she has felt the goosebumps. One wonders whether these experiences might not be similar to features of the altered states of consciousness associated with apparition experiences, such as the feelings of cold that accompany the hypnagogic and hypnopompic states.[251]

PART VII

THE MEANING OF MEDIUMSHIP

The purpose of this part of the book is to give an overview of different types of interpretations of the significance of spirit mediumship. Keep in mind that the main focus of this book is to analyze the processes by which some people in modern society manage to become and to perform as mediums. There is a great deal more to be said about the larger context of how society evaluates this mediumship, some of which you might like to explore through bibliographical references provided here.

It is convenient to divide the literature on spirit mediums into interpretations that fit roughly along a continuum from scientific to paranormal to spiritual. Finally we shall present our own personal views on the subject.

71

"Crazy but Useful:"
Social and Behavioral Science

Traditionally the social and behavioral sciences (including especially sociology, anthropology and psychology) have attempted to explain human behavior in general and mystical/paranormal experience in particular within a natural-science framework. As Julia Howell[252] points out, this includes the following implicit assumptions: there is an objective material world, mind is generated by the brain, and mental experiences are internal products of the brain communicated and shared symbolically with others.

This means that allegedly other-worldly experiences tend to be explained by social/behavioral scientists either as delusional or (more charitably) as having social functions independent of whether they are objectively real or not. Howell points to new models of mind and "reality" that suggest that some human experience may actually occur outside of the materially real and culturally symbolic realms. Until recently, very few social and behavioral scientists have cared or dared to question the old assumptions or to consider these new models. Anthropologist Edith Turner[253] is a good example of an exception in her own work on spirit phenomena in Northern Alaska, and she gives several other examples of anthropologists who have written about their own spiritual experiences in the field.

We should add, however, that at least most social/behavioral scientists who have studied spirit mediumship have seen the phenomenon as socially significant rather than ridiculing it. Ridicule becomes an issue in the next chapter, under the debunking perspective.

From a sociological and anthropological perspective the most obvious importance of spirit mediumship in the United States is its central role in religious social movements. For an overview of Spiritualism as a social movement, including how it originated and diffused throughout the U.S. and

Europe (especially the UK) see Braude, Cross, Carroll, and Moore.[254] Braden and Melton[255] give good history-of-religion material on Spiritualism. Channeling, which is a modern variant on spirit mediumship, is central to the New Age Movement, for which you can read Brown and Riordan.[256]

Some treatments focus on the internal structure of the movement. For example, Carroll argues that mid-nineteenth century Spiritualism in America was more theologically and organizationally structured than is generally thought.[257] For studies of twentieth-century Spiritualist organization see Skultans (on churches in the UK), Lawton (on Lily Dale in the early 1930s), Richard and Adato (on Lily Dale in the 1970s), and Lloyd (on the group legitimation of altered-state experiences).[258]

What makes spirit mediumship so potentially powerful and liberating (or dangerous, depending on your point of view) is that it purports to be a privileged channel to new revelation from the spirit world. If new revelation can emerge through just anyone, rather than through legitimated, powerful sources, this threatens the status quo. In other words, mediumship can provide the ideology for a social movement (an attempt to change the existing social arrangement).

I.M. Lewis establishes a good general, cross-cultural theoretical framework for understanding the rebellious potential of spirit mediumship in the article "Spirit Possession and Deprivation Cults."[259] Deprived groups, such as women, tend to be overrepresented among people who are "possessed" by spirits, as in spirit mediumship (especially in a trance state). Although dominant groups tend to label such possessed people as pathological, "Women and other depressed categories exert mystical pressures upon their superiors in circumstances of deprivation and frustration when few other sanctions are available to them."[260] Before launching into specific examples it is worth noting that Gillen[261] reminds us that deprivation theories fail to consider the pleasures involved in cult movements like spiritualism, including sociability and the attempt by individuals to understand spiritual phenomena on a personal level.

As Lewis suggests, women are the main deprived group in many societies that uses spirit mediumship as an attempt to gain a voice. Ann Braude[262] (*Radical Spirits*) deserves prime mention for her discussion of the role of women in American spiritualism: how they managed to speak in public before other feminists dared to, and how they became the most radical of feminists not only in feminist causes but also in slavery abolitionism and other radical movements. Other sources emphasize the connection between spiritualism and women's power or leadership, e.g. Owen, Haywood, Baer (on black women spiritualists), and Lerch (on women spirit mediums in Brazil).[263]

Not unrelated to this gender discussion, of course, is the issue of political power for deprived groups, women included. See Barrow (for England), Dann (for Brazil), and Lain (for Zimbabwe).[264] Backing up farther, let us not forget that the ostensible basis of this protest is religious. Both Braude and Moore[265] remind us that American Spiritualism was essentially an alternative to orthodox Christianity. It was founded by a loose confederacy of free-thinking Swedenborgians and fallen-away Quakers, by women who rejected many aspects of mainstream nineteenth-century American society, including the popular religious notion that their infants who died unbaptized would forfeit the opportunity to go to Heaven.

Another way to state the significance of Spiritualism is to see it as a populist movement. This means that lower-class people in general (as a deprived group) could use Spiritualism as a way to challenge elite culture. In fact, Prothero[266] explains Theosophy as a later "uplifting" of the democratic tradition of Spiritualism into a more elitist framework by Helena Blavatsky and others.

It is also important to note that spirit mediumship has been studied in many societies throughout the world. As mentioned above, Lewis[267] gives many cross-cultural examples of mediumship within the context of "deprivation cults." Lerch and Dann[268] both provide analysis of spirit mediumship in Brazil. Lain[269] discusses it in the context of Zimbabwe.

Probably spirit mediumship exists in some form in virtually all societies, at least in the broad sense of some type of spirit possession or contact. However, we should not expect mediumship to have the same meaning in all societies, in spite of Lewis' general theory about mediumship and deprived groups. In traditional Chinese culture, for example, Emmons[270] points out that ancestor worship contains an institutionalized form of mediumship designed for ascertaining the needs of one's ancestors (to be satisfied through ancestor worship and sacrifices) and for communicating one's own desires to the ancestors. Chinese ancestor cults were hardly just for deprived groups, and it appears that ancestor worship trickled down from nobility to commoners since ancient times.

Variation or change within a single cultural tradition is also important to consider. Morris[271], to take another Asian example, discusses the new meanings of mediumship within the situation of modernization in Northern Thailand. Let us also not assume that all spiritualism in the Western world is equally discounted as irrational. Swatos and Gissurarson[272] delineate the special historical circumstances in Iceland that have given spirit mediumship greater respectability there and a different relationship to science.

Recalling Howell's[273] statement that paranormal experiences are often assumed by social scientists to be delusional, even if they are not explicitly labeled as such, let us see what types of psychological analysis have been applied to spirit mediumship. Moore[274] and Owen[275] show how the medical profession sometimes labeled spirit mediums as hysterical or victims of "mediomania". Hysteria was a diagnosis often used in Victorian times to put rebellious wives away; it could also be used in an attempt to control the rebellious doings of Spiritualist women.

Brown[276] considers channeling within the context of a multiple-personality interpretation, or more precisely shows parallels between channeling and the multiple-personality perspective. For a wider historical treatment of mediumship and other psychological phenomena in terms of multiple personality, see Kenny.[277]

Not all psychological investigation into spirit mediumship sees it necessarily in terms of a pathological condition like split or multiple personality, or as a dissociative disorder. Buhrman[278] has investigated different types of trance states and analyzed them in terms of memory for both Spiritualist mediums and yogis.

Some psychologists have valued the study of mediumship, including automatic writing, for what it might reveal about the unconscious mind.[279] Although Freud was interested in the paranormal, both Thuillier and Palfreman[280] point out that the interest of Freud and of other investigators tended to move away from mediumship and toward telepathy.

Linking the psychology and sociology of paranormal experiences to the physiology of the brain, McClenon[281] examines evidence for the altered-states-of-consciousness correlates of anomalous and religious experiences in humans over the millennia. He then proposes the theory that psychophysiological structures in the brain that were conducive to hypnotizability were selected for over time due to the fact that they facilitate shamanistic healing of various types. Spirit mediumship is just one of the altered-state activities that might be related to such brain physiology, and some persons might be more genetically predisposed to mediumship than others.

Underwood[282] discusses the development of "neurotheology" as studied by researchers like Andrew Newberg. This is the examination of brain function changes that occur during altered states like meditation and mediumship. For example, dissociation, which is the disengaging of one region of the brain from others, may allow anomalous experiences.

In particular, for example, a medium's clairaudience ("clear hearing") may occur when the Broca's area connected with generating speech is active simultaneously with a reduction in outer sensory input (due to being in a mild trance state). The medium may then interpret the voice not as her own inner voice but as a voice from elsewhere. Of course this physiological explanation does not explain away any accurate evidential information that might be produced.

Shortly we shall examine the perspectives that debunkers and then parapsychologists take on spirit mediumship. However, as a transition from the social/behavioral science view we have been examining, it is important to note that there is also an interesting literature that tries to describe and account sociologically for the very existence of the debunking and parapsychological subcultures themselves.

Moore and Carlton[283] give an historical overview of the development of interest in examining the phenomena of spiritualism scientifically in the nineteenth and twentieth centuries. McClenon, Hess, and Goode[284] present sociological and anthropological frameworks for understanding the knowledge subcultures of science, parapsychology and the "new age" (or more generally, various religious/spiritual perspectives, including spiritual and/or new age).

A great many of the pronouncements from these subcultures represent attempts at boundary maintenance. For example, parapsychology has to struggle to be included within science because it tends to be defined as dangerously close to spiritual or religious when it examines questions like mediumship and whether there is a survival of consciousness after death.

Palfreman[285] comments that psychical research was motivated partly by an attempt to show that there was still a spiritual aspect to nature after the crisis in religion caused by Darwinism. Garroutte[286] presents a fascinating interpretation of the struggle by Spiritualists to make knowledge claims about science. Spiritualism still claims to be a religion, a philosophy, and a science.

However, according to Garroutte, Spiritualists' popular, amateur science (showing evidence for the survival of the spirit after death through seances etc.) was marginalized as science became increasingly professionalized throughout the nineteenth century. Amateurs lost the ability to contribute to science as science required professional credentials and the financial backing of major institutions.

72

"Crazy and Deceptive":
Scientific Debunking

By "debunking" we mean the perspective of trying to discredit paranormal claims. By far the most important work in this area is done by the Committee for Scientific Investigation of Claims of the Paranormal (CSICOP), especially in their journal *Skeptical Inquirer*. Although CSICOP emphasizes the term "skeptical," their critics label the work of CSICOP as "debunking". In other words, a skeptical attitude is consistent with the scientific value of careful examination of evidence, whereas debunking (when used with a negative connotation) implies a greater interest in guarding against deviant challenges to normal science than in finding the truth.

It is difficult for us to give a fair treatment of this view due to our attitudes about those who zealously defend normal science (see Emmons, *At the Threshold*[287]). However, we shall attempt to do so at this time and to save our critique for later. We should also hasten to add that *Skeptical Inquirer* has published material on mediumship that is well worth considering.

Notice that skeptical/debunking scientific views of spirit mediumship are somewhat continuous with the social/behavioral scientific view discussed above, especially in terms of Howell's comment that paranormal experiences are traditionally assumed to be delusional or invalid. However, at least the debunkers are willing to consider the question more explicitly about whether the paranormal has an objective existence. Of course they are also much more likely to see paranormal beliefs as dangerously irrational rather than having positive social functions.

Looking in the other direction, debunkers share something with the parapsychologists and even with Spiritualists (to be considered later). All of these groups acknowledge that at least part of the time there have been delusional or fraudulent practices in mediumship.

When CSICOP and other debunkers turn their attention to spirit mediumship they generally frame it within the assumption that there can be no such thing because there is no evidence for the continuity of consciousness. On an abstract level they would have to agree that it is impossible to prove that there is *not* a surviving spirit. Therefore the emphasis is upon a rational, material explanation as being sufficient for all human behavior and thought (as in Howell's statement about the nature of mind discussed earlier), and upon there being demonstrably irrational and fraudulent aspects of mediumship as it is practiced.

Sometimes *Skeptical Inquirer* articles on mediumship analyze the "cold reading" techniques of mediums who apparently manage to extract information from the sitter (person getting a reading) through body language or conversational cues, or by asking "fishing" questions and manipulating the conversation. A good example of this is found in a piece by Peter Greasley.[288]

Greasley observed a 1998 BBC television documentary about a spirit medium and noticed seven techniques for eliciting positive responses and managing negative ones. One was to make statements with a high probability of being true. Another was to make indefinite references that a cooperative sitter might identify and fill in the interpretation. On the negative side, statements could be "attenuated" or reduced in emphasis to make them more acceptable, or "extended" to apply to someone close to the sitter for example.

In our own study we have observed hundreds of public message services and have certainly seen all of these techniques and more besides. One that Greasley doesn't mention, which actually deals with ignoring rather than managing negative responses, is for the medium to claim to know information that the sitter does not. For example, "You say you don't plan to take a trip, but you're going to take one anyway." This usually gets a laugh from the crowd (congregation) and may provide the impression that the medium is daring and all-knowing (whether it is true or not cannot be confirmed at the moment).

Other *Skeptical Inquirer* articles attack the paranormal by demonstrating that the phenomena can be produced by fraudulent means. In other words, if a trick magician can produce the same effects, this suggests that a spirit medium (for example) may be using fraudulent means as well. This seems to be a reasonable substitute for catching mediums in the act of fraud (although many mediums have indeed been caught in the past century and a half). Richard Wiseman and his colleagues have demonstrated how faulty eyewitness testimony can be in reporting on the paranormal, and how especially believers can be duped into seeing fraudulent seance phenomena (such as the movement of objects) as real.[289]

Not all debunking appears in the *Skeptical Inquirier.* Sybo Schouten[290] wrote a virtually debunking article on mediumship ("An Overview of Quantitatively Evaluated Studies with Mediums and Psychics") that appeared in *The Journal of the American Society for Psychical Research.* This provides a good transition into our next section on the parapsychological perspective on mediumship.

From the perspective of parapsychology today (the article appeared in 1994), it would be preferable to emphasize the possible existence of ESP without necessarily attributing it to survival, and without lending legitimacy to people who occupy the dubious roles of medium or psychic. We cannot necessarily attribute this "politically correct" attitude to Schouten, but it is interesting that one could see this article as a type of debunking from the perspective of mainstream parapsychology.

Schouten appreciates the methodological difficulties involved in establishing a quantitative probability framework for testing the largely qualitative statements of mediums, and he gives an historical overview of such attempts. However, he comments that most research testing the accuracy of the statements of mediums and psychics found insignificant results, perhaps one in three being significant, often only marginally significant statistically. He even says that the mediums/psychics have not been more successful than mainly nongifted subjects have been in laboratory tests of ESP. We should point out that Schouten may be comparing apples and oranges here and that the methodological difficulties in the testing of mediums are formidable.

But to continue, Schouten goes on to present an analysis of the interactive process between medium/psychic and sitter involved in a reading. Essentially a cooperative sitter helps the reader manipulate the material to make it appear legitimately paranormal and accurate. This is similar to the perspective taken by Greasley referred to above (on the manipulation of positive and negative responses from sitters).

Interestingly Schouten thinks that mediums/psychics might be so constrained by the professionalization of the role and by the drama of it that they block the spontaneous impressions they might get normally, making them "even less paranormally sensitive than nonpsychics."[291] Of course CSICOP would be likely to embrace Schouten's analysis of how readings are made to seem more impressive than they are, but not Schouten's willingness to concede that "It might well be that occasionally paranormal elements emerge."[292] And like a good skeptical social scientist, Schouten hastens to add that mediums/psychics might provide useful therapy even if they have little or no access to the paranormal, because they often have good psychological insights derived from their own difficult lives and because their clients may trust in their alleged paranormal abilities.

73

Searching for Survival: Parapsychology

We have already dipped into parapsychology by reviewing the article by Schouten above, in which he argued that quantitative studies have generally not provided statistically significant evidence for the accuracy of spirit mediums. Now we need to go back to a time when spirit mediumship was given much more positive attention by parapsychologists. In fact parapsychology emerged in the latter half of the nineteenth century out of the curiosity of scientists and Spiritualists about mediumship. Moore[293] explores this history including the founding of the Society for Psychical Research in London in 1882, a very prestigious organization including eight Fellows of the Royal Society (for example, Alfred Russel Wallace) and literary people like Alfred Tennyson.

Arthur Conan Doyle[294] wrote a sympathetic review of spiritualist mediumship and the controversies involved in its investigation in a two-volume work first published in 1926. For a more recent parapsychological overview see the 1982 book by Gauld.[295]

For those mediums who did not appear to be frauds and who provided impressive evidential material, there were essentially two explanations offered: telepathy and survival of the spirit. The most thorny theoretical problem arose when the concept of super-ESP (ESP without limitations of time or space and independent of thought transference or telepathy) seemed to account for everything that might be thought to come from contact with the spirit world. After a fascinating and complex examination of the evidence, Gauld[296] concludes that the super-ESP hypothesis seems unconvincing in a number of cases and that there is "a sprinkling of cases which rather forcefully suggest some form of survival."

However, other modern parapsychologists have been rather dismissive of spirit mediumship as evidence for survival. Becker[297], for example, in his book on the paranormal and survival spends only two pages explaining that spirit mediumship provides poor evidence for reincarnation, then fails to discuss it at all in other sections of the book. Kastenbaum[298], in his book on survival (life after death) is dismissive of the Fox Sisters case in 1848 (which is typical of the superficial treatment given this very complex story) but later provides a good forty pages covering mediumship and channeling.

One reason for the recent neglect of mediumship by parapsychologists is that "legitimate" parapsychology now takes place largely in laboratories under controlled experimental conditions. It is very difficult to study spirit mediumship in a lab setting. However, Schwartz and Russek[299] provide an interesting example of an experimental design for testing mediumship and a study involving two mediums and three experimenters, the results from which suggested spirit contact.

Schwartz[300] has also now (2002) produced a book, The Afterlife Experiments, in which he reports highly significant results above chance, testing prominent spirit mediums like John Edward in a laboratory setting. The procedures are progressively refined from one experiment to the next in order to eliminate alternative explanations such as fraud or various forms of information leakage. Providing a probability frame for judging results is still difficult, but Schwartz devises interesting techniques for doing this and uses control groups of nonmediums to establish a baseline for chance guessing within the same framework.

Although the evidence is very strong for his "dream team" of mediums performing generally far above the chance level, the question remains whether super-ESP could explain the results. Schwartz suggests that the continuation of consciousness after death is the simpler explanation (the principle of Occam's razor, prefer the simpler theory).

Another fascinating part of Schwartz's book deals with the HBO television special on his research.[301] He was dismayed that the final product was edited for emotional entertainment effects without making a scientific statement. This was followed by a show on Fox that used one of the mediums in Schwartz's study but favored a debunking perspective and failed to use evidential footage of her from a Schwartz experiment that he had sent them.

The entertainment industry is indeed a double-edged sword for serious mediums and parapsychological researchers. It airs "forbidden" research but also tends to either sensationalize it or (sometimes) debunk it, both for entertainment "values" (in order to make money of course). John Edward's books *One Last Time* and *Crossing Over* (especially the latter)[302] are excellent not only for the insights they provide into his life as a medium but also for understanding how he has had to fight to bring mediumship into the media without manipulation and distortion.

Back to the survival question again, although I am not a parapsychologist, when I conducted my study of *Chinese Ghosts and ESP*[303], I was really thinking more in terms of telepathy than survival of the spirit when I observed a spirit medium in Hong Kong giving rather convincing evidential information about my relatives and others. By now I am more likely to consider spiritual interpretations, as in the book *Body, Mind, Spirit: Exploring the Parapsychology of Spirituality* edited by Tart[304].

Keep in mind that the issue of whether there is really communication going on with an external, nonmaterial consciousness outside of the medium's own brain also comes up in the broader concept of channeling. Hastings and Klimo[305] give interesting, extensive analyses in their books on channeling, considering a variety of interpretations.

As one might expect in a book review appearing in *The Journal of the American Society for Psychical Research* in the 1990s, Anderson[306] is glad that Hastings included at least some examples of ridiculous channeling that might be titled "*Dumb Things My Voices Have Said.*" Anderson goes on to say that "in the aggregate I find very little indication (in channeled writings) that there is anything…transcending our normal capacities, unless it be in the direction of the pretentious and verbose, the outlandish and the inane….The vast bulk of it is just so much dingy twaddle…." Having read a number of popular books that were allegedly channeled, I am inclined to smile and agree with Anderson. However, the social scientist in me wants to deemphasize the ridicule and dismissal of channeling present in Anderson's review (although he likes Hastings' book for the most part), to suspend judgment on things I cannot test, and to appreciate more the social/cultural significance of channeling.

74

Rating the Spirits:
Spiritual Perspectives

On the surface it might appear that a Spiritualist view of mediumship would be obvious: the purpose of spirit mediumship is to demonstrate the continuity of life by establishing recognizable contact with the spirit world. However, it is not quite so simple as that.

To begin with, Spiritualists have been bothered with one of the central problems parapsychologists encountered with mediumship. Even if the process is paranormal (not just the imagination of the medium or some type of hoax or leakage of normal information), how do we know that the medium is not accessing the information through mental telepathy or some other type of ESP (clairvoyance, not to be confused with "clairvoyance" as a synonym for any message from a medium)?

This is important for two reasons. First of all, if it is telepathy, then this doesn't necessarily demonstrate continuity of life. The medium could simply be reading the mind of the sitter. Second, "merely" using telepathy would not distinguish a medium from a psychic or fortune teller.

Sometimes parapsychologists have been able to rule out telepathy when the sitter has no knowledge of material that is later confirmed[307], although this doesn't rule out super-ESP (something that we don't hear Spiritualists talking about). Colville[308], a Spiritualist writing in 1906, offered a solution to the problem for fellow Spiritualists, saying that we ought to understand telepathy as the fundamental process for communicating with other humans spiritually both before and after death.

Another problem for Spiritualists is the possibility of unreliable, even deceitful messages from the other side. Swedenborg, the intellectual forerunner of much Spiritualist thought, wrote in 1748 that a person "must beware lest he believe them in anything. For they (the spirits) say almost anything."[309] We were told something similar by a modern-day Swedenborgian author. It is also common to hear some Spiritualists today arguing against taking advice from spirit friends and relatives. "If they were jerks when they were alive, why would you think they would become so smart just because they died?"

This is certainly a controversial point. Probably most spiritualist mediums deemphasize the problem of visitation by evil or imposter spirits ("wicked personating spirits," Colville[310]), yet they feel protected by saying a prayer, setting the intention for only "the highest and best," and often by asking for the "white light of protection." They are also inclined to believe that most spirits do in fact become improved after death, having no pain of course, but also seeing things more peacefully and clearly. A hidden assumption is that spirits (or "Spirit", which is a vague reference to spirits and/or God) can tell the future, which mediums will often deny in spite of the fact that they often do bring through messages about the future.

Without going into detail about all of the modern versions of channeling in general, we should remember that channeling has been attacked by skeptics as containing a lot of drivel (see Anderson's comments above in connection with the studies by Hastings and Klimo). It is especially difficult to truth-test channeled material, since channeling can be from a wide variety of alleged beings, not just friends and relatives as typically in Spiritualism in particular, but also higher teachers and guides, discarnate spirits who may never have incarnated, aliens, group thought forms etc.

The most common response to this is that good channeled material "feels right." As Beard[311] says, valid material "resonates in a sure way to the inner in ourselves." This is a good reflection upon the psychological and spiritual function of channeling, but not very useful from a scientific perspective. Once I attended a channeling lecture in which the alleged outer-space beings coming through the channel (living person doing the channeling) said, "We are not your encyclopedia. Once you think you have us figured out, we'll tell you something different." One could perceive this statement as a convenient way to evade truth-testing.

On another occasion I asked the allegedly channeled being (a deceased medium) a question about a detail of his life that I knew but very probably the channel did not. The spirit could not remember. Of course this negative evidence cannot be used to disprove the validity of the spirit contact.

Going back to the nineteenth century, there were of course other spiritual movements afoot besides Spiritualism. As noted before, Spiritualists took much from Swedenborg (through Andrew Jackson Davis), although Swedenborgians have been wary of mediumship. They also borrowed from the Transcendentalists, who ironically also scorned them back. Moore[312] refers to the disdain that Thoreau and Emerson had for the mediumistic phenomena of Spiritualism, which Emerson referred to as the "rat hole of revelation." Not very nice. Not very "spiritual."

Probably the rise of Theosophy clarifies better than anything else the reason for the rejection of spirit mediumship and Spiritualism by nonSpiritualist spiritual groups. Prothero[313] explains that the Theosophical Society grew out of the Spiritualist movement but was an attempt by elites to reform it. Spiritualists, along with Methodists and Baptists, criticized both the elite clergy and the power structure of the rest of society. This is why they also supported such causes as the women's movement and the abolition of slavery (remember the deprivation theory in Chapter 71).

On closer examination the story of Theosophy is complicated by the fact that one founder Henry Steel Olcott was rooted in the U.S. metropolitan gentry, which wanted to uplift the masses, but the other founder Helena Petrovna Blavatsky was more oriented toward a Russian aristocratic view. Although Blavatsky was more attached to esoteric phenomena than Olcott, both ridiculed Spirtitualists for dealing with "elementary spirits" (ranking above animals but below humans) who were capable of deceiving mediums by impersonating spirits of the dead, when they should be seeking revelation from higher spirits. For a detailed and fascinating, though uncharitable, treatment of the history of Theosophy, see Washington's book *Madame Blavatsky's Baboon.*[314]

At any rate, according to social scientists like Prothero, the spiritual debates over mediumship seem to be more a struggle for respectability and prestige than an argument about the actual validity of mediumship. Indeed, one could frame the entire debate over mediumship that way. Spiritualists want to preserve a boundary between mediumship and psychic or fortune-telling activities. Parapsychologists are more willing to see mediumship in terms of ESP than to accept it as evidence for survival (which seems more religious and less scientific). Normal scientists (including most social scientists) prefer to reject mediumship as a valid way of knowing because it is deviant from a rational perspective.

75

Charlie's View

Let me begin by saying that I find some "truth" or usefulness in all of these perspectives: social/behavioral scientific, debunking, parapsychological, and spiritual. I do not think that this represents a "relativization of knowledge," in which anything can be true if you believe in it. I just mean that taken literally each perspective offers interesting possible explanations, some of which may be valid at certain times.

Taken at a deeper level, each of these perspectives tends to become a dogmatic, competitive belief system conducive neither to science nor spirituality. Practitioners of them tend to lose sight of the alleged purposes of systems: to explain reality and to enrich our lives. Every organized belief system is really a social construct created in part to serve the political ends of the group, or at least of the elite members of the group.

What I would like to do is to extract some wisdom from each perspective (giving it a sympathetic reading), and leave the competitive interests and dogmatic structures behind. This (ideally) approaches a multifaceted or pluralistic (and not merely relativized) approach.

I feel good about having played the role of practitioner in each of these systems, so that I can use each without being overly committed to any. The one I have least experience with is debunking, because I cannot accept the narrow view of debunking and its attempt to demolish "ignorance" rather than to engage in open-ended inquiry. If members of CSICOP should hasten to claim that I have an incorrect view of their purpose, which is actually to be skeptical, providing a counterbalance to uncritical belief, then I would happily concur that I have been a "skeptic" in this sense too. And in fact some pieces in *Skeptical Inquirer* and by members of CSICOP published elsewhere have been fair. Susan Blackmore is my favorite example of such fairness.

I anticipate that some of my colleagues in sociology and anthropology will say that I have taken participant observation too far and have "gone native" by actually learning to do spirit mediumship. I was supposed to study spirit mediums, not become one. This is a valid criticism that must be considered, but I see what I have done as "participatory science," becoming involved fully in the phenomenon itself, which has made it much more understandable to me on a personal level. Of course this becomes more controversial when the phenomenon is considered deviant or dubious by the scientific community.

I say that I have become fully involved, but actually I have not become a registered medium or done mediumship for personal financial gain. I *have* joined a Spiritualist Church and done "student" mediumship.

Having said all of that, let me now reflect on each of these perspectives and share what I think about spirit mediumship as a phenomenon.

First, there cannot be much doubt about spirit mediumship having social and psychological functions (or being involved in power or conflict, not to slight conflict theory). In my own research in Hong Kong[315] I was able to observe people consulting a spirit medium in order to make contact with relatives who might help them with practical matters like winning the lottery to get into public housing. Traditional Chinese ancestor worship culture requires mediums to facilitate the communication between ancestors and descendants who are supposed to help each other. Going deeper, ancestor worship has held together large kinship groups who worship common ancestors going back several generations, especially in areas of south China where wet-rice cultivation was managed by the clan.

As for psychological functions (and dysfunctions), mediumship certainly has a psychological base in terms of altered states of consciousness (which I have also experienced myself), even for mediums today who tend to go into only a light trance. There is no general strong correlation between mediumship and mental illness, although this has been an issue in the literature. Some mediums quite apparently have multiple personality or experience other dissociative states. I think that labeling all of these as pathological is problematic and prematurely judgmental. As we have seen, one of the ways to control especially women in Victorian times was to threaten to commit them to insane asylums after diagnosing them as hysterical or mediomaniacal.

McClenon's theory of the genetic foundation of religion based on the evolution of humans toward hypnotizability (discussed above) is certainly an interesting view that suggests a promising way into studying the physiology and psychology of anomalous or paranormal experiences. I think that scientists who see the connection between brain patterns and anomalous experience as an obvious refutation of the "reality" of the paranormal, and the psychospiritual folks who are upset with this research are both mistaken.

Just because such experiences have a brain component doesn't mean that they don't have "evidential" (containing evidence of paranormal knowledge or experience) aspects as well. If people do have a spiritual or surviving-consciousness component, they also need a physical component in order to experience life on the physical plane and to make connections between the two. Although it seems plausible to claim that a spirit medium, for example, is merely dissociating when he/she experiences a spirit message, it could also be that the brain needs to disconnect from normal patterns in order to get the information more clearly. A parapsychologist would test the evidentiality of the message in order to distinguish between these two interpretations.

Now I am ready for my most difficult task: finding useful elements in the debunking perspective to help understand spirit mediumship. I recall when I was doing my book on UFO researchers[316] how some of them pointed out that UFO debunkers were good for keeping serious ufologists on their toes. Even if some debunkers often were scornful and disrespectful of UFO experiencer claims and often refused to look at the evidence, there were also times when some of them came up with good alternative theories for sightings, such as radar malfunctioning and earthquake lights. Most UFO researchers recognize that the bulk of UFO reports in fact can be "explained away" through mundane explanations. Therefore their own scientific skepticism about any particular report actually coincides with the perspective assumed by debunkers.

Moving to the issue of spirit mediumship, the same sort of overlap exists between debunkers and parapsychologists and even spirit mediums. As pointed out earlier in this book, many of the mediums we interviewed, and even many of the famous mediums in history have had considerable skepticism even about their own personal work. Although many late nineteenth-century Spiritualists became impatient with the scientists who studied mediumship, they did share a desire to root out and expose fraudulent mediums.

CSICOP proclaims the worthy objective of promoting scientific literacy and reducing gullibility in the general population. When it comes to mediumship, this would involve pointing out various tricks used by fraudulent mediums. Even mediums who are not intentionally fraudulent can engage in guesswork through observing body language and other cues. As Schouten noted (discussed above), medium and sitter can cooperate in creating an illusion of appropriateness in the reading. With a greater wariness, people might be less likely to accept readings necessarily as communications from the spirit world.

Now I must show some distance from this perspective. First, it is difficult to judge that believing in the reading is a bad thing, even if it is not really from "spirit". Going to a spirit medium or psychic may be very therapeutic, as even Schouten admits. Mediums often say in a public message service that messages given to one person may contain some good lessons for others present.

Next, I think it is very difficult to pass judgment on particular mediums. Partly this is because it is so difficult to establish a probability frame for scoring a medium's accuracy. Even when a medium is rather general, she or he may be very good at identifying the person's personal issues and do a good service. As I say elsewhere, just when I get a feeling from observation that a medium is not very good, I get a very positive report from someone about what a good reading she/he gave, or I witness it for myself at a public service.

One thing that I definitely oppose is the unscrupulous gouging of clients. There are stories of mediums or psychics who tell people that they will remove a curse for a $3,000 fee (although I do not have any first-hand evidence of this). There are also a very few mediums who charge very high fees; but this would be a problem if we were talking about doctors or attorneys as well.

At any rate, debunkers help sound a note of caution for those who are ready to believe in anything allegedly miraculous. In my experience I do not think that many of the people who frequent Lily Dale or who attend the Spiritualist churches I have observed are seriously absent of judgment. They are not participating in some cult that is taking away all of their worldly goods. Good mediums also remind people that they have free will and should use their common sense.

Moving to parapsychology, which shares a scientific skepticism with the debunkers, especially when it comes to mediumship as noted above, I think that it requires a great deal of reading to sort out the evidence on mediumship. From reading the sources referred to above and many more, I think that the evidence for mediumship is very supportive of a core of truly remarkable phenomena that cannot be dismissed.

It was often the case that famous mediums mixed legitimate phenomena with cheating (perhaps unconsciously). These tended to be prematurely dismissed by some even though there was good evidence for the nonhoaxed portion. Also, complex cases like that of the Fox Sisters, who at one point admitted to cheating but then recanted, should not be dealt with stereotypically and simplistically as they often are in popular publications or debunking literature.

From the beginning I realized that this study could not hope to set the validity issues in mediumship straight when a century and a half of research had failed to do so. No one should accept the last two paragraphs above without doing some research. It is not a very efficient way to do things, but in a field that has not been legitimated by mainstream science, one almost has to do one's own study to decide the issue for oneself. I believe that I have done enough research of my own to appreciate the fact that some phenomena in mediumship are genuine (which is not to say that I can explain it). This is apart from my own experiences as a medium. What I am referring to here is my study of mediums that was part of the larger study *Chinese Ghosts and ESP*.[317] It was clear to me that some sessions were so accurate that they were remarkably beyond what could be reasonably attributed to chance.

What parapsychology contributes is a relatively open-minded exploration of the truth claims of spirit mediumship, something that social scientists and debunkers do not do (if they are performing their expected roles). Certainly there was much more attention directed to mediumship by parapsychologists in the nineteenth and early twentieth centuries than since, but there may well be a revival of interest due to the popularity of mediums and psychics in current popular culture. I have not studied it much, but there is also an amateur parapsychology subculture, made up of "ghost hunters" especially, who use electronic equipment as well as mediums/psychics to investigate hauntings. Perhaps they will discover something due to the democratization of technology.

Last I need to comment on the spiritual perspective on spirit mediumship. In part this is where my own "participatory science" belongs, insofar as my attempt to do mediumship represents a direct experience of an allegedly spiritual phenomenon.

Most of my experience is not directly a test of whether spirit mediumship is really a communication with the spirit world. Most of it is learning to understand the role of spirit medium, how one becomes recruited and socialized to it, and how one performs it and feels about it. Previously in this book we have discussed all of that, including the persistent problem of doing something intuitive in a rational culture.

In a larger sense I feel that mediumship in this society is just one piece of a larger spiritual attempt to find meaning in an increasingly meaningless, technologically dominated mass society (the subject of my next study probably). I could probably explain my own involvement in mediumship since 1993 (when my mother died and I started hearing her voice in my left ear) in those terms.

However, I do not want to just get lost in a spiritual subculture to feel good about my place in modern society and to be at peace with my dead relatives. I also have a curiosity addiction fed by the scientific side of me, which is continually laughing at the "spiritual" side of me. On the other hand, my skeptical side is also fair enough to consider the subjective evidence provided through my own experience. The price my spiritual side pays for this tolerance is that it needs to come up with some pretty good evidence to my skeptical side that I am not just being deluded by wishful thinking.

In an earlier chapter I shared my own experiences that convinced me that the messages I was getting were highly evidential. One involved two "watch out" warnings in my left ear just before coming close to u-turning kids on tricycle and bicycle, separated by ten or fifteen seconds. Another involved getting two detailed messages complete with directions on who should receive them, then going to a message service in which those (nearly) identical messages were given by two other mediums to the very people I knew should get them.

The parapsychologist in me is very sure that I have received intuitive messages that are correct way beyond any reasonable chance explanation. This satisfies the skeptical side of me, to a point. However, I cannot prove that there isn't some explanation other than spiritual communication. It could be super-ESP, or the one mind, or whatever.

My spiritual side is convinced (sort of) that I really am communicating with my parents and other people, and that my mother is my spirit guide when I do mediumship. How do I know? I just know. But that's not good enough for my skeptical side. I really don't know of a critical experiment that could settle the matter. Right now I'm content to go on marveling and seeking, and acting as if it's true. I think I've already discovered more than I ever expected to.

But there's more. From my observations I think that spirit mediumship is a great mystery, of which we know only a little. I find it both amusing and annoying when people think they have it all figured out. "It's nonsense." "It's real, but you have to do it this way." From interviewing many mediums and from doing it myself, I think that it happens in a great many ways, not just one way. And of course lots of times people try to do it without very good results.

Trying to force it into a social mold with rigid rules doesn't always work. Some spirits seem to be very confused, or communicate to the wrong people (I don't blame all displacement on the medium). Some people just don't come through when you want them to; or the sitter can't get it when you deliver it. Trying to get the spirits to cue up and behave might work to some extent, but the concept amuses me.

At any rate, we have very little knowledge of the process, apart from some understanding of the conditions that help people get into altered states, and how the brain works differently when it happens. Subjectively mediums working in a variety of ways get to recognize the experience and learn to pass on what they are getting.

In my own mediumship I have learned to be less analytical (difficult for a college professor) and to bring things forth with less editing. I have learned to set a good intention and to worry about it less. I continue to marvel when I get things right, more right than would seem possible by chance. Any more than that I shall probably have to tell you after I die.

76

Penelope's View

Our consciousness is energy. Holistic medicine and the new science have begun to express this paradigm shift, but I think it could be another twenty years until we will have a handle on how it is all connected. So my simple answer for how does mediumship happen is that we "know", communicate, and transfer energy in ways yet unknown to us. All can be known and can unfold once we stop directing the energy in ways we were taught, such as through believing only in cause and effect.

I have read that the Aboriginal people of Australia refer to humans as "forever beings." I think that we were created and that we are creators forever. We don't die. One hundred and forty years ago some people (Spiritualists) thought that to know something from another plane of existence, our deceased loved ones had to tell us. It also satisfied a longing for continued connection with the person, as one developed a new relationship that focused on the soul instead of the physical form.

I have received such meaningful, healing messages. Once I spent the day and evening with an older couple who ran an addiction recovery house. They reminisced about Bill W. and other people they had known through AA. After I went home, that night they were both murdered by an ex-client.

The next morning I stopped to return a book and was shocked to learn of the events. I volunteered to help with details and to clean up the bloody sheets. I looked at the mess and thought it should be done, but I felt frozen in shock and horror. Suddenly a warm golden light (probably sunlight) came through a window from behind my right shoulder and shone on the bloody bed-sheets. I clearly heard my friend say, "Just see it and do it, don't make a big deal out of it. I am fine, and we are with more people that we loved here than we knew and loved there. Now we will live here. It was *fast*, quite a trip, like 'Beam me up, Scotty.' Thank you, and I love you."

Two months later a medium from Canada (who had no way of knowing about the event) said to me, "I have a woman here. She identifies herself as 'Bloody Mary'. She hopes everyone will forgive and move on. She hopes that there will not be a trial. She says, 'Thank you, and I love you.'" I knew it was my friend Mary, whom I identified with "bloody" and who was 40 years in recovery when she died, thus the name "Bloody Mary." That was the one time in my life that I *needed* to hear from a specific spirit. I had never before (nor have I since) experienced gun violence or murder. During the grief and loss I was comforted by those brief communications.

I have also performed as the medium who hears from spirits who identify themselves to the sitter and gives meaningful messages to others. The way I know that the spirits are individualized expressions of consciousness is that I will sense particular energy personalities, and feel love and other deep emotions toward the sitters as if they were my own children, partners or friends. For the length of time I am communicating I care so deeply, yet I have just met the sitter, and the feeling is gone as soon as the message is over.

But there is often more going on than a discarnate spirit showing up. More often I just know things. Call it super-ESP or being a reishi (a knower or seer). I have "read" others' minds, and I have observed my mind from a consciousness beyond it.

Once I spent the day with a physicist who was so excited after getting a reading and interviewing me that he enthusiastically drew a whole page of symbols to explain to me what I had just done. It made sense as he wrote formulas and talked. But when he left it just looked like a page full of squiggles. Just as a physicist can understand concepts that are unknown to me, perhaps the future will reveal new "laws" of consciousness to humanity.

We can study the concepts of chi and chakras that Eastern sages have explored for thousands of years and "know" that as it is within us, so it is out in the world. Just as a cell can be cloned to create a reproduction of the whole, so we are a microcosm of the macrocosm. Why shouldn't all be known even though our Western science has yet to develop the measuring tools? After all, electricity existed before we could understand it.

A remembering could also occur. I have observed what my mind has called reincarnation (or parallel lives, life in a spiral continuum) where we spirits create a consensus that says this is 2003. But in a past-life regression my mind has visited another point in time and space. I have seen an image of past times imposed translucently upon today's landscape. Clairvoyantly I have also experienced visions where I watched a moving picture with my eyes open and received a knowing insight without hearing words. Sometimes I have been invited by spirit teachers to a mystical plane of existence, where everything that is, and has been, is known.

Yet I have had more ordinary days and ways of knowing than extraordinary ones. Each is a gift. I am blessed to know that life is forever, the universe and humans are so remarkable, and there is much for me to discover on my journey. Appreciating, marveling, discovery and adventure, healing, transforming, service, loving and being loved are what mediumship means to me.

Bibliography

Alcoholics Anonymous Staff
1993 *Alcoholics Anonymous*. New York: AA World Services, Inc.

Allen, James
1994 *As a Man Thinketh*. Brownlow Pub. Co.

Altea, Rosemary
1995 *The Eagle and the Rose: A Remarkable True Story*. New York: Warner Books, Inc.

Anderson, Rodger
1993 Review of Arthur Hastings, *With the Tongues of Men and Angels: A Study of Channeling*. The Journal of the American Society for Psychical Research, vol. 87, January, pp. 117–121.
1994 Review of Paul Beard, *Inner Eye, Listening Ear: An Exploration into Mediumship*. The Journal of the American Society for Psychical Research, vol. 88, pp. 287–291.

Angoff, Allan
1974 *Eileen Garrett and the World Beyond the Senses*. N.Y.: William Morrow & Co. Inc.

Ashlay-Lehrer, Pamla
1993 *The Soul Book*. Minneapolis, Minnesota: All One Journey.

Baer, Hans A.
1993 "The Limited Empowerment of Women in Black Spiritual Churches: An Alternative to Religious Leadership," *Sociology of Religion*, 54, 1, spring, pp. 65–82.

Barrett, Harrison D.
1895 *Life Work of Mrs. Cora L.V. Richmond*. Chicago: National Spiritualists Association of the USA.

Barrow, Logie
> 1980 "Socialism in Eternity: The Ideology of Plebeian Spiritualists, 1853–1913," *History Workshop*, 9, spring, pp. 37–69.

Beard, Paul
> 1992 *Inner Eye, Listening Ear: An Exploration into Mediumship.* Norwich, England: Pilgrim Books.

Becker, Carl B.
> 1993 *Paranormal Experience and Survival of Death.* Albany, NY: State University of New York Press.

Braden, Charles S.
> 1949 *These Also Believe: A Study of Modern American Cults and Minority Religious Movements.* N.Y.: The Macmillan Company.

Braude, Ann
> 1989 *Radical Spirits: Spiritualism and Women's Rights in Nineteenth-Century America.* Boston: Beacon Press.

Britten, Emma Hardinge
> 1900 *Autobiography of Emma Hardinge Britten*, (edited posthumously by Mrs. Margaret Wilkinson). London: John Keywood.

Brown, Michael
> 1997 *The Channeling Zone: American Spirituality in an Anxious Age.* Cambridge, MA: Harvard U. Press.

Buckland, Raymond
> 1997 *Doors to Other Worlds: A Practical Guide to Communicating with Spirits.* St. Paul, Minnesota: Llewellyn Publications.

Buhrman, Sarasvati
> 1997 "Trance Types and Amnesia Revisited: Using Detailed Interviews to Fill in the Gaps," *Anthropology of Consciousness*, 8,1: pp.10–21.

Burton, Jean
> 1948 *Heyday of a Wizard: Daniel Home the Medium.* London: George G. Harrap & Co., Ltd.

Carlton, Eric
2000 *The Paranormal: Research and the Quest for Meaning*. Aldershot, UK: Ashgate Publishing, Ltd.

Carroll, Bret E.
1997 *Spiritualism in Antebellum America*. Bloomington: Indiana U. Press. Colville, W.J.
1906 *Universal Spiritualism: Spirit Communion in All Ages Among All Nations*. New York: R.F. Fenno and Company.

Carroll, Lee and Jan Tober
2001 *The Indigo Children*. Carlsbad, CA: Hay House, Inc.

Cook, Mrs. Cecil M.
1919 *How I Discovered My Mediumship*. Chicago: The William T. Stead Memorial Center.
1931 *The Voice Triumphant: The Revelations of a Medium*. New York: Alfred A. Knopf.

Cooke, Grace
1965 *The New Mediumship*. Liss, Hampshire, England: The White Eagle Publishing Trust.

Cory, Charles E.
1919 "Patience Worth," *Psychological Review*, Sept., pp. 397–407.

Crinita, Joey
1982 *The Medium Touch: A New Approach to Mediumship*. West Chester, PA: Whitford Press.

Cross, Whitney R.
1981 *The Burned-over District: the Social and Intellectual History of Enthusiastic Religion in Western New York, 1800–1850*. New York: Octagon Books.

Dailey, Abram H.
1894 *Molly Fancher, The Brooklyn Enigma*. Brooklyn, New York: Eagle Book Printing Dept.

Dann, Graham M.S.
    1979 "Religion and Cultural Identity: The Case of Umbanda," *Socio-logical Analysis*, 40, 3, fall, pp. 208–225.

Davis, Andrew Jackson
    1859 *The Magic Staff; An Autobiography of Amdrew Jackson Davis*. New York: J.S. Brown and Co.

D'Esperance, E.
    1897 *Shadow Land, or light from the Other Side*. London: George Redway.

Dixon, Joy
    1997 "Sexology and the Occult: Sexuality and Subjectivity in Theosophy's New Age," *Journal of the History of Sexuality*, 7, 3, January, pp. 409–433.

Doyle, Arthur Conan
    1975 *The History of Spiritualism*, 2 vols. New York: Arno Press.

Dunninger, Joseph
    1971 "Joseph Dunninger Discusses the Houdini-Ford Controversy," *Fate*, Nov., pp. 74–82.

Edward, John
    1999 *One Last Time: A Psychic Medium Speaks to Those We Have Loved and Lost*. New York: Berkley Books.
    2001 *Crossing Over: The Stories Behind the Stories*. N.Y.: Princess Books.

Emmons, Charles F.
    1982 *Chinese Ghosts and ESP: A Study of Paranormal Beliefs and Experiences*. Metuchen, New Jersey: The Scarecrow Press, Inc.
    1987 *Hong Kong Prepares for 1997*. Hong Kong: Centre of Asian Studies.
    1997 *At the Threshold: UFOs, Science and the New Age*. Mill Spring, North Carolina: Wild Flower Press.
    1999 "Recruitment and Socialization to Spirit Mediumship." Unpublished paper.

Farmer, John S.
    1886 *Twixt Two Worlds: A Narrative of the Life and Work of William Eglinton*. London: The Psychological Press.

Foght, Paul
    1962 "Seance with D.D. Home," *Fate*, June, pp. 68–72.

Ford, Arthur
    1958 *Nothing So Strange: The Autobiography of Arthur Ford*, in collaboration with Margueritte Harmon Bro. New York: Harper & Row.

Foundation for Inner Peace Staff
    1997 *A Course in Miracles*. Arkana.

Galanti, Geri-Ann
    1987 "Why Do People Go to Psychics?" *Fate*, May, pp. 68–75.

Garrett, Eileen J.
    1938 *My Life as a Search for the Meaning of Mediumship*. New York: Oquaga Press.
    1968 *Many Voices: The Autobiography of a Medium*. New York: G.P. Putnam's Sons.

Garroutte, Eva Marie
    1993 "When Scientists Saw Ghosts and Why They Stopped." In *Vocabularies of Public Life*, edited by Robert Wuthnow. New York, NY: Routledge.

Gauld, Alan
    1982 *Mediumship and Survival: A Century of Investigations*. London: Paladin Books.

Gawain, Shakti
    1993 *Living in the Light*. NY: Bantam Books.

Gibson, Edmond P.
    1961 "Is This Houdini's Telepathic Code?" *Fate*, April, pp. 53–57.

Gillen, Paul
    1987 "The Pleasures of Spiritualism." *Australian and New Zealand Journal of Sociology*, 23,22, pp. 217–232.

Goode, Erich
    2000 *Paranormal Beliefs: A Sociological Introduction.* Prospect Heights, Illinois: Waveland Press, Inc.

Greasley, Peter
    2000 "Management of Positive and Negative Responses in a Spiritualist Medium Consultation," *Skeptical Inquirer*, Sept/Oct., pp. 45–49.

Guggenheim, Bill and Judy
    1996 *Hello from Heaven.* New York: Bantam.

Hastings, Arthur
    1991 *With the Tongue of Men and Angels: A Study of Channeling.* Fort Worth, TX: Holt, Rinehart and Winston, Inc.

Hay, Louise L.
    1999 *You Can Heal Your Life.* Carlsbad, CA: Hay House.

Haywood, Carol Lois
    1983 "The Authority and Empowerment of Women among Spiritualist Groups," *Journal for the Scientific Study of Religion*, 22, 2, June, pp. 157–166.

Hess, David J.
    1993 *Science in the New Age: The Paranormal, Its Defenders and Debunkers, and American Culture.* Madison, Wisconsin: University of Wisconsin Press.

Home, D.D.
    1864 *Incidents in My Life.* Secaucus, New Jersey: University Books, Inc.

Howell, Julia D.
    1989 "The Social Sciences and Mystical Experience." In *Exploring the Paranormal: Perspectives on Belief and Experience,* edited by George K. Zollschan *et al.*, pp. 77–94. Dorset, UK: Prism Press.

Kardec, Allan
1874 *Book on Mediums; Or, Guide for Mediums and Invocators.* York Beach, Maine: Samuel Weiser, Inc.

Kastenbaum, Robert
1995 *Is There Life After Death? The Latest Evidence Analyzed.* London, UK: Prion.

Kenny, Michael G.
1986 *The Passion of Ansel Bourne: Multiple Personality in American Culture.* Washington, DC: Smithsonian Institution Press.

King, Lotus Ray
1999 *The "I Am" Discourses.* Chicago, IL: Saint Germain Press.

Klimo, Jon
1987 *Channeling: Investigations on Receiving Information from Paranormal Sources.* New York: Jeremy P. Tarcher, Inc.

Lain, David
1985 *Guns and Rain: Guerillas and Spirit Mediums in Zimbabwe.* Berkeley: U. Of California Press.

Lauck, Joanne Elizabeth
1998 *The Voice of the Infinite in the Small: Revisioning the Insect-Human Connection.* Mill Spring, North Carolina: Swan.Raven & Co.

Lawton, George
1932 *The Drama of Life after Death.* New York: Henry Holt.

Leonesio, Mary E.
1989 "Psychics and 'Fortunetellers,'" *Fate*, July, pp. 90–96.

Lerch, Patricia B.
1982 "An Explanation for the Predominance of Women in the Umbanda Cults of Porto Alegre, Brazil," *Urban Anthropology*, 11, 2, summer, pp. 237–261.

Lewis, I.M.
1966 "Spirit Possession and Deprivation Cults," *Man*, 1,3, pp. 307–329.

Litchfield, Beals E.
1893 *Autobiography of Beals E. Litchfield, or Forty Years Intercourse with the Denizens of the Spirit World.* Jamestown, New York: F.H. & W.A. White.

Literary Digest, The
1916 "Fifty Years of Spiritual Victory," February 26, p. 507.

Lloyd, John
1986 "The Sociability of Sensations," *Sociological Review*, 34, 4, Nov., pp. 773–796.

Lone Dog, Louise
1964 *Strange Journey: The Vision Life of a Psychic Indian Woman.* Healdsburg, California: Naturegraph Publishers.

Lord-Drake, Mrs. Maud
1904 *Psychic Light: The Continuity of Law and Life.* Kansas City, Missouri: The Frank T. Riley Publishing Company.

Mandino, Og
1985 *The Greatest Salesman in the World.* New York: Bantam Books.

Marryat, Florence (ed.)
1893 *The Clairvoyance of Bessie Williams (Mrs. Russell Davies).* London: Bliss, Sands and Foster.

Martin, Joel and Patricia Romanowski
1988 *We Don't Die: George Anderson's Conversations with the Other Side.* New York: Berkley Books.
1997 *Love Beyond Life: The Healing Power of After-Death Communications.* New York: Dell Publishing.

Mattey, Angela M.
1993 *The Key to Spiritual and Psychic Development: Table Tipping.* Phoenix, Arizona: Tam Enterprises Publishing Co.

McClenon, James
1984 *Deviant Science: The Case of Parapsychology.* Philadelphia, PA: University of Pennsylvania Press.
1997 "Shamanic Healing, Human Evolution, and the Origin of Religion," *Journal for the Scientific Study of Religion,* 36, 3: pp. 345–354.
2000 "Content Analysis of an Anomalous Memorate Collection: Testing Hypotheses Regarding Universal Features," *Sociology of Religion,* 61, 2: pp.155–169.
2001 "Mathematical Models of the Ritual Healing Theory: Shamanism, Anomalous Experience, and the Origin of Religion," paper presented at Southern Sociological Society meetings, Atlanta, GA, April.
2002 *Wondrous Healing: Shamanism, Human Evolution, and the Origin of Religion.* DeKalb, IL: Northern Illinois University Press.

McCoy, Edain
1994 *How to Do Automatic Writing.* St. Paul, MN: Llewellyn Publications.

McDowell, Bill
1992 *The Lily Dale Portraits: Interview Transcripts.* Unpublished.

Melton, J. Gordon (ed.)
1990 *Spiritualism I: Spiritualist Thought.* N.Y.: Garland Publishing.

Moody, Raymond with Paul Perry
1993 *Reunions: Visionary Encounters with Departed Loved Ones.* New York: Ivy Books.

Moore, Dorothy (as told to Maxine Lampshire)
1976 *Fifty Years of Mediumship: The Dorothy Moore Story: Not Bread Alone.* Washington, D.C.: ESPress, Inc.

Moore, R. Laurence
1977 *In Search of White Crows: Spiritualism, Parapsychology, and American Culture.* New York: Oxford U. Press.

Morris, Rosalind C.
2000 *In the Place of Origins: Modernity and Its Mediums in Northern Thailand.* Durham, NC: Duke University Press.

Newport, Frank and Maura Strausberg
2001 "Americans' Belief in Psychic and Paranormal Phenomena Is Up Over Last Decade." Princeton, NJ: Gallup News Service, 8 June.

Northrop, Suzane Northrop with Kate McLoughlin
1994 *The Seance: Healing Messages from Beyond.* New York: Dell Publishing.

Owen, Alex
1990 *The Darkened Room: Women, Power and Spiritualism in Late Victorian England.* Philadelphia: University of Pennsylvania Press.

Palfreman, Jon
1979 "The Seances and the Scientists," *New Society,* 48, 872, June 21: pp. 709–711.

Prince, Walter Franklin
1927 *The Case of Patience Worth: A Critical Study of Certain Unusual Phenomena.* Boston Society for Psychic Research.

Prothero, Stephen
1993 "From Spiritualism to Theosophy: 'Uplifting' a Democratic Tradition," *Religion and American Culture: A Journal of Interpretation,* Summer, vol.3, no.2, pp.197–216.

Putnam, Allen
1873 *Biography of Mrs. J.H. Conant, the World's Medium of the Nineteenth Century.* Boston: William White & Co.

Randolph, P.B.
1869 *The Davenport Brothers, The World-Renowned Spiritual Mediums: Their Biography and Adventures in Europe and America.* Boston: William White and Co.

Richard, Michael P. And Alberto Adato
1980 "The Medium and Her Message: A Study of Spiritualism at Lily Dale, New York," *Review of Religious Research*, 22,2, Dec., pp.186–197.

Riordan, Suzanne
1991 "Channeling: A New Revelation?" In *Perspectives on the New Age*, edited by James R. Lewis and J. Gordon Melton (eds.). Albany, NY: SUNY Press.

Roberts, Estelle
1959 *Forty Years a Medium*. London: Herbert Jenkins, Ltd.

Roman, Sanaya, and Duane Packer
1987 *Opening to Channel: How to Connect with Your Guide*. Tiburon, California: H.J. Kramer, Inc.

Schouten, Sybo A.
1994 "An Overview of Quantitatively Evaluated Studies with Mediums and Psychics," *The Journal of the American Society for Psychical Research*, vol. 88, pp. 221–254.

Schwartz, Gary E.
2002 *The Afterlife Experiments: Breakthrough Evidence of Life After Death*. New York: Pocket Books.

Schwartz, Gary E.R. And Linda G.S. Russek
1999 *The Living Energy Universe*. Charlottesville, VA: Hampton Roads Publishing Co., Inc.

Shupe, Anson and Jeffrey K. Hadden
1988 "Spiritual Healing and the Medical Model." Paper presented to the North Central Sociological Association.

Skultans, Vieda
1974 *Intimacy and Ritual: A Study of Spiritualism, Mediums and Groups*. London: Routledge & Kegan Paul.

Stoff, Jesse A. and Charles R. Pellegrino
    1992 *Chronic Fatigue Syndrome*. HarperTrade.

Swatos, William H., Jr. and Loftur Reimar Gissurarson
    1997 *Icelandic Spiritualism: Mediumship and Modernity in Iceland*. New Brunswick, NJ: Transaction Publishers.

Sway, Marlene B.
    1987 "Fortune Telling Practice among American Gypsies," *Free Inquiry in Creative Sociology*,15,1, pp. 3–6.

Targ, Russell, and Jane Katra
    1998 *Miracles of Mind: Exploring Nonlocal Consciousness and Spiritual Healing*. Novato, California: New World Library.

Tart, Charles T. (Ed.)
    1997 *Body, Mind, Spirit: Exploring the Parapsychology of Spirituality*. Charlottesville, VA: Hampton Roads Publishing Co., Inc.

Thuillier, Pierre
    1983 "Spiritualism and the Science of the Unconscious," *Recherche*, 14, 149, Nov.: pp.1358–1368.

Turner, Edith
    1996 *The Hands Feel It: Healing and Spirit Presence among a Northern Alaskan People*. DeKalb, Illinois: Northern Illinois University Press.

Underwood, Anne
    2001 "Religion and the Brain," *Newsweek*, May 7: pp. 50–57.

Van Praagh, James
    1997 *Talking to Heaven: A Medium's Message of Life after Death*. New York: Dutton.

Wallis, E.W. and M.H.
    no date *A Guide to Mediumship and Psychical Unfoldment*. Summit, New Jersey: Stow Memorial Foundation Inc.

Washington, Peter
    1996 *Madame Blavatsky's Baboon: A History of the Mystics, Mediums,*

and Misfits Who Brought Spiritualism to America. New York: Schocken Books, Inc.

Weldon, Warren
1970 *A Happy Medium: The Life of Caroline Randolph Chapman*. Englewood Cliffs, New Jersey: Prentice Hall, Inc.

Wiseman, Richard *et al.*
1995 "Eyewitness Testimony and the Paranormal," *Skeptical Inquirer*, Nov./Dec., pp. 29–32.
1999 "The Psychology of the Seance, From Experiment to Drama," *Skeptical Inquirer*, March/April, pp. 30–32.

World, The
1898 "Molly Fancher, Famous Invalid, Hears a Concert by Telephone," Thursday, March 24.

Worth, Patience
1917 *A Sorry Tale: A Story of the Time of Christ*, communicated through Mrs. John H. Curran. New York: Henry Holt & Co.
1918 *Hope Trueblood*, communicated through Mrs. John H. Curran. New York: Henry Holt & Co.

Endnotes

1. Newport and Strausberg, 2001.
2. McClenon, 2002, pp. 60–61; Turner, 1996.
3. Emmons, 1999.
4. Cook, 1919, pp. 15–55.
5. Cook, 1931.
6. Cook, 1919, pp. 23–24.
7. Roberts, 1959, p.15–17.
8. Roberts, 1959, p. 31.
9. Home, 1864, pp. 1–3.
10. Foght, 1962, p.69.
11. Moore, 1977, p. 105.
12. Angoff, 1974, pp. 47–50; Garrett, 1939, pp. 16–19.
13. Garrett, 1939, pp. 23–28; Angoff, 1974, pp. 50–52.
14. Garrett, 1968, p. 48.
15. Garrett, 1968, pp. 91–94.
16. Davis, 1859, pp. 57–59.
17. Davis, 1859, pp. 63–65.
18. Davis, 1859, pp. 66–67, 91–95, 107–120.
19. Davis, 1859, pp. 98, 126, 164–176.
20. Davis, 1859, pp. 181–184.
21. Davis, 1859, pp. 181–186.
22. Davis, 1859, pp. 201–212.
23. Davis, 1859, pp. 213–248.

24. Davis, 1859, pp. 296–307, 420–436.

25. Moore, 1977, p. 11.

26. Cross, 1981, p. 344.

27. Britten, 1900, p. 4.

28. Britten, 1900, p. 6.

29. Britten, 1900, p. 15

30. Britten, 1900, pp. 17–27.

31. Britten, 1900, pp. 28–36.

32. Britten, 1900, pp. 39–40.

33. Britten, 1900, p. 42.

34. Ford, 1958, pp. 1–5.

35. Ford, 1958, pp. 5–32.

36. Ford, 1958, p.29.

37. Ford, 1958, pp. 58–59.

38. Ford, 1958, pp. 67–75.

39. Dunninger, 1971.

40. Gibson, 1961.

41. Ford, 1958, pp. 67–74; Dunninger, 1971.

42. Litchfield, 1893, pp. 17–24.

43. Litchfield, 1893, pp. 40–46.

44. Litchfield, 1893, pp. 56–66.

45. Barrett, 1895, pp. 8–14.

46. Barrett, 1895, pp. 8–14.

47. Barrett, 1895, pp. 21, 137–138, 172.

48. *The World*, 1898.

49. Dailey, 1894, pp. 11–27.

50. *The World*, 1898.

51. Dailey, 1894, pp. 28–58.

52. Dailey, 1894, pp. 57–66.

53. Dailey, 1894, p. 68.

54. Dailey, 1894, pp. 69–75.

55. Dailey, 1894, pp. 146–149, 178–180; *The World*, 1898.

56. *The Literary Digest*, 1916.

57. Prince, 1927, pp. 11–14.

58. Prince, 1927, pp. 15, 21.

59. Prince, 1927, pp. 21–29.

60. Prince, 1927, pp. 29–30.

61. Prince, 1927, pp. 22, 31.

62. Prince, 1927, pp. 33–35.

63. Prince, 1927, pp. 42, 57.

64. Prince, 1927, p. 59.

65. Prince, 1927, pp. 336–338.

66. Prince, 1927, pp. 62, 78.

67. Prince, 1927, p. 44.

68. Prince, 1927, p. 156–176.

69. Prince, 1927, 185.

70. Prince, 1927, p. 187.

71. Prince, 1927, pp. 198–200.

72. Prince, 1927, pp. 55–56.

73. Prince, 1927, pp. 206–207.

74. Prince, 1927, p.344.

75. Prince, 1927, p. 344.

76. Prince, 1927, pp. 345–350.

77. Prince, 1927, pp. 321–329, 397.

78. Prince, 1927, p. 398.

79. Prince, 1927, pp. 295–297.

80. Cory, 1919.

81. Prince, 1927, pp. 428–442.

82. Prince, 1927, p. 509.

83. Prince, 1927, pp. 353–354.

84. Prince, 1927, pp. 212, 252.

85. McDowell, 1992.

86. McDowell, 1992.

87. Emmons, 1982, pp. 187–224.

88. Carroll and Tober, 2001.

89. Allen, 1994.

90. King, 1999.

91. Alcoholics Anonymous Staff, 1993.

92. Foundation for Inner Peace Staff, 1997.

93. Mandino, 1985.

94. Hay, 1999.

95. Gawain, 1993.

96. Stoff and Pelegrino, 1992.

97. Lauck, 1998; Emmons, 1982.

98. Guggenheim, 1996.

99. Guggenheim, 1996, p. 276.

100. Lone Dog, 1964, pp. 33–35.

101. Lain, 1985.

102. Marryat, 1893, p. 167.

103. Britten, 1900, p. 46.

104. Randolph, 1869.

105. Gillen, 1987.

106. Van Praag, 1997, p. 161.

107. Burton, 1948, p. 48.

108. Lord-Drake, 1904, pp. 25–28.

109. McDowell, 1992.

110. Britten, 1900, p. 36.

111. Weldon, 1970, p. 95.

112. Moore and Lampshire, 1976, pp. 16–18.

113. Lawton, 1932, pp. 333–336, 342–344, 350–353, 365–367.

114. Richard and Adato, 1980, pp. 190–194.

115. McDowell, 1992.

116. McDowell, 1992.

117. Prince, 1927, p. 296.

118. McDowell, 1992.

119. Galanti, 1987, p. 74.

120. Davis, 1859, pp. 248–255.

121. Lawton, 1932, pp. 337–343.

122. Shupe and Hadden, 1988; McClenon, 2002.

123. Skultans, 1974, pp. 5–7, 27–44.

124. Braude, 1989, pp. 32–55.

125. Martin and Romanowski, 1988.

126. Van Praag, 1997.

127. Altea, 1995.

128. Edward, 1999 and 2002.

129. Guggenheim, 1996; Martin and Romanowski, 1997.

130. Lord-Drake, 1904, p. 88.

131. Putnam, 1873, pp. 37–38.

132. Lone Dog, 1964, pp. 47.

133. Edward, 2001, p. 51.

134. Altea, 1995, p. 96.

135. Van Praagh, 1997, pp. 103–119.

136. Britten, 1900, p. 46.

137. Gauld, 1982, pp. 32–44.

138. Farmer, 1886, p. 49.

139. d'Esperance, 1897, pp. 188–381.

140. Richard and Adato, 1980, p. 191.

141. Lawton, 1932, p. 146.

142. Galanti, 1987, pp. 73–74.

143. Carroll, 1997.

144. Brown, 1997.

145. Skultans, 1974, pp. 61–74.

146. Leonesio, 1989.

147. Leonesio, 1989, p. 92.

148. Sway, 1987.

149. Eliade, 1964; Nicholson, 1987; Drury, 1991.

150. Merkur, 1992; Peters, 1987; Lain, 1985; King, 1987, pp. 193–195.

151. Emmons, 1982, p. 39.

152. Emmons, 1982, pp. 225, 39.

153. Twigg and Brod, 1972, p.24.

154. d'Esperance, 1897, pp. 4–23.

155. Lone Dog, 1964, p. 13.

156. Roberts, 1959, p. 16.

157. Chaney, 1946, p. 125–126.

158. Chaney, 1946, pp. 158–161.

159. Lord-Drake, 1904, pp. 22–23.

160. Martin and Romanowski, 1988, pp. 40, 50.

161. Browne and May, 1998, pp. 6–7.

162. Brown, 1893, pp. 19–20.

163. Hoyle, 1975, v. 1, pp. 60–118.

164. Randolph, 1869, pp. 22–31.

165. Doyle, 1975, v. 1, p. 212.

166. Vlerebome, 1911, pp. 10, 16.

167. "Herself" (sic), 1921, pp. 31–32, 38–40.

168. d'Esperance, 1897, pp. 60–69.

169. Doyle, 1975, p. 12.

170. Braude, 1989, p. 25.

171. Richard and Adato, 1980, p. 189.

172. Hulberd, 1909, p. 9, 11.

173. Prince, 1927, pp. 12–13, 15, 21.

174. Wehner, 1929, pp. 59–60.

175. Browne and May, 1998, p. 15.

176. Weldon, 1970, pp. 17–18.

177. Barrett, 1895, pp. 5–7.

178. Edward, 1999, pp. 5–12.

179. Edward, 1999, pp. 104–110.

180. Crinita, 1982, p. 127–128.

181. Perriman, 1936, p. 14.

182. Twigg, 1972, pp. 24–26.

183. d'Esperance, 1897, pp. 9–11, 22, 45–52.

184. Whiting, 1872, pp. 30–31.

185. Moore and Lampshire, 1976, pp. 8–10.

186. Wehner, 1929, pp. 60–61, 65.

187. Burton, 1948, pp. 46–47.

188. Altea, 1995, p. 12.

189. Smith, 1964, pp. 13–14.

190. Hulberd, 1909, pp. 10–12.

191. Doyle, 1975, v. 1, pp. 70–74.

192. Doyle, 1975, pp. 82–83.

193. Randolph, 1869, pp. 24–36.

194. Hulberd, 1909, p. 11.

195. Vlerebome, 1911, p. 10.

196. Crinita, 1982, p. 128.

197. Lord-Drake, 1904, p. 20.

198. Burton, 1948, pp. 47–48.

199. Putnam, 1873, pp. 17–29.

200. Pittsburg Headlight, no date, pp. 6–10.

201. Perriman, 1936, pp. 17–20.

202. Martin and Romanowski, 1988, pp. 40–47.

203. Van Praagh, 1997, pp. 3–4.

204. Chaney, 1946, pp. 40–41.

205. McDowell, 1992, p. 1.

206. Farmer, 1886, pp. 1–3.

207. "Herself," 1921, pp. 68, 77, 91–92.

208. Putnam, 1873, pp. 37–38.

209. Lond Dog, 1964, p. 32.

210. Twigg and Brod, 1972, pp. 38–41.

211. Putnam, 1873, pp. 39–41.

212. Snow and Machalek, 1984; Lewis and Melton, 1991.

213. Wright, 1946, p.8.

214. Putnam, 1873, pp. 35–37.

215. Doyle, 1975, v. 2, pp 28–29; Gauld, 1982, p. 32.

216. Doyle, 1975, v. 2, p. 29.

217. Vlerebome, 1911, pp. 18–23.

218. Braude, 1989, pp. 82–98.

219. Owen, 1990, pp. 143–167.

220. Emmons, 1982, p. 187.

221. Buhrman, 1997.

222. Smith, 1964, p. 16.

223. Smith, 1964, p. 35.

224. Gauld, 1982, p. 33.

225. Owen, 1990, p. 145.

226. Gauld, 1982, p. 33.

227. Emmons, 1982, pp. 198–199.

228. Ford, 1958, p. 32.

229. Cook, 1919, pp. 22–23.

230. Moore and Lampshire, 1976, p. 35.

231. Vlerebome, 1911, p. 30.

232. Wehner, 1929, pp. 261–268.

233. Prince, 1927, pp. 350–351.

234. Gauld, 1982, p. 35.

235. Putnam, 1873, p. 57.

236. Taylor, 1933, pp. 65, 88.

237. Smith, 1964, pp. 202–204.

238. Ford, 1958, p. 30.

239. Ford, 1958, p. 40.

240. Braude, 1869, pp. 162–169.

241. Browne and May, 1998, pp. 6, 22.

242. Davis, 1859, pp. 215–216.

243. Prince, 1927, pp. 394–395.

244. Prince, 1927, p. 397.

245. Tietze, 1973, p. 22.

246. Doyle, 1975, v.2, pp. 24–25.

247. Stern, 1974, p. 161.

248. Warren, 1970, p. Ix.

249. Twigg and Brod, 1972, p. 42.

250. Garrett, 1943, p. 274.

251. Emmons, 1982, pp. 150–156.

252. Howell, 1989, pp. 78, 91.

253. Turner, 1996.

254. Braude, 1989; Cross, 1981; Carroll, 1997; Moore, 1977.

255. Braden, 1949; Melton, 1990.

256. Brown, 1997; Riordan, 1991.

257. Carroll, 1997.

258. Carroll, 1997; Skultans, 1974; Lawton, 1932; Richard and Adato, 1980; Lloyd, 1986.

259. Lewis, 1966.

260. Lewis, 1966, p. 318.

261. Gillen, 1987.

262. Braude, 1989.

263. Owen, 1990; Haywood, 1983; Baer, 1993; Lerch, 1982.

264. Barrow, 1980, Dann, 1979; Lain, 1985.

265. Braude, 1989; Moore, 1977.

266. Prothero, 1993.

267. Lewis, 1966.

268. Lerch, 1982; Dann, 1979.

269. Lain, 1985.

270. Emmons, 1982.

271. Morris, 2000.

272. Swatos and Gissurarson, 1997.

273. Howell, 1989.

274. Moore, R. Laurence, 1977, pp. 127–128.

275. Owen, 1990: pp. 144–151.

276. Brown, 1997, pp. 174–191.

277. Kenny, 1986.

278. Buhrman, 1997.

279. Thuillier, 1983.

280. Thuiller, 1983; Palfreman, 1979.

281. McClenon, 1997, 2000, 2001,2002.

282. Underwood, 2001.

283. Moore, 1977; Carlton, 2000, pp. 16–20.

284. McClenon, 1984; Hess, 1993; Goode, 2000.

285. Palfreman, 1979.

286. Garroutte, 1993.

287. Emmons, 1997.

288. Greasley, 2000.

289. Wiseman *et al.*, 1999, 1995.

290. Schouten, 1994.

291. Schouten, 1994, p. 249.

292. Schouten, 1994, p. 246.

293. Moore, 1977.

294. Doyle, 1975.

295. Gauld, 1982.

296. Gauld, 1982, pp. 261–267.

297. Becker, 1993, pp. 9–10.

298. Kastenbaum, 1995, pp. 116–120, 141–184.

299. Schwartz and Russek, 1999, pp. 113–119.

300. Schwartz, 2002.

301. Schwartz, pp. 208–213.

302. Edward, 1999, 2001.

303. Emmons, 1982.

304. Tart, 1997.

305. Hastings, 1991; Klimo, 1987.

306. Anderson, 1993, pp. 119, 121.

307. Gauld, 1982.

308. Colville, 1906, pp. 39–56.

309. Anderson, 1994, p. 289.

310. Colville, 1906, p. 45.

311. Beard, 1992, p. 115.

312. Moore, 1977, pp. 25, 38, 52–54.

313. Prothero, 1993.

314. Washington, 1996.

315. Emmons, 1982.

316. Emmons, 1997.

317. Emmons, 1982.

Index

0-595-26805-6

Printed in the United States
20041LVS00004B/59

9 780595 268054